Interdisciplinary Education in K–12 and College

A Foundation for K–16 Dialogue

Julie Thompson Klein, Editor

College Entrance Examination Board
New York

The College Board: Expanding College Opportunity

The College Board is a national nonprofit membership association dedicated to preparing, inspiring, and connecting students to college and opportunity. Founded in 1900, the association is composed of more than 4,200 schools, colleges, universities, and other educational organizations. Each year, the College Board serves over three million students and their parents, 22,000 high schools, and 3,500 colleges through major programs and services in college admissions, guidance, assessment, financial aid, enrollment, and teaching and learning. Among its best-known programs are the SAT®, the PSAT/NMSQT®, and the Advanced Placement Program® (AP®). The College Board is committed to the principles of equity and excellence, and that commitment is embodied in all of its programs, services, activities, and concerns.

For further information, contact www.collegeboard.com.

Copies of this book may be ordered from:
College Board Publications
Box 886, New York, NY 10101-0886
(800) 323-7155 or online at www.collegeboard.com.
The price of this book is $22.95, plus $5.00 for postage and handling.

Editorial inquiries should be addressed to Office of Academic Initiatives,
The College Board, 45 Columbus Avenue, New York, NY 10023-6992.

Library of Congress Cataloging-in-Publication Data

Interdisciplinary education in K-12 and college : a foundation for K-16 dialogue / Julie Thomson Klein, editor.
    p. cm.
    Includes bibliographical references (p.).
    ISBN 0-87447-679-8
    1. Curriculum planning. 2. Interdisciplinary approach in education. I. Klein, Julie Thomson.

LB2806.15 .I58 2002
375_.001—dc21
                                                                2002019152
International Standard Book Number: 0-87447-679-8

Printed in the United States of America.

Contents

Contributors v
Acknowledgments vii

Introduction: Interdisciplinarity Today: Why? What? And How?
Julie Thompson Klein 1

PART I: Current Issues in K–12
Chapter 1: Integrated Curriculum Design
Heidi Hayes Jacobs..21

Chapter 2: Interdisciplinary Teamed Instruction
Rebecca Crawford Burns..45

Chapter 3: Politics and Possibilities Beyond the Separate Subjects
James A. Beane 71

Chapter 4: Interdisciplinary High School Learning in an Information Age
Russell M. Agne and John H. Clarke 91

PART II: Current Issues in College
Chapter 5: Integrating the College Curriculum
William H. Newell 117

Chapter 6: The Joys and Pitfalls of Team Teaching
James R. Davis..139

Chapter 7: Developing and Administering Interdisciplinary Programs
Beth A. Casey 157

PART III: Toward a K–16 Dialogue
Chapter 8: Assessing Interdisciplinary Learning K–16
Julie Thompson Klein 179

Epilogue: Imperatives for Dialogue on Interdisciplinarity K–16
Julie Thompson Klein 197

A Beginning Library..203
References..205

For Gordon Vars,
who exemplifies K–16 dialogue

Contributors

Russell M. Agne teaches science methods and curriculum topics at the University of Vermont. A former high school science teacher and university administrator, he now works on curriculum and instruction with schools, K–12. He has directed grants to support improvement of instruction in K–12 and worked with Teacher Enhancement Programs of the National Science Foundation. He is the author of numerous articles and was coauthor with John H. Clarke of *Interdisciplinary High School Teaching: Strategies for Integrated Learning* (1997).

James A. Beane is a Professor in the Department of Interdisciplinary Studies in Curriculum, National College of Education, National-Louis University. He has taught in junior, middle, and high schools and was a project director for the New York State Regional Education Planning Centers. His books include *Affect in the Curriculum: Toward Democracy, Dignity, and Diversity* (1990), *A Middle School Curriculum: From Rhetoric to Reality* (1993), and *Curriculum Integration: Designing the Core of Democratic Education* (1997).

Rebecca Crawford Burns is affiliated with the Appalachia Educational Laboratory, which serves as the Regional Educational Laboratory for Kentucky, Tennessee, Virginia, and West Virginia. She consults widely on curriculum integration and the design and implementation of interdisciplinary teamed instruction. She is the author of *Dissolving the Boundaries: Planning for Curriculum Integration in Middle and Secondary Schools* (1999) and coauthor with Beth D. Sattes of an accompanying *Facilitators Guide* (1995).

Beth A. Casey is Director of General Education at Bowling Green State University, where she teaches American and English Canadian literature. She consults on development and administration of interdisciplinary studies in higher education and was previously an associate dean at Hobart and William Smith Colleges. She is a former president of the Association for Integrative Studies and the Association of General and Liberal Studies and publishes on general education, academic administration, and humanities.

John H. Clarke taught reading and curriculum design in the secondary education program at the University of Vermont and helped coordinate Professional

Development Schools throughout Vermont. He has conducted workshops and presentations across the country and worked to integrate teacher preparation programs and school-restructuring efforts in development institutes and centers in high schools. His books include works on thinking instruction and, with Russell M. Agne, *Interdisciplinary High School Teaching: Strategies for Integrated Learning* (1997).

James R. Davis is Director of the Center for Academic Quality, Assistant to the Provost, and Professor of Higher Education at the University of Denver. He has conducted workshops on college teaching throughout the United States and in Brazil. He is the author of several books, including two works in the American Council on Education/Oryx Series on Higher Education, *Better Teaching, More Learning: Strategies for Success in Postsecondary Settings* (1993) and *Interdisciplinary Courses and Team Teaching: New Arrangements for Learning* (1995).

Heidi Hayes Jacobs is a Professor at Teachers College of Columbia University. She consults frequently on curriculum planning and integrated and interdisciplinary design models. She has written widely on interdisciplinary education and worked closely with the Association for Supervision and Curriculum Development, which published her books on *Interdisciplinary Curriculum: Design and Implementation* (1989) and *Mapping the Big Picture: Integrating Curriculum and Assessment, K–12*.

Julie Thompson Klein is Professor of Humanities in the Interdisciplinary Studies Program at Wayne State University. She consults widely on interdisciplinarity. Her books include *Interdisciplinarity: History, Theory, and Practice* (1990) and *Crossing Boundaries: Knowledge, Disciplinarities, and Interdisciplinarities* (1996), the AACU monograph *Mapping Interdisciplinary Studies Today* (1999), and the coedited *Interdisciplinary Studies Today* (1994) and *Transdisciplinarity: Joint Problem Solving among Science, Technology and Society* (2000).

William H. Newell is Professor of Interdisciplinary Studies and Director of the Institute in Integrative Studies at Miami University in Oxford, Ohio. He serves as Executive Director of the Association for Integrative Studies and has been a consultant and external evaluator at over 85 colleges and universities in the United States, Canada, and New Zealand. He was editor of the first edition of *Interdisciplinary Undergraduate Programs: A Directory* (1986) and *Interdisciplinarity: Essays from the Literature* (1998).

Acknowledgments

This book began with a deceptively simple question. Robert Orrill, former Executive Director of the Office of Academic Affairs and former director of the National Center for Crossdisciplinary Teaching and Learning at the College Board, asked what I thought about interdisciplinarity in K–12. Like most of my counterparts in college, I knew little about what was happening in schools. This exploration of interdisciplinarity across the K–16 continuum has been an extended way of answering his question.

It has also been collaborative. My greatest debt is to the authors, for participating in this effort to build a foundation for dialogue across the continuum: to Heidi Jacobs, Russ Agne, John Clarke, Becky Burns, and Jim Beane for their contributions on K–12 and to Beth Casey, Bill Newell, and Jim Davis for their chapters on college.

I am also indebted to several individuals at the College Board. Joanne Daniels, formerly a consultant for the Office of Academic Affairs, helped shape the initial prospectus. The College Board librarian Lianna Kelly helped locate resources, and Renée Savin provided valuable office support. Most of all, I thank Diane Foster, for her skillful guiding of the volume through final editing and production, and Howard Everson, Vice President for Academic Initiatives and Chief Research Scientist, and Edmund Gordon, Senior Visiting Scholar in Residence, for their instrumental roles in the book's publication.

Finally, I thank George Klein, for his steadfast support throughout this project.

Julie Thompson Klein
Detroit, Michigan 2001

Introduction

Interdisciplinarity Today: Why? What? And How?

Julie Thompson Klein

At the beginning of the twentieth century, the word "interdisciplinarity" was not even in the English language. Today, it is in wide use throughout grades K–12 and college. Many educators, in fact, regard interdisciplinarity as essential for teaching and learning in the twenty-first century. A profusion of publications, conferences, and messages on electronic bulletin boards and listservs for teachers document the current level of interest (Siskin 2000). Many educators, though, are unsure about where to begin, and even veterans of interdisciplinary teaching are not aware of the abundant resources. The College Board's publication of *Interdisciplinary Education: A Guide to Resources* (1999) was an important step toward meeting the needs of newcomers and veterans alike. Edited by Joan Fiscella and Stacey Kimmel, it is the first annotated bibliography of the literature throughout the K–16 continuum of primary, secondary, and postsecondary education. The contributors in this book take the next step.

The purpose of this volume is to inform curriculum change in two ways: by examining current issues in K–12 and college and by providing a foundation for dialogue across K–16. It is a timely project. Creating connections across K–16 has become a major topic in education. The discourse of K–16, however, is dominated by subjects and disciplines. The term "K–16" appears in many contexts. It is linked with new technologies, multicultural and environmental education, skills across the curriculum, systematic assessment, teacher training, a coordinated national education policy, and school partnerships with colleges, corporations, communities, and government agencies. The term was popularized in the early 1990s when the Education Trust, with support from the American Association for Higher Education, launched an effort to coordinate reforms around benchmark standards for particular subjects (Haycock and Brown 1993, 4–5; Gross 1988, xi, 1–5).

With the exception of the school-to-work movement and individual school/college partnerships, interdisciplinarity has been a relatively neglected topic in K–16 discourse. This effort to include interdisciplinarity in the discussion is aimed at the key change agents in education—teachers, administrators, and curriculum planning groups. The book focuses on definitions, guiding principles, and current models and practices. In doing so, it draws deeply on the contributors' experiences as consultants, researchers, administrators, and teachers. Spending as much time as we do in classrooms and meeting rooms across the country, we are keenly aware of the need for a common framework. Educators come to interdisciplinarity and curriculum integration at different points of entry. Some are experienced at particular parts of the continuum, but many are not. Some are familiar with the literature that Fiscella and Kimmel identified, but the majority are not or have only limited familiarity. As a result, they lack awareness of the tradition, vocabulary, methods, and theory of interdisciplinary education. Lack of shared knowledge impedes work at all levels, from individual classrooms to national forums.

The problem is not limited to the United States. In studying interdisciplinary teaching in Brazilian schools, Ivani Fazenda discovered an indiscriminate proliferation of practices. In Brazil, the U.S., and Europe, the number of educational projects with the word "integration" and "interdisciplinary" in their titles has increased dramatically. Yet, many usages arise from intuition or trendiness. "In the name of interdisciplinarity," Fazenda lamented, "established routines are condemned and abandoned, and slogans, nicknames, and working hypotheses are created which many times are improvised and ill-considered" (1995, 7). Contributors to the present study concur. "I can't tell you how many times," Heidi Jacobs echoes, "I've been in a school and seen good intentions gone astray" ("Curriculum Integration," 2; in ASCD, 76). Klein and Newell report the same problems in college (1997, 408). One of the major purposes of this book, then, is to enable everyone, in the parlance of the day, to start out "on the same page" with a shared understanding of what interdisciplinarity and integration entail.

Extending dialogue across K–16 does not ignore differences. Student ages and cognitive development, institutional structures, and professional mandates vary greatly across the continuum. In a rare reflection on differences in notions of interdisciplinarity in K–12 and university settings, Grossman, Wineburg, and Beers (2000) report that the greatest inroads in K–12 have been in elementary and middle schools, where a "generalist ethos" has wide support and teaching often does not have strong disciplinary commitments. Curricula tend to be "predisciplinary," in contrast to the more self-conscious focus on disciplines found in high school and college. Moreover, there is a "different flavor" to discussions of interdisciplinarity across K–16. The conversation about disciplinary tools and ways of knowing and about interdisciplinarity as a intellectual problem may not be heard in elementary or middle schools, where interdisciplinarity is more often conceived as a practical solution to organizational and administrative problems of increasing motivation and creating a healthier social and psychological environment.

Even with these differences, though, there is also a substantive basis for K–16 comparison. The effort begins by answering three of the most immediate questions that arise in both K–12 and college:

1. Why is interdisciplinarity important now?
2. What is interdisciplinary education?
3. How do you do it?

1. Why Is Interdisciplinarity Important Now?

In descriptions of contemporary education and research, interdisciplinarity is often called "cutting edge" work and is located at the "frontiers" of current knowledge. The concept is not new. Underlying ideas of integration, synthesis, and general knowledge date to ancient philosophy. Nevertheless, the first explicit interdisciplinary approaches did not appear until the opening decades of the twentieth century, primarily in the areas of core curriculum and general education. During the 1960s and early 1970s a new momentum for educational innovation, coupled with the rise of interdisciplinary fields, heightened awareness. Later into the 1970s economic retrenchments crippled many celebrated experiments, marginalizing interdisciplinary programs across K–16. The past two decades, however, have been a time of renewed interest in interdisciplinarity and curriculum integration. There are four major reasons for the resurgence of interest during the 1980s and 1990s:

- Knowledge Change
- Educational Reform
- Problem Solving
- Critique

Knowledge Change

The entire curriculum, from K–12 through college, is bulging at the seams. The most popular image of this phenomenon is a "knowledge explosion." A staggering increase in the amount of knowledge and information has made it impossible to teach everything, even in a single subject. Evidence abounds in both disciplines and interdisciplinary fields.

Disciplines

As recently as the 1970s, disciplines were not associated with interdisciplinarity. They were considered the major obstacles to integrating curriculum. Yet, in surveying the current literature on interdisciplinary education, Fiscella and Kimmel found the "contemporary life" of disciplines and school subjects to be a major topic of discussion (1999, 10). Judith Rényi, executive director of the National Foundation for the Improvement of Education, likens the disciplines to "a moving target" (2000, 53). New research on the mind, the body, the family, the earth, and the solar system has blurred traditional boundaries of school subjects and college majors. Powerful concepts and related methods also cross-fertilize the disciplines. The concepts of narrative and interpretation are used in literary studies, history, art history, religion, anthropology, law, and psychiatry. Similarly, the concepts of information and communication appear in media studies, social psychology, engineering, and cognitive science.

Educators are keenly aware of these changes. Their disciplines have changed since they were in college and even over the course of their careers. As a result, interdisciplinarity has become a major topic across subject journals, from *Chemical Education* to *Teaching History* to *American Music Teacher.* Classroom practices are changing as well. English teachers across K–16 are adding a diversity of texts while drawing on social history and postmodern approaches to the study of language and culture. Social science and sociology teachers are bringing interdisciplinary research on human behavior into the traditional curriculum. History teachers are applying quantitative methods from the social sciences and borrowing qualitative strategies of understanding texts from literary theory. Geography teachers are using both scientific and humanistic approaches to studying interactions between humans and their environments. And science teachers are incorporating new research on genetics, evolution, and geoscience, while integrating mathematics and computers into the teaching of science.

The knowledge explosion is also the result of another major development: the emergence of interdisciplinary fields.

Interdisciplinary Fields

Over the course of the twentieth century, the emergence of interdisciplinary fields has altered the landscape of knowledge. During the 1930s and 1940s, the fields of American studies and areas studies began to be developed. In the 1960s and 1970s, women's studies, ethnic studies, urban studies, environmental studies, and studies of science, technology, and society entered the academy. In the 1980s and 1990s, the field of cultural studies expanded rapidly, along with new and older fields of cognitive and information sciences, neuroscience, molecular biology, and international and global studies. Policy studies, marine biology, comparative literature, gerontology, and criminology also have strong interdisciplinary identities.

The knowledge produced in such fields enters the curriculum in three ways: as the intellectual foundation for interdisciplinary programs, as new topics in the core curriculum and general education, and as new foci within traditional subjects and disciplines. Environmental studies illustrates all three effects. In both K–12 and college, environmental themes and problems, such as ecology and pollution, are popular topics in general education. They also have a growing presence in science education. Depending on the institution, a college student can major in environmental studies, complete a minor or concentration, or take individual courses as electives. The concept of cultural diversity followed a similar pattern as it entered the curriculum. In college, interdisciplinary programs are offered in women's studies, African American studies, ethnic studies, international studies, and postcolonial studies. Theory and content from these fields have been incorporated into a variety of disciplines and, across K–16, general education and core curricula are forums for teaching multiculturalism and global diversity.

For many educators, the motivation for changing the curriculum is simply to keep up with these changes in knowledge, though a number of additional concerns are addressed in educational reform.

Educational Reform

"An interdisciplinary curriculum," Ellis and Stuen explain in their book on the subject, "is an integrated curriculum" (1998, 30). Not all forms of integration are the same, however. In K–12 the tradition of curriculum integration dates to the 1800s. The most prominent early movement was named after German philosopher and educator Johann Friedrich Herbart. In the late 1880s, Herbart developed ideas of "correlation" of subjects that were sometimes called "integration of studies." During the 1920s, the Progressivists' social democratic vision of integration placed students' personal and social concerns at the center of educational experience. The term "integrated curriculum" was used in other contexts as well, including the project approach in the 1920s, the core curriculum movement in the 1930s, and problem-centered core curricula in the 1940s and 1950s. The word "integration" also appeared in conjunction with the psychological process of holistic learning; personal and social integration; moral education; an experience-based curriculum and merging learning and work; a child-centered curriculum and teacher-student planning; and a broad-fields approach (Clarke and Agne 1997, 13; for an extensive history of "integration" see Beane 1997, ix–37).

During the 1980s and 1990s, the term "curriculum integration" reappeared in K–12, as a generic label for any approach that draws on more than one subject or discipline. The major examples include thematic studies, multidisciplinary and multisubject designs, integrated units, skills across the curriculum, a social-problems approach to science education, and familiar integrated constructs such as social studies and whole language. Several interest groups also voiced support. Early childhood educators advocated integration, and some proponents of outcomes-based education argued that sophisticated levels of learning cannot be attained by studying subjects separately. The concept of the "teacher as generalist" and the project approach in the work of Theodore Sizer and the Coalition of Essential Schools was a further stimulus, as well as the movement toward a "brain-based" approach. The brain-based argument is not new. The belief that integration arises from a basic human inclination or need appeared in the 1920s in organismic and Gestalt psychology, in the concept of an integrated personality (Beane 1997, 2). Recent research in neuroscience, however—which suggests that the brain is a parallel processor that makes meaning through patterning, by discerning and creating connections among isolated pieces of information—strengthens the argument. Even in the absence of extensive empirical proof, there is mounting evidence that integrative and cooperative approaches enhance learning and retention.

In K–12, Grossman, Wineburg, and Beers report, interdisciplinarity has also become "synonymous" with school reform. In one recent study, three-fourths of "restructuring schools" were engaged in interdisciplinary reorganization of their curricula (2000, 1). In the middle school literature, Fiscella and Kimmel found the topic to be converging with discussions of not only school reform but also teacher autonomy, educational values, school-community relations, and the purpose of education (1999, 11). High school has traditionally been more resistant to interdisciplinarity. Restrictive time schedules and requirements for graduation narrow the room for innovation. Teachers also tend to identify more closely with specialized disciplines. Nonetheless, constructivist and project learning, problem-solving, new work on learning process, integrations of subject-matter knowledge, and new approaches to teaching and learning have enhanced the visibility of interdisciplinary approaches in high school. Across K–16, educators also share a conviction that all students deserve integrative learning experiences, making general education a primary site of curriculum reform.

General Education

Recent campaigns to establish common cores of learning in K–12 and in college are the latest in a history of efforts to foster integration in the part of the curriculum that does not concentrate on a single subject or major—general education. Like "integration," the term "core curriculum" is used both generically, as an umbrella label for any common learning experience, and technically, as a concept with distinctive characteristics. In the latter case, "interdisciplinary" is sometimes a code word in K–12 for particular approaches such as inquiry-based or active learning, projects, and constructivism (Hammerness and Moffett 2000, 137–38, 147). The meaning of "core" and assumptions about "common" knowledge have changed over time, though some traditions persist. Blocktime core classes and team teaching have been features of middle schools since their inception around the turn of the century.

In college, general education is the fastest growing site of interdisciplinary approaches today, making it a major sector of innovation in the postsecondary part of the continuum. The first interdisciplinary core courses in college arose in the early twentieth century. Founded in 1919, Columbia University's Contemporary Civilization program promoted shared interdisciplinary knowledge through study of contemporary problems and reflection on the process of knowing. Great Books programs at the University of Chicago and St. John's College differed. They centered on a canon of books or ideas thought to embody unified and universal knowledge (Klein 2001, 392–93).

In recent decades, the meaning of interdisciplinarity has broadened as campuses replace traditional distribution models of general education with integrated models. "Integration" is a profoundly different metaphor for education than "distribution." In a distribution model, existing subjects or disciplinary courses are learned separately. Across K–16, integrative models of general education restructure curriculum, promoting multidisciplinary breadth of knowledge and the integrative skills needed to understand complex themes and problems. In college, individual courses are also being clustered together, and collaborative learning communities are being created. And in the past two decades an added need has contributed to the resurgence of interest in interdisciplinarity across K–16—problem solving.

Problem Solving

Interdisciplinarity is often justified by the "real-world" argument. Life, the argument goes, is not divided into school subjects and academic disciplines. The premise is overstated, ignoring the functional walls that separate departments in business, industry, and government. It is not new either. During the late 1940s and early 1950s, life problems were a central feature of the integrated curriculum movement in schools. Contemporary problems were also a focal point of the Contemporary Civilization program at Columbia. Today, however, problem-focus has attained center stage across the curriculum. There are several reasons.

The heightened demand for solving economic and technological problems is an impetus for interdisciplinary research in areas of intense international competition, such as engineering and industrial production, computers, molecular biology, and biomedicine. Complex problems of practice in law, medicine, social work, education, and business have also fostered interdisciplinary approaches in professional education. Meanwhile, curricular boundaries are shifting in vocational education. Biology and chemistry are being studied as they apply to health care and chemical engineering, not as sciences in themselves (J. Farmer 1997, 477). Elsewhere on the continuum, the school-to-work movement prepares high school students for high-skill careers in project- and service-based learning, youth apprenticeship programs, community programs, and career academy programs organized around industrial or occupational themes. Emphasis is placed on themes, collaboration, problem-solving skills, critical thinking, and connections among disciplines and between academic and vocational programs.

The workplace is not the only problem context. In K–12, the demand for interdisciplinary approaches is being reinforced by state mandates to include in the curriculum problems of drug use, AIDS prevention, sex education, and family life. In college, new disciplinary partnerships in undergraduate education are focusing on problems such as crime, juvenile violence, infant mortality, AIDS, ethnic tensions, and pollution (Jacobs 1989, 3–4; Hendershott and Wright 1997, 314). As this list suggests, all "problems" are not the same. Courses centered on equality and crime stem from a different motivation than improving economic competition or workplace skills. Labor and democracy, James Beane cautions, are different reasons for integrating the curriculum (1997, 21–22). Disagreements about the definition of interdisciplinarity and curriculum integration often center on which problems should be the focus of study. This difference raises the fourth and final reason for the current resurgence of interest in interdisciplinarity: the expanding critique of knowledge and education.

Critique

In a number of new fields, the purpose of interdisciplinarity is not simply to combine existing disciplines. Interdisciplinarity interrogates and even disturbs existing categories of knowledge and institutional structures. Women's studies and cultural studies, for example, are changing the ways that gender and culture are understood and taught. During the late 1980s and 1990s, a number of academic movements, including multiculturalism and postmodernism, further challenged the dominance and authority of traditional subjects and disciplines. Their cumulative effect has been to call into question all forms of knowledge, while generating new categories of knowledge and education.

Critique also raises the most fundamental question of all. What is the purpose of education? In its highest form, interdisciplinarity is not a finite set of skills or a logistic wrinkle in the schedule. The ultimate goal is to reconstruct what is taught and how it is taught (Panaritis 1995, 624, 628 in ERS). Clarke and

Agne's description of the implications of thematic and interdisciplinary teaching apply across K–16. All components of the system are affected, from philosophy, organizational structure, management style, institutional culture, curriculum, and instruction to scheduling, tracking and sequencing, budgets, certification and licensure, teacher education, in-service training, and professional development. Introducing new courses and requirements into a curriculum often means running two systems at once. An older system holds fast, while a new one struggles into being (1997, 84–85).

Interdisciplinarity, to sum up, has become more important because the needs it serves, although varied and even conflicting, are pervasive. Responding to those needs requires answering the second question: What is interdisciplinary education?

2. What Is Interdisciplinary Education?

Basic definitions are similar across the continuum. Heidi Jacobs describes K–12 interdisciplinary education as a view of knowledge and curriculum that applies methodology and language from more than one discipline to the study of a particular theme, issue, problem, topic, or experience (1989, 8). Clarke and Agne describe integrated teaching in high school as a movement that lets questioning and problem solving direct the process of acquiring knowledge and skills (1997, 1). Klein and Newell describe interdisciplinary studies in college as a process of answering a question, solving a problem, or addressing a topic that is too broad or complex to be dealt with by a single discipline or profession (1997, 393). The connecting link among these definitions is process, not a fixed body of content.

The conventional picture of the curriculum is a set of boxes, each box containing credits in particular subjects or disciplines. Divisions of knowledge are matched by segments of time—separate hours of the day, weeks of the semester, and months of the year—and domains of space—separate rooms and buildings. Interdisciplinarity redraws the boundaries of the boxes by creating new structures. Subjects and disciplines are no longer isolated or self-justified; they become tools for a new purpose. To understand the new structures, readers need to be familiar with basic terminology. Unfortunately, the "mind-boggling flotilla of terms," to echo Heidi Jacobs's description, can be confusing. Even major terms such as "integrated" and "interdisciplinary" are used differently. So it is no surprise that terminology was the number one issue Fiscella and Kimmel identified in the literature on foundations of interdisciplinarity. Terminology is not merely a semantic game, James Beane advises. Different terms reflect different views of the purpose of curriculum, the best use of knowledge, and the place of disciplines. These differences are apparent even in this book, particularly on the role of disciplines and choice of design models. Nevertheless, some basic distinctions can be recognized.

Design Models

The major distinction among design models is degree of integration. In K–12, the lowest degree of integration is found in the model of "parallel disciplines," also called "correlated" and "sequenced" design. Rebecca Burns offers keywords for thinking about different models, beginning with *sequencing*. When disciplines have a "parallel" relationship, content does not change, only the order of presentation. Class schedules are reconfigured so that students can explore similar themes, topics, issues, or problems simultaneously. However, they are usually left to uncover connections by themselves, the content and procedures of disciplines remain intact, and the dynamic of team teaching is often missing.

In K–12, an English teacher might present a historical novel while a history teacher is working with the same era in another class. Or, a unit on hurricanes might be taught simultaneously in separate English, geography, and science classes. In college, students might take separate courses in twentieth-century literature and history during the same semester, or separate courses dealing with particular subjects, such as women, the environment, or urban affairs. This model is common; it is easy, inexpensive, and does not disrupt the status quo. Both practical and philosophical reasons come into play. For some teachers, it is the most they can do. They lack sufficient knowledge of other disciplines to teach them. Over time, as they gain more familiarity, they move to a greater degree of integration. Others do not go further, because their philosophy of education is deeply rooted in disciplines. In their minds, integration is only a technique for enhancing the teaching of subjects and disciplines. (For a three-tier continuum and helpful illustration of differences, see Applebee, Burroughs, and Cruz 2000).

A "multidisciplinary" approach goes beyond sequencing to intentionally align courses. The keyword is *coordinating*. A theme, a problem, or a question is woven through complementary disciplines, creating an integrative "overlay" for separate concepts and activities. In K–12, historical periods and events—such as the Renaissance or the U.S. Civil War—are typical overlays. So are problems of the environment and concepts such as change. In college, courses from separate departments may be explicitly aligned, as they are in an American studies program. However, students do not necessarily experience integrative seminars or projects. Even when team teaching occurs, individuals still present their disciplinary perspectives separately, in a fashion dubbed "turn" or "tag" teaching. Students gain breadth of knowledge but do not engage in explicit analysis of disciplinary perspectives or interdisciplinary synthesis. Many so-called "interdisciplinary" models are actually "multidisciplinary." They fall short of more integrated design for several reasons, though the "potpourri problem" is common. "Potpourri" is Heidi Jacobs's term for putting together bits and pieces of knowledge from different disciplines. Courses exhibiting this problem lack focus, direction, conceptual clarity, and clear goals and objectives. Basic skills also tend to be neglected, the teaching of subjects may be superficial, and students do not necessarily perceive connections, even if their teachers do.

Integrated designs go further. They do not simply build bridges: they restructure the curriculum. Burns's keywords are *focusing* and *blending.* Content is revised, a new "connective depth" is created, and true team teaching may occur. In K–12, the terms "curriculum integration," "unified studies," and "fusion" model are common labels for this degree of integration. In both K–12 and college, "interdisciplinary" is also used as a technical label for this level of integration. Formats vary, from a single unit or course to a year-long program and, in rare cases, a student's entire educational experience in an "academy," "whole school," "school-within-a-school," or autonomous program or college. In high school, English and history are combined in a "fusion" model that facilitates broad study of American cultural history. Subjects and disciplines become tools for studying themes such as culture, identity, ethnicity, and regionalism. In college, an American studies program moves beyond multidisciplinary juxtaposition of separate disciplines to include core interdisciplinary seminars.

At the highest level of integration, the keyword is *transcending.* Boundaries blur and connections are magnified. Robin Fogarty likens this level to a kaleidoscope. Varied and shifting images produce a new complexity of design (1991, 64; ASCD). Generic use of the term "integration" to describe any model that uses more than one subject or discipline obscures an important difference. At this level of the design continuum, integration becomes the purpose of education, not simply a tool. The most comprehensive examples of integration in this book—Rebecca Burns's scheme of "transdisciplinary" education and James Beane's model of "curriculum integration"—reconceptualize the nature of education. A student's world, not a school or a state syllabus, becomes the heart of learning. Furthermore, in contrast to the tendency for teachers to choose themes, students participate in selecting the themes and problems they will study, and they work collaboratively. Students become full partners in learning, enacting a genuinely democratic concept of education. In college, the term "transdisciplinary" also appears as a label for a new organizational and intellectual framework, such as the overarching paradigms of feminism or general systems theory.

Organization of Courses

In both K–12 and college, interdisciplinary courses are most commonly organized around a theme, a problem, a question, or an idea. The word "theme" is a generic term in the literature for these new organizing principles. Thematic studies vary in length, from a single class period or week to a semester to an entire program. A theme is not an automatic guarantee of integration. Wineburg and Grossman's book *Interdisciplinary Curriculum* (2000) is full of cautionary tales of inappropriate themes, disciplines forced to fit a particular theme, and other problems.

Actual themes vary widely, from personal issues of identity and the body to social problems and abstract intellectual questions. In K–12, annual events are popular foci, such as Christmas and Thanksgiving, President's Day and Election Day, Martin Luther King Jr. Day, and Earth Day. The seasons and special events, such as the Olympics, are common topics as well. In working with younger children, teachers select themes related to animals and marine ecology, the planetary system and space exploration. At varying levels of complexity, students of different ages explore topics in history (immigration, genealogy, exploration, and war), social problems (violence, hunger, poverty, and racism), institutions (the family, the community, and government), systems (transportation, the economy, and ecology), and abstract concepts (conflict, change, democracy, and responsibility).

In college, typical themes in general education include the individual and community, authority, values, and democracy; cultural diversity and globalism; the environment, and topics in science and technology. The fastest growing subject areas in general education, Beth Casey reports, are international studies, American multicultural and gender studies, and the inherently synoptic, broadly encompassing areas of historical consciousness and ethics (1994, 56). Reflecting the history of general education, "great" books and ideas still anchor many courses, and theme-based surveys of humanities, social sciences, and science continue to provide multidisciplinary breadth. Both national trends and local missions influence choice of themes. A religious college may select topics related to spirituality and values, such as Judeo-Christian history or ethical decision making. At a public university, humanities faculty with an interest in aesthetics and philosophical ideas may choose the relationship of beauty and goodness.

In interdisciplinary fields, major organizing themes are drawn both from relevant disciplines and from core interdisciplinary concepts. In American studies, for example, culture and society are core concepts, along with such topics as diversity or the American dream. In women's studies, gender and sexuality are defining concepts of the field, while major topics include the family, ethnicity, and feminist theory and methodologies. In peace and justice studies, peace and justice are core concepts, and topics include nonviolence, power, conflict resolution, and international relations. In neuroscience, students take courses in foundational disciplines of science, math, and computers, while studying topics in cellular and molecular neuroscience, systems neuroscience, cognitive science, neuropsychology, electrophysiology, and genetics.

The value of thinking in terms of K–16 is underscored by two striking parallels in high school and college. The first is cultural history. The most common structures of fused courses in high school are cultural perspective and historical change. Early on, world history and American history found a place in the high school curriculum because they create contexts in which art, artifacts, historical events, philosophical positions, political trends, and beliefs can be questioned and meaning explored (Clarke and Agne 1997, 52). They also draw on knowledge produced in university research settings. Historical themes tap interdisciplinary subfields of history and new cross-fertilizations of research in humanities and social sciences. Culture-based themes incorporate research in area studies, international studies, and American cultural studies.

The second parallel is science, technology, and the environment. The field of science, technology, and society studies (STS) dates from the 1960s when environmental studies was also gaining an institutional foothold. In K–12, the themes of space, computers, and health are popular, and many projects focus on water quality in local rivers and lakes. In college, science- and technology-related themes are becoming more prominent in general education, and students can major in STS at undergraduate and graduate levels. Courses focus on the nature of scientific inquiry and the implications of increasing reliance on science and technology. STS is also a vigorous field of research on the history of science and technology, the sociology of scientific practices, and critiques of the economics, politics, and epistemology of science and technology.

3. How Do You Do It?

In and of themselves, curriculum designs and themes are inert. The third question—How do you actually *do* interdisciplinary teaching?—focuses on the actual process of integration. The remainder of this book is devoted in significant part to answering this question. First, though, some basic definitions are needed. Interdisciplinary pedagogy is active, dynamic, and process-oriented. Application of knowledge takes precedence over acquisition alone, accentuating development of skills of analysis and critical thinking. There is no unique pedagogy or formula for integration. The "best practices" affirm the premise Agne and Clarke voice in this book: When teachers go beyond subject knowledge they prepare lessons based on a contemporary view of pedagogy.

Pedagogy

There is no unique interdisciplinary pedagogy. Across K–16, teachers tend to use innovative approaches that promote dialogue and community, synthesis, critical thinking, problem posing and problem solving. Collaborative work, projects, and case studies are common and, in undergraduate general education, larger lectures are often combined with smaller workshops and discussion groups. Team teaching is often equated with interdisciplinary teaching, though there is more team planning than actual teaching together. Team teaching not only fosters integrative learning among students, it is a source of intellectual revitalization for teachers. The collaborative curriculum design that occurs in team teaching also promotes a greater sense of community and involvement in decision making.

Interdisciplinarity reconceptualizes the roles of teacher and student alike. Group work is common, involving students in cooperative learning and collaborative problem solving. The traditional teaching functions of telling, delivering, directing, and being a "sage on the stage" are replaced by the role models of mentor, mediator, facilitator, coach, and guide. Teachers in an integrated school, Burns discovered, no longer think of themselves only as subject specialists but also as generalists who organize learning activities around essential questions, themes, or concepts. Their subject areas become sources of knowledge and skills applied to larger purposes. They become "experts" at making connections, a vision that Clarke and Agne extend to high school and William Newell to college.

When instruction becomes more integrative, it also becomes constructivist. K–12 authors Burns and Agne and Clarke ground the theory of integrated learning in a constructivist view of how learners make meaning. The constructivist approach emphasizes active involvement, exploration, and higher-level thinking skills of reflection. Students are engaged in the actual *doing* of a subject or discipline. They also grapple with the cognitive conflict that occurs when working with alternative perspectives. For that reason, project work is common in K–12. In fact, Ellis and Stuen identify projects and theme-based units as the two major approaches to interdisciplinary curriculum. The project approach is linked historically to the Progressivists, who emphasized questions and "real-life" theme-oriented projects. In the 1950s, it was reinvigorated in the work of Jean Piaget. In recent years, the project approach has gained new momentum because of heightened interest in problem-solving and decision-making skills and, from a theoretical standpoint, widening use of constructivist pedagogy (1998, 59–61, 64).

As these examples suggest, innovative pedagogies are complementary. Burns considers innovative pedagogies a major factor in the current resurgence of interest in integration in secondary schools. In addition to constructivist learning, interdisciplinarity complements inquiry- and discovery-based learning. All of these approaches emphasize thinking skills, not just mastery of facts. By engaging students in the actual *doing* of a subject or discipline, the inquiry approach heightens learning and retention through posing of questions and gathering of knowledge and information. The search for meaning becomes active, not passive. Moreover, inquiry-based learning is often conducted in an interdisciplinary manner. A new book, *Innovations in Interdisciplinary Teaching* (Haynes 2002), explores further correspondences with collaborative learning and learning communities, feminist pedagogy and multicultural pedagogy, team teaching, writing-intensive teaching, inquiry-based and performance-based teaching and learning. Interdisciplinarity also intersects with new thinking about advising, assessment, technology, lifelong learning, and study abroad.

Skills

As the discussion of pedagogy suggests, process and skills are inextricably linked. Once again, basic definitions furnish valuable clues to the meaning of learning across the continuum. In Clarke and Agne's vision of the emergent interdisciplinary high school curricula, the fundamental learning actions are asking questions and constructing answers. In K–12 curriculum integration, James Beane identifies the critical skills of reflective thinking, critical ethics, problem solving, valuing, self-concepting and self-esteem, and searching for completeness and meaning. In college, Newell links integrative study with exploration and question posing, active-experiential learning, decision making and problem solving, comparing and contrasting different perspectives and synthesizing them. To reiterate, these skills are not unique to interdisciplinary teaching and learning. Inquiry- and discovery-based learning develop comparable skills. However, they are central to integrative thinking.

In keeping with the interrogative character of interdisciplinary learning, questioning plays an important role. From a conceptual standpoint, essential questions are powerful themes. They are "essential" because they focus on the meaning, value, and purpose of life. "If the questions are large," Clarke and Agne explain, "the sources will have to be interdisciplinary" (1997, 9). Questions are also organizational devices for teaching relational thinking. Heidi Jacobs describes essential questions as the "connectors" for integration. In K–12, the pedagogical tools of curriculum wheels, webs, and concept maps are graphic devices for organizing ideas, activities, and subjects. A question or a theme, topic, problem, or concept is placed at the center in a brainstorming exercise. Then, connections across disciplinary spokes and lines can be identified and focused on the task at hand.

Interdisciplinary teaching also promotes higher-level critical thinking. Making meaning from diverse and conflicting sources is a higher-level challenge. It is a questioning process, not a simple transmission of codified bodies of knowledge.

The key skills that Clarke and Agne identified in high school models are grappling with uncertainty, working with multiple criteria, and arriving at nuanced judgments and interpretations. Students in college, Newell adds, go beyond logical skills to become critically reflexive about the nature of disciplines and themselves. They develop the capacity to locate and work with pertinent information, to compare and contrast different methods and approaches, to clarify how differences and similarities relate to a task, and to create an integrative framework and a more holistic understanding of a theme, question, or problem.

Using This Book

This book spans past, present, and future. Part I (Chapters 1-4) explores current issues in K–12 and Part II (Chapters 5-7) in college. The topics include course and program design, team teaching, integrative process, pedagogy, assessment, administration, and teaching with technology. I preface each chapter with an introduction that situates the author's earlier work in the field in relation to this project. The actual chapter begins with the author's reflection on what has happened in the intervening years. This unique bridging of past and present provides rare insight into how interdisciplinary education has evolved from the standpoint of individuals at the forefront of change. The authors' "Recommended Readings" close each chapter. Part III (Chapter 8 and the Epilogue) looks toward the future and the prospect of K–16 dialogue. Chapter 8 is the first comparative discussion of interdisciplinary assessment in K–12 and college. The Epilogue presents five imperatives for a dialogue. The book ends with a "Beginning Library" for individuals, schools, and colleges, followed by a composite list of references for all chapters.

The book may be used in several ways. Individuals can read it to become familiar with the nature of interdisciplinary education. In school or college workshops and teacher training sessions, groups can read individual chapters or parts to acquire a common vocabulary and understanding of the subject, as well as practical ideas and guidelines for curriculum design and delivery. Along with the Fiscella and Kimmel bibliography, this volume also gives schools, colleges, and libraries a standard reference set. Without a basic foundation, valuable time is lost searching for materials and struggling with questions that are already answered in the literature. In addition to its primary purpose—to inform and support curriculum change—this volume can be used as a textbook in education courses. Researchers interested in the concepts of interdisciplinarity and integration will also benefit from the account of current issues and models. And, finally, it can inform K–16 initiatives in local communities, regional networks, and national professional organizations.

As recently as 1991, Nathalie Gehrke commented that integrative curriculum is like the weather: "Everyone talks about it, but no one ever does anything about it—or almost no one" (107; in ASCD, 125). This is no longer the case. Moreover, the current resurgence of interest has heightened awareness of interdisciplinarity and curriculum integration. This is not the first time that interest has run high, and obstacles to implementation continue. What has changed, however, is the existence of a large body of resources, strategies, and wisdom gained from practice. The challenge now is to put the lessons that have been learned to wider use both within and across K–16.

Part I

Current Issues in K–12

1

Introduction to *Integrated Curriculum Design*

In 1988, a poll conducted by the Association for Supervision and Curriculum Development (ASCD) suggested that curriculum integration was the number one issue among educators. ASCD's national polling panel was composed of a sample of the organization's members, invited guests, state school officers, and deans of schools of education. They offered several reasons for the level of interest in integration. The knowledge explosion was high on the list, along with fragmented class schedules, the need to make connections between school and students' lives, and new demands for workers skilled at dealing with multiple forms of knowledge. The following year, ASCD published a book intended to help K–12 educators understand and respond to this changing educational environment.

The book, *Interdisciplinary Curriculum: Design and Implementation* (1989), became a defining work. Edited by Heidi Hayes Jacobs, it contained essays on design options, basic terminology, criteria for integration, and guidelines for developing units, selecting themes, and integrating thinking and learning skills. In an early chapter on "Design Options for an Integrated Curriculum," Jacobs laid out a continuum of design models that ranged from no integration ("discipline-based") to alignment of disciplines ("parallel" and "multidisciplinary") to fully integrated formats ("interdisciplinary" units and courses, an "integrated day," and a "complete program"). There is no right or wrong choice, she emphasized. She weighed the advantages and disadvantages of each option, and illustrated how they might even be combined in revised schedules for elementary, middle, and high schools. Not everyone may be ready for greater degrees of integration, she cautioned. In some schools, an incremental approach may be more appropriate, starting with "parallel" and "complementary" models.

Since the ASCD book, Jacobs has continued to work with K–12 educators. She still advocates a choice of models, not a single approach. In recent years, however, the context of practice has changed. In Chapter 1, Jacobs describes the new context. Planners today, she notes, have three major choices of content design: discipline-based, interdisciplinary, and student-centered. Each content source, in turn, can be shaped into focus areas centered on topics, issues, problems, works, themes, or events. The meaning of "integration" has changed as well. In interdisciplinary contexts, it no longer refers primarily to fusing subject matter from two or more disciplines. It now encompasses content, skills, and assessment. Jacobs provides a checklist of questions for evaluating how well the three elements are integrated in design models. The determining factor is what best serves the learner. The conversation about assessment has changed too, a shift evident in the immense variety of tangible products and performances that are being used across K–16. Neither the stages of learning characteristics that Jacobs presents nor the rosters of assessment tools are rigid prescriptions. They are guidelines for improved practice. A clear picture of options, Jacobs urged in 1989 and reiterates today, facilitates informed discussion of what is possible in a particular school. The option of interdisciplinarity, she proposes, is no longer unusual; interdisciplinary courses are no longer special events. In the new context of practice, they should be viewed as a "normal" consideration in the planning process and a common curricular experience.

Integrated Curriculum Design

Heidi Hayes Jacobs

Ten years ago, the curriculum battlefield featured a tug-of-war over the territory of content. Polarized into ideological camps, teachers were pitted against one another: the discipline-based purists versus the interdisciplinary libertarians. Given the entrenched nature of discipline-field based specialists and schedules in our schools, the discipline-field squadron appeared to be winning the battle. I wanted to encourage interdisciplinary work as a legitimate option. But when educators argued for interdisciplinarity as an inherently better approach to learning, the polarization only continued. My goal in the 1989 ASCD book was to move teachers beyond an either/or proposition of viewing disciplines versus interdisciplinary work and to consider a range of options. Indeed, the very existence of a battle was the core problem. An interdisciplinary curriculum could be viewed as an ordinary choice, not a contentious one. I wrote to eliminate the battle and have moved over the past 10 years to a design view of curriculum making.

A flexible array of design options is the basis for composition in a range of fields: architecture, engineering, physics, literature, and music. Effective results emerge when the designer manipulates elements, producing a plan that fulfills the specific needs of the target population. The same premise holds true in instructional planning. Curriculum integration has taken on a more dynamic definition than it had 10 or 25 years ago when I first began studying its application. This dynamism has emerged in several ways. Interdisciplinary work is no longer primarily about content. Skills and assessment are two other elements requiring equal attention for thoughtful integration across fields of knowledge.

Given that the majority of standards developed by state education departments declare a need for cross-disciplinary linkages, connections in skills, assessment, and content are being emphasized. As a result, interdisciplinary courses are no longer the novelties they were 10 or 20 years ago. The work in curriculum design now should be on integration. An integrated curriculum is a coherent match among the key elements of content, skills, and assessment meeting the needs of a specific group of learners.

Curriculum Integration

Curriculum integration should be planned over time with a thoughtful eye to changes in the learner's development. Although educators have been keenly aware of the work of Piaget and other developmentalists, there is often a curious gap between what we know about how children learn and the integration of this knowledge with the three basic curriculum design elements. There should be a direct correspondence between the needs of the student and the design of the curriculum at each stage of development. Working for the past decade on K–12 curriculum mapping has been the impetus for looking at curriculum through a developmental lens. Looking to the next decade, it is exciting to consider how new knowledge, new technology, and new forums will expand the curriculum design dynamic. In our classrooms today are future designers: architects, engineers, composers, and curriculum planners.

A curriculum is a design genre. As an architect examines many elements while drawing the blueprint that leads to the construction of a new building, the curriculum planner must weigh many choices while designing the plan that leads to the construction of student learning. The architect takes into account the purpose of the building, the existing foundation, the available materials, and budgetary realities. Aesthetics and style are key. Zoning laws and standards must be met. But ultimately, the architect must consider the most important question of all: Who will the building serve? What are the constituents' needs? What are their characteristics? What are their patterns of use? Only with informed answers to these questions can the architect can pull together the elements of building design and make the best choices for a coherent lasting outcome.

In the same spirit of design, the curriculum writer should consider the available resources, restrictions, and possibilities of building on an existing foundation. In order for a curriculum to achieve the best results, it should be targeted to the precise needs and characteristics of a specific constituency in a specific setting. A curriculum design based on integration is more than a simple fusion of two disciplines. It is a deliberate attempt to integrate specific data about the nature and needs of the learners in the initial phases of curriculum design. Unfortunately, a conspicuous lack of attention to developmental characteristics of the specific learners involved is curiously apparent in the planning of many curriculum projects. Historically, interdisciplinary projects and syllabi have focused on subject matter. Today, the curriculum designer can incorporate a century of data regarding how learners learn at different levels in their journey through schooling. These data assist the designer in making discriminating choices of elements for the curriculum composition.

Let us return to our architect. When planning a building, the architect directs his or her attention to the choice and melding of critical elements: choice of materials, size, and shape; number of floors, entryways, and passageways; an architectural style that not only suits the building's purpose but works with the surrounding landscape. And then, in order to make intelligent decisions about each of these elements, the architect must also consider the characteristics of the users of the future building in relation to each element too.

The curriculum designer also must consider critical elements in the planning of future learning: content, skills, and assessment. The successful selection and integration of these elements produce desired results in our learners. Rather than singling out interdisciplinary curriculum design, the contention here is that learners are better served when interdisciplinary curriculum is viewed as one option on the designer's palette. The planning process should start with the learner's needs, followed by the selection of design elements integrated to serve the learner.

This chapter examines the choice of content, skills, and assessment in light of developmental characteristics of the learner from kindergarten through college. A case is made for this choice supported by numerous examples from the field. The ultimate purpose is to help curriculum planners in any educational setting design their blueprints for learning. Therefore, interdisciplinarity should be viewed as a "normal" consideration in the planning process rather than an unusual one. Interdisciplinary courses should not be viewed as special events, but rather as common curricular experiences.

The chapter is organized in two parts: first, a section that clarifies the nature of curriculum design elements and discusses the role standards play in curriculum integration; and, second, an extension of each developmental stage with corresponding curriculum guidelines to assist designers as they provide integrative learning experiences.

1. Integrating Curriculum Design Elements

There are three fundamental design elements in the development of curriculum, each of which offers an enormous menu of choices. Our architect wrestles with decisions that may seem overwhelming; there are so many materials and styles to consider before homing in on the appropriate choice. Similarly, creative curriculum designers wrestle with complex and subtle choices when laying out initial sketches for the future curriculum plan. The basic design elements of content, skills, and assessment may be considered in any order. A planner might begin with skills or assessment, or perhaps all three elements are crystallized at once. When the design is complete, however, there must be coherence among the three elements. The first to be reviewed here is content.

The Element of Content

Content is the element that determines the subject matter to be parlayed by the learner. Matter is the operative word. Content can be presented in a range of forms but it cannot be exhaustive for there is a limit to the "matter" and it should matter. On the most fundamental level the element of content can be configured by discipline, by interdisciplinary linkages, or derived directly from learner interest. All of these sources of content can be viable options for the designer. No one choice is intrinsically better than the others, any more than any one style is better for our architect. This central design issue is selecting the option that will best serve the purpose for the learner.

A discipline-based choice suggests that the learner will examine subject matter predicated on a specific field of knowledge. As Lawton (1975) points out, a discipline is characterized by a distinctive set of problem-solving strategies, terminology, and practitioners. In school life we institutionalize the disciplines into scheduled instructional times of day such as Math, Science, Art, and English. A discipline has potential value for the learner when there is design integrity; that is, when the dynamic qualities of the discipline are integrated into the curriculum. This means the student becomes a practitioner of the field utilizing specialized problem-solving strategies and terminology. For example, rather than simply studying history, the student employs the strategies and vernacular of the historian. When this kind of design integration is planned the implications for the learner are significant because the other elements of design are immediately affected. The skills of the historian are taught, such as artifact analysis and primary source research. The resulting assessments are the products and performances rendered by historians, such as histories.

When an interdisciplinary format is chosen for content formation, the designer brings together two or more disciplines in a deliberate fusion of content. There is a flotilla of terms for this format floating through the pages of curriculum journals and guides in part because educators have discovered some genuinely subtle and intriguing variations on the approach. The number of prefixes can be mind-boggling: transdisciplinary, omnidisciplinary, cross-disciplinary, interdisciplinary, and multidisciplinary. The most crucial and obvious point to note is that all of the terms come with the root word discipline. For the purposes of this chapter, an operational definition is proposed based on the realities of school programs that directly impact the potential of speculative epistemologies.

Educators may debate the merits of various philosophies of knowledge, but in reality they are most frequently influenced by the school's schedule and the way departments are organized. The designer is taking a perspective and knowledge from specific disciplines and fusing them to provide insight and power in the examination of the subject matter. Eventually the designer might choose full integration, completely dissolving subject area boundaries as Beane (1995) advocates. In his view subjects, serving as tools, can be brought into instruction as needed. On the other hand, the designer might elect to maintain a parallel design with the concurrent teaching of mutually compatible subjects.

In each instance there are differences between the interdisciplinary terms that potentially can affect learning outcomes. What is most critical is that the designer selects the format for presenting the subject matter that best suits the conceptual aims for the learner. In other words, if the goal is to gain understanding about a work of literature then it makes infinitely good sense to present the book as the student examines the historical context of the author or the setting within the story. When the English and social studies teachers collaborate they are designing a multidisciplinary unit. If a third-grade teacher introducing the concept of "life cycles" in natural science elects to bring in social studies, mathematics, and the arts, then the designer feels that a fully interdisciplinary unit of study is the appropriate choice. There can also be power in the collaboration when college professor in biology and a colleague teaching ethics develop a seminar on the Ethics of Genetic Engineering.

This picture of options marks another change. The battle zone between discipline-field based curriculum and interdisciplinary has been erased. The adage that the "pendulum swings" from one pole to the other in educational history is tiresome and dated. Certainly the polarization between interdisciplinary and disciplinary has been real enough in the past. Whether it was the Herbartians in 1890s versus the Committee of Fifteen, or Dewey's Experimental School versus the Classicists, or the open classroom versus the closed classroom, debate has tended to split fiercely into ideological camps. Evolving steadily has been a more sophisticated and dynamic approach to curriculum reform based on a range of design configurations (Jacobs 1989; Fogarty 1991). A continuum of options is available to today's designer.

When the source of content is derived from the individual learner's interests, then the subject matter is constructed by the student based on intrinsic need. The difference between this design option and the others is that the starting point does not come from a field of knowledge or from the fusion of fields.

The starting point for the content is the child. This approach has a philosophical root in Rousseau's *Emile*, written in the 1800s. That is not to say discipline-based or interdisciplinary content should not be geared toward the child, for certainly student engagement would be the shared goal. Rather the student-centered content option is based on a specific problem or issue coming directly from the learner. This approach is most common in the United States in early-childhood classes and in certain private schools and public charter schools committed to this philosophy. In high schools, curriculum integration around student-selected work appears most frequently in senior independent-study projects (Jacobs 1997). An offshoot of student-centered work, the field experience model, is common in specialized junior and senior courses in undergraduate colleges. Usually these are part of off-campus programs in which students learn from their interactions in the new milieu. Here the curriculum content is predicated on integrating the curriculum experiences in a specific environment.

Each of the three content sources can be shaped into different types of focus areas:

Topics are basic areas of investigation, akin to listings in a text or an encyclopedia (Ancient Rome, Insects, DNA);

Issues are irresolvable points of controversy facing society or individuals. If they could be resolved they would not be issues. (Euthanasia, Abortion);

Problems are hypotheses to be tested or pivotal points of investigation requiring solutions (How can we design a solar collector to run our school?);

Works are specific works of literature, art, or objects that can be used as vehicles for content exploration (*Hamlet*, the Chrysler Building, the *Titanic*);

Themes are broad-based concepts that are used to link a range of disciplines (Patterns, Conflict);

Events are critical turning points and occurrences that have had long-term impact (the Holocaust, the Renaissance).

Successful integration of curriculum content requires the selection of both a configuration of the content and a type of presentation that will best suit the learner. It may be that working within the focused and purposeful lens of the disciplines in a science class makes the most sense in enabling the learner. The curriculum designer then might choose to focus the course unit on a topic, such as Genetics; or an issue, the Ethics of Genetic Engineering; or a problem, How to Design a Bird Feeder for our First-Grade Playground; or a theme, Flight. These are as real and noticeable design choices as the architect's decision to change from a modern style to French Provincial.

The task of determining content can be daunting because there is so much "matter" to deal with. Rather than attempting to cover the total content, teachers can frame the curriculum around a set of essential questions. This is a promising strategy because coverage is a "no win" type of planning style. Wiggins (1989) wrote a provocative article entitled "The Futility of Trying to Teach Everything of Importance," which suggested the fruitlessness and frustration of coverage. Focusing and connecting content through essential questions is a useful solution to the dilemma. Most state syllabi are vastly overwritten, creating problems for teachers who feel rushed and pressured to present all the material. The alternative is to reshape curriculum around a set of concepts that are the most critical for learners. This allows students to focus their work and projects on essential concepts, factual knowledge, and skills (Jacobs 1997). Whether explicitly or covertly, every time a teacher begins instruction, he or she is choosing the focus of content. The critical issue is whether the choice is essential or nonessential to the learner. A state may issue curriculum guides recommending concepts to be highlighted, but there is no guarantee that the teacher will adhere or should adhere to the focus. In practice, the effectiveness of essential questions will depend on the individual instructor and his or her relationship with the learners.

The use of essential questions is a central feature of integration. It is of particular importance when the designer elects an interdisciplinary approach so that the student will have a coherent experience rather than a potpourri of assorted activities. For example, English, science, and social studies teachers might work together on an interdisciplinary unit called Ancient Egypt. They could ask their students to investigate the following questions: Why did Egypt come to power? What were major contributions of the Egyptians? What was their legacy to subsequent civilizations? Students will gather knowledge and insight into the essential questions utilizing the disciplines involved and the work that emerges in the explorations of the questions.

The essential questions become the connectors. They maintain an integrated focus for all classroom activity regardless of the class or type of content choice. Essential questions also serve to unify and revitalize the curriculum experience for the designer. There is a sense of ownership and choice rather than a manic sense of trying "to cover Ancient Egypt," which would obviously require more than the allotted six weeks.

The Element of Skills

A skill is always a verb. It is a learning action. The element of skills will be defined here as the designated techniques and processes the learner is expected to employ when engaged in educational activity. Skills can be discussed in isolation but in practice they are always applied to some kind of content. In other words, if a student is engaged in a discrete composition skill, such as writing the opening sentence to an essay, then the skill has to be about something. But this is not simply stating the obvious, for the nature of the "something" has everything to do with the nature of the skill. Here are some factors about different types of skills a planner might consider when composing an integrated curriculum plan:

Some skills are clearly discipline-based. Solving an algebraic equation, for instance, or computing long division of two-digit integers are actions that are carried out in the field of mathematics. As noted earlier—and the point is a powerful one—in such cases curriculum planners will want to maintain the integrity of the disciplines. In this way, the specific skills of the historian can be underscored, or the skills of the professional journalist or the skills of the mathematician.

Some skills are cross-disciplinary and do not reside within the domain of a given field. An example here is analyzing cause-and-effect relationships. Cross-disciplinary skills deal with a range of areas such as reading, researching, organizing, and technological data gathering. These skills would be present in the science class, art studio, and journalism seminar. They are present throughout the day of the kindergarten child and the graduate student.

Some skills—such as analysis, synthesis, problem solving, brainstorming, conjecturing, and comprehending—are presented in the form of abstractions. These skills are usually cross-disciplinary and are difficult to perceive without a context for application. In short, people don't go around "analyzing all day"; they have to be analyzing in a specific context. A third grader might examine the course of change in a plant's growth while an eighth grader might present his or her view on the inevitability of World War II.

Some skills—such as interviewing, listing, categorizing, and paraphrasing—are presented as more concrete techniques linked to an observable action. In each of these instances there is a clear and precise link to a contextual outcome with the product or performance embedded. For example, an interview requires a specific individual or group of people to practice the skill with intent. When a junior interviews five employers about the qualities they consider necessary in potential employees, the result will be observed in the actual dialogue and in a transcript of the interview.

Some skills—such as learning skills, reading, writing, and researching—are presented in a generic format with broad-based meaning. These skills are simply too large in scope to allow for incremental skill development of the individual learner. The following discussion details this critical problem.

The difficulty with broad generic skills is that when applied to classroom work they can become so broad as to defy instruction. One might just as well say someone is working on living skills or breathing skills. A hazardous practice in curriculum integration is the overgeneralization of skills because they are so difficult to assess when they are so large in their range. The converse practice of precision skill development creates more dynamic learning. Two areas that are particularly effective at this kind of specific and precise skill articulation are athletics and the arts. One would never hear basketball coaches request that the learners in their charge work on "playing" skills. Rather, there are highly specific and technical skills to be addressed. "Today, team, we're working on driving to the basket and making a lay-up"; "Today we're going to shoot three-point perimeter shots"; or, "Today we're going to work on making assists and passing" are far more likely commands. These skills are specific and technical and can be assessed. Increased performance and acumen can be observed. The "content" for applying these skills will ultimately be games against different teams in which the assessment process can be elaborated further.

In the arts, reliance on specific skills and techniques is the hallmark of learning. Whether it is a music teacher who drills a piano student on the techniques of employing pacing and staccato in a passage of Mozart, or the drama coach who asks actors to modulate inflection in *Hamlet*, the key to proficiency in both the arts and athletics is their emphasis on the specific skill.

Of great importance in both fields is the notion that each skill can be directed toward increased proficiency through three tiers:

- drill and practice
- rehearsal and scrimmage
- authentic performance skills

All of these tiers are interrelated and all are critical, but it is noteworthy that in the arts and athletics students work on precise skills that ultimately transfer to an increasing larger context. This movement is exemplified when the piano student moves from the drill of the staccato to the rehearsal session and then to the live uninterrupted recital; the student progresses in the application of the technique.

The case for precision skill work is of great concern when designing interdisciplinary curricula. Because interdisciplinary negotiations often entail meetings between departments, content often becomes the focus of discussion. Planners should be vigilant and dig deep into discussions about the shared processes and skills students will need to employ. Frequently, teachers talk with genuine frustration about how their students "need skills." Their frustration stems in part from the imprecision of skills instruction in academic areas over the course of time. Integration of curriculum requires the integration of appropriate techniques taught through the vehicle of powerfully formatted content. Educators face the constant dilemma of determining which specific skill to work on given the myriad possibilities. Perhaps the key is our final element, assessment, because it is through the performance that the coach determines whether the requisite skill has been achieved and the degree to which more sophisticated techniques can evolve.

The Element of Assessment and the Role of Standards

Assessment is evidence. Assessment is a demonstration of learning. A student's performance is the basis for examining the quality and nature of learning. The only way to know that a student has accomplished or learned to develop a skill is through a product or performance. In the past, the common view of assessment was restricted to a primary emphasis on standardized testing. Over the past few years educational institutions ranging from state governments to local agencies, business circles, and other societal groups have recognized that more comprehensive assessment is needed than standardized tests can provide.

The curriculum designer can conceive of assessment on the most fundamental level as two types of evidence. The first type is a tangible product. These are permanent in nature and can be held, manipulated, and examined. Whether a product is a piece of writing, a sculpture, a painting, a model, a spreadsheet, a blueprint, a puppet, or a replica, it demonstrates student skill and insight. The second type of assessment is a performance. These are temporal in nature. A dance, an athletic event, a debate, an oral presentation, and a play are all examples of a performed outcome that can be observed. It is critical to note that the teacher and the learner have an opportunity to monitor, revise, and improve the specific skills evidenced in the performance and/or product. Just as the skill is always a verb, the assessment is always a noun. Teachers can only know if their students are learning by what those learners say, write, draw, and produce . . . certainly not by what the teacher "covers." Dynamic assessment is the cornerstone of interdisciplinary design.

A central concern in the past has been the integration of assessment and curriculum. Previously, educators had a tendency to view assessment as an afterthought. Teachers would present courses of study, cover the curriculum, and then give thought to a test of some kind to look back on the process. The newer look on assessment is quite different. Instruction and curriculum planning begin with the assessment in mind. Assessment is part of the curriculum. A teacher might say to the student: "As a result of our interdisciplinary experience in our interdisciplinary course study on the nature of the immigrant experience, you're going to be able to produce a position paper, examine points of view, and conduct extensive research. You will interview a range of people and use a CD-ROM to produce this position paper which will not only give insight into the changing nature of immigration over this century but also demonstrate your ability to carry out these skills." Students realize that the beginning point is the assessment, because they know that the paper will ultimately be evidence of conceptual insight, interdisciplinary linkages, knowledge of key facts, and technical skills addressed in the course of study.

With younger children, the same holds true. If a teacher asks first-grade students to produce a story so that they can become cogent and creative writers, ultimately that will be the goal. The teacher will explain that they will study what makes a good story—the choice of words, a logical sequence, and exciting and vivid imagery. The students realize that the reason they are studying these factors is to help them produce the story. Assessment gives meaning and voice to the curriculum and integrates the purpose of the learning. It explains to learners why they are doing what they are doing. In interdisciplinary programs, there also needs to be direct and palpable evidence of cross-disciplinary connections produced by learners in the work. If they cannot demonstrate these connections then it is difficult to justify the development of interdisciplinary programs.

The links among assessment, skills, and content are clear. Through the curriculum, teachers are asking learners to produce tangible products or observed performances that reveal skill development and content understanding. Each of the elements can be discussed and unpacked, but it is the effective integration of the elements that creates lasting learning. If one of the elements is "mismatched" with the others there will be problems in the curriculum design. Coherent design is achieved when the following questions can be answered in the affirmative:

- Is the content format (discipline-field-based, interdisciplinary, student-centered) best suited to the core concepts? *Should the math teacher work within the field of math or collaborate with science? Is it time for our fifth-grade teachers to design an independent project based on their students' interests?*
- Does the content type (topic, issue, work, problem, theme, event) best serve purposes of the curriculum? *Should my students focus on the Civil War as a topic or on the issue: Is the Civil War Still Going On?*
- Are the content concepts and factual data base framed around essential questions? *Is the second-grade study of oceans an assorted cluster of random activities or is it focused on investigating a set of essential questions?*
- Are the targeted skills precise? *Are students interviewing to understand point of view or interviewing to develop speaking skills?*
- Do the skills serve the investigation of the essential questions? *What are the regional differences in France? Do the specific research, listening, reading, and speaking skills learned in French class help answer the essential question?*

- Do the choices of assessment products and performances provide authentic evidence of the targeted skill? *If we are assessing taking a stand to affect others, would an appropriate product be a letter to a newspaper editor?*
- Do the choices of assessment products and performances provide authentic evidence of conceptual insight and knowledge of the essential questions? *If we are trying to ascertain student understanding of the question, "What was the legacy of the Ancient Greeks?," would a model of the Parthenon be a sufficient product, or do we need written or oral work in which the student describes present-day evidence of Greek architecture?*

The standards to be met by the learner are a critical influence on assessment choices. If we return to our architectural analogy there is one other external force that holds the designer and the overall design accountable: standards. In every community there are building codes that must be met and are used as a kind of point-counterpoint to any design. Generally, these codes provide some latitude on the specifics of a design but they also set a level of quality assurance for anyone using the finished building.

In contemporary education in the United States, standards exist on the national level and are emerging on state and local levels at a rapid pace. Almost without exception these standards are based on student performance. On the national level professional organizations such as NCTM (National Council of Teachers of Mathematics 1989) or the Geography Education Standards Project (1994) have created sets of standards to guide teachers and assess students. Of particular interest here is the fact that the majority of standards have explicitly declared the need for interdisciplinary or integrated curricula. Science standards require applications of principles integrated in real-world contexts; some states have standards written in an integrative format. For example, New York State's Math, Science, and Technology benchmarks are written as one set of standards. I do not know of one state that does not promote English, Language Arts, reading, writing, speaking, and listening across the disciplines.

Each state has been grappling with and/or producing sets of standards all public schools in that state must meet. The standards—seen as a monitoring device measuring the quality of public education—are written in the form of benchmarks at developmental levels. Students at the elementary, intermediate, and commencement levels will need to demonstrate their competency by performing specific tasks in the area of writing skills across disciplines with resulting assessments. These assessments will be examined to see if they meet a specified level of quality on a writing rubric. There is a great deal of room for individual teachers and local school districts to create curriculum and design instruction to help their learners achieve the standards. In this way the analogy to architecture holds true. There is no one best architectural style or blueprint, but all designs must meet the standards.

When standards are well written they can inspire educators to revise and improve their existing curriculum. Many schools have been expanding their design options to include interdisciplinary work because of new standards, and given the emphasis on quality assessment, the results are often rigorous. When working with teachers on the design of curriculum, a practical use of standards is to consider them as editorial criteria. This is in keeping with the way that publishing houses ask potential writers to review their manuscripts. The standards are the basis of checking whether there is a level of quality in a book that the publisher elects to produce. In the past there has been a sense of bureaucratic inundation in public education, but the new work on standards has a refreshing combination of oversight and flexibility. Interdisciplinary connections are evident in many of the assessment tasks used to determine whether a standard has been met. A physics student might be asked to plan a bridge to an actual setting and must consider social values, environmental concerns, and budgetary interests. A fourth grader might write and essay explaining supply and demand in a specific area of the world.

Standards represent an agreement by professionals and the community about what learning outcomes are critical for children. The curriculum is the plan to enable children to reach those outcomes through the investigation and assimilation of content, the exercise and development of skills, and the resulting product and performance assessments. Integration of these choices lies at the heart of powerful design. Within each element of curriculum design are specific and subtle distinctions that can create a dynamic and meaningful learning experience in school. The integration of curriculum is the effective fusion of all three elements by the designer to meet the needs of learners in a specific setting addressing designated standards of excellence. Poor or inappropriate choices will correspondingly generate robotic, dreary, and lifeless classrooms. To return to the initial analogy of this chapter, we have all walked into bland, depressing, and boring buildings. Like our architect, the builder of curriculum creates a model that is most useful when it is most effectively designed.

2. Integrating a Developmental Perspective in Curriculum Design

Designing is making choices. It is weaving together selected and compatible elements. When a design is to serve a practical purpose—as curriculum design must do—it is incumbent upon the planner to take into account the most salient information about the design's eventual consumer. Among the most fundamental factors that should influence instructional choices are the age and stage of the learners. When the developmental perspective is neglected in curriculum design, the resulting plan may be a poor match for the learning constituency. Of particular concern is a lack of developmental planning in interdisciplinary work. Perhaps because the opportunity to expand on content choices is so liberating, it is easy to neglect developmental considerations.

Certainly there is abundant reference in educational circles to developmental thinking since the early writings of Piaget. Yet a problem keeps emerging in practice. Extensive fieldwork in curriculum mapping K–12 (Jacobs 1997) indicates a lack of consistent focused developmental design in each of the three elements: content, skills, and assessment. In other words, a unit or course of study may have a coherent mix of content, skills, and assessment, but the design does not reflect the basic characteristics of the learner. The architectural equivalent of this problem would be a beautifully designed building that does not meet the needs of the users. Recently I landed at a newly built airport in a major city in the United States. The terminal was aesthetically striking with modern and exciting features, but unfortunately it was one long—very long—walkway. It took about 45 minutes to walk the length of the terminal, creating the very real possibility that one might miss a connecting flight. The human species generally does not walk this far burdened with carry-on luggage. I concluded that it was designed for the Olympic track team.

This section of the chapter suggests curriculum design options to match the characteristics and developmental stages of learners in schools. These characteristics are drawn from a range of sources in the developmental literature: Piaget (1932), Kohlberg (1981), Selman (1980), Gilligan (1982), and Lickona (1983). Stage theorists have based and continue to base their suppositions about how human beings learn on extensive cross-cultural observations. Although the approach has been criticized as potentially being too linear, most educators find they can remain sensitive to individual progress while still relying on stage theory as a realistic and helpful teaching tool. At each developmental stage the three elements of curriculum design will be revisited with recommendations for the curriculum designer and with a particular eye to interdisciplinary connections. Developmental assessments for each stage (Jacobs 1997) are articulated in this section, but content and skills are not ignored.

The goal is to clarify and refine design practice in order to integrate the learner fully into the choices the designer makes. The guidelines are in four developmental clusters, grouping learners to correspond to the realities of most school programs. This is a practical choice. It should be stated that these categories are not "hard and fast" and could easily be adjusted to reflect the nature of a specific institution. Each of the developmental clusters will be viewed in light of the curriculum designer's optimum choices for the three elements of content, skills, and assessment. Interdisciplinary connections will be highlighted in the discussion.

Integrated Curriculum Design Responses to the Early Childhood Learner: Grades K–2

The Learner: Cognitive level is concrete operations; sensory-motor modalities dominate; student is egocentric; parallel play still dominates with the beginning signs of social interaction with peers; there is a strong need for primary affiliation with a key adult at school and parental surrogates; student is willing to experiment and take risks; verbal skills are generally more pronounced in girls; spatial-motor skills are generally more pronounced in boys; there are evident disparities between various areas of development as in fine/gross motor differences; uneven development in reading, writing, and speaking skills emerges at this level with the learner's fascination with sound-symbol relations.

Content: All three content formats have application at this level. Given the self-centered nature of the learner, student-centered content driven by the interests of the learners has particular resonance here. Young learners bring in the results of their personal investigations in the world as fodder in the classroom. Whether the content is based on disciplines or is interdisciplinary, the topics, themes, issues, problems, works, and events should be concrete in nature; clear and tangible to the child; relevant and immediate in their environment. Rather than selecting the abstract theme of Seasonal Change as an area for study, it is more sensible to study something concrete such as Apple Picking or Leaves in autumn. The selection of content is critical. As adults we sometimes fail to realize that young learners really do take things literally, and if they do not have access to the language, then the content is beyond their grasp. In an interdisciplinary unit on Snow, first-grade teachers in a suburban New York school posed the following essential questions to focus the content: "What is snow?" "How does snow affect people?" The questions are deceptively simple. When answering "What is snow," the first graders will be learning about seasonal change, the snow cycle, and the difference between New York slushy snow and Utah powder snow. It is a significant difference for the learner.

Skills: The great majority of skills the young learner must master are beginnings of a lifelong foundation. There is a pronounced focus on reading, writing, speaking, and listening. These skills are inherently interdisciplinary as children explore all the arenas of their lives. Given their new interest in social interaction, interpersonal learning bounds. It is important to note that there is a raging debate over the best approach for language acquisition, but there can be little question that communication skills are necessary. Precision skills work should be thoughtfully communicated between teachers in the most careful incremental ways possible. The danger in early childhood education is a lack of clarity concerning the types of skills required and when they should be addressed.

Assessment: The following products and performances match the learning characteristics of the early childhood learner:

captions	story boards
labels	story lines
simple research	graphs/charts
interview with key question	joke telling
diorama	
observational drawing	

These examples reflect the concrete and accessible assessment genre that will integrate with the early childhood learners' abilities and interests. It is noteworthy that these are interdisciplinary assessments. The total integration of a cogent content, skill, and assessment choice creates the most coherent learning experience.

Integrated Curriculum Design Responses to the Learner in Latency: Grades 3–5

The Learner: Cognitive operations are moving through concrete functions with early signs of simple abstract thinking; students able to combine several concepts and perceive cause-and-effect relationships; fascination with the world; excellent "reporters" and seekers of interesting information; social skills related strongly to peers and to teachers; enjoy large group projects; social concern for others emerging; physical stability and agility more consistent.

Content: Given their developmental turn toward the world around them, upper elementary children are stimulated by fascinating new topics and bodies of information that can come from the disciplines or from interdisciplinary connections. It is always a pleasant surprise to see a group of fourth graders studying Colonial America and displaying genuine enthusiasm when they make their maps, models, and colonial newspapers. The content in most schools moves toward a more densely packed set of required subject matter, and the key for teachers is to form and reform the concepts and facts into units that will prove engaging. Interdisciplinary work is a natural outgrowth of this age group's interests. Themes and topics that bring students to the natural world or the larger human world are generally well received. Regions of the World, Inventors and Inventions, Local Environmental Issues, and Legends and Folktales are examples of rich and common interdisciplinary units.

Skills: Skills should evolve steadily from the primary grades, always building on the base of fundamentals. Techniques should become increasingly complex. In basketball, an early learner begins with the dribble, and as he or she progresses the skill evolves into more complex dribbling patterns that can be combined with a bounce pass to another teammate. So it is in academic skills as well. The student begins in first grade by writing and recognizing a complete sentence. In the fifth grade that same student should be able to embellish the sentence with prepositional phrases, imagery, and adjectives. The most critical variable is the real and authentic communication between teachers about precisely what skills are addressed and how students are progressing in those skills.

Assessment: The following examples reflect the data-gathering and investigative-reporting nature of the upper elementary learner:

simple research report	extended research report
note cards	interview: question series
short stories	photo essay with text
artifact analysis	comparative observations
newspaper articles	math matrix with two factors

Integrated Curriculum Design Responses to the Early Adolescent: Grades 6–8

The Learner: Labile period of development; surge into formal operations; quest for personal identity; heightened sensitivity to ego; heightened awareness of peers; fascination with issues of fairness, justice, and trust; pronounced surges in physical development; uneven development among peers; self-consciousness about physical presence; concern for others conflicting with concern for self.

Content: This age group thrives when content is cast as issues and problems. This should not be surprising given the characteristics of the most trying period in the growth pattern of childhood into adulthood. For example, a unit in science on DNA and Genetics can be made more engaging by creating an interdisciplinary title: The Ethics of Genetic Engineering. In the humanities a literature study might be focused on finding modern-day classics: Does Any Writer in this Century Match Shakespeare? This age group is naturally predisposed to investigating problems. More conceptual themes work well here too, as in James Beane's provocative curricular focus asking middle school learners to examine themes reflecting their age such as conflict and identity.

Skills: There is a natural movement toward more sophistication in the level of skills. As this age group is moving into more formal operations, students need meta-level skills, a kind of strategic oversight. It is important that they move from immediate tasks to organizational and structuring skills. The many roving inner thoughts of the adolescent need to be focused on communication in all subjects. Consistent and penetrating work on reading, writing, speaking, and listening skills in all subjects requires professional articulation across departments. It can be daunting to formulate these skills, but it is critical that this take place across disciplines. In many ways, the greatest obstacle here is the diversification of staff that commonly occurs during these years. Emphasizing team teaching, the middle school collaborative approach among faculty is of critical importance for this particular age group. The close articulation of cross-disciplinary skills is crucial.

Assessment: The following examples of more advanced genres reflect the early adolescent learner's need to declare personal identity:

persuasive essays	descriptive essays
analytic essays	personal essays
hypothesis testing	issue-based forums
blueprints and models	original plays
museum text/captions	note-taking forms

Integrated Curriculum Design Responses to the Midadolescent and Pre-adult Learner: Grades 9–12

The Learner: Significant differences among ninth and twelfth graders progressing from midadolescent concerns to pre-adult education; formal operations involving abstract concepts; projections; social life focused on smaller groupings and pairings; sexuality an issue; physical maturity rapidly paces; focus on future and next steps.

Content: The obvious change in preparation for adult experience should be a major contributor to the framing and selection of content. High schools that provide students with a perspective on the world in their courses, with an integrated view of practical problems, with a grounded sense of the future of each area they study, will best serve learners. Interdisciplinary courses that provide authentic context for real-world applications do well at this level, such as Global Economics, Media Production, Legal Issues in Science. Discipline-field-based courses should be predicated on the most direct link to real-world problem-solving applications with mentorships and site-based work. Student-centered content should be the hallmark of senior projects and independent studies.

Skills: The root of all skills at this level should be independence in personal work. An example of this independence is the ability to edit and revise any kind of product or performance without the continual intervention of the teacher. There should also be an equal emphasis on the interdependent skills of teamwork and group planning. Both of these will be required in almost every work situation. The level of sophistication should move to more nuanced and subtle skills, from the first-grade complete sentence to the development of a vast array of sentence structures to provide variety while keeping an eye on paragraph transition. Skills for long-range planning and self-monitoring must be built and layered through each year of the high school experience.

Assessment: The following examples reflect the pre-adult learner's independence and long-range planning skills.

position papers	legal briefs
business plans	anthologies
choreography	game book
film and literary criticism	senior project and defense
work-study analysis	factor analysis
interview simulations	case studies
original musical compositions	original product designs

Conclusion: Toward K–16

In the spirit of considering a student's pathway through elementary and secondary institutions, the following postsecondary implications for curriculum design are offered. The intention is to build thoughtfully on the student's previous experience in a more seamless fashion and to provoke discussion among planners as to sensible next steps toward moving from K–12 to K–16.

Integrated Curriculum Design Responses to Pre-Adult and Young Adult Learners: Undergraduate College Students and/or Entry-Level Workers

The Learner: Consistent ability to deal with formal operations and abstract concepts; sorting out conflicts between idealistic expectations and reality of engagement with college or workforce; quest for personal identity frequently has been physicalized by leaving home environment; fears for achieving fulfillment emerging; emotionally trying; social life continuing toward smaller groupings and pairings; physically and sexually maturing; experimentation for testing out personal choices may be occurring; selecting of more refined and focused aspirations possibly creating satisfaction or frustration.

Content: When students leave high school they embark on their personal journey into adulthood. If a student moves directly into the undergraduate environment then a significant change occurs where personal independence now means personal responsibility. The young adult selects courses, relationships, study habits, career directions, and living situations. If the student moves directly into the workforce there will be a similar adjustment to freedom and responsibility. The consequences of the choices made in early adult development can prove lasting. It is critical in undergraduate institutions or job training programs that students be engaged in problem-based content and exposed to more complex essential questions and issues that take advantage of their desire to become independent adult thinkers and doers. Interdisciplinary contexts can provide natural and rigorous opportunities for this engagement.

Skills: The skills to be emphasized are independent problem solving and habits of mind that will bring long-term success in career and personal situations. Long-term planning and small work groups are of great benefit to the entering freshman who comes in often as a stranger to the campus. In the workforce situation, the young adult needs guidance and support to become a more responsible employee. Making decisions, taking stands, analyzing problems in real contexts, and posing solutions are high-powered attributes of the young adult mind.

Assessment: As with the high school learner, the types of assessment should reflect adult and professional-level experience. The young adult should approach projects with increased finesse and detail, taking into account complex variables and applications. Professors should become advocates for their students by assisting in the display of excellent student products and performances and providing opportunities for students to launch their work in the actual career world. By the same token, results that reveal problems should be used diagnostically to assist learners. Our finest professors teach as well as profess. They learn from their students' work and assist them in meeting adult-level expectations. Some assessments include:

policy statements	television scripts
designs for new products	responses to current journal articles
scientific proofs	mathematical proofs
plans to take over a business	internships
on-site residencies	
long-term observations at field sites	

Teachers across K–16 should reflect on the characteristics of learners from the commencement of their journey at the kindergarten door through the sprawl of the college campus. Clearly communication among educational designers about other levels of instruction will help them understand the context from which the learner arrives and to which the learner departs. If we are not informed in our curricular choices about the learner's curricular context, we are working in a vacuum under possibly erroneous assumptions. If interdisciplinary programs are selected for ideological reasons to satisfy a trend or personal preference, then a token program is in the works. Interdisciplinary designs should be chosen when they are the best designs for a specific population to achieve a specific purpose.

There is much to be learned about curriculum development and the preparation of teachers and professors from our architect. When young people enter a professional school of architecture, training will provide the aspiring architects with a range of options and techniques to suit an extensive array of situations. They will be prepared to evaluate each new construction and design viable and engaging plans to meet the needs of those using their buildings. Trained to examine the existing foundation, they will also be sensitized to the adjacent buildings and landscapes in each context. They will study the great and striking buildings in the world crafted by architects who have woven together separate elements of design in their creations. They will learn that no single design is best in all situations. Discussion will be lively as classmates and professors debate the merits of the designs, the architects, and the concepts behind them. Ultimately, discussion will be grounded in reality, for theirs is an applied field of practice. Ideas are proven in concrete contexts.

In our field the master curriculum designer pulls together the elements of content, skills, and assessment, gearing his or her choices directly to the constituency the design is to serve. The existing foundation must be scrupulously examined in order to select the best options. Standards should be utilized to evaluate the quality of the design. In this way integration of elements is matched to the needs of the students at their developmental stage in a coherent and creative plan.

Unlike the work of the architect, the results of the master curriculum designer's efforts are not physically apparent. Yet great and striking structures can occur when thoughtful integration is brought to the curricular blueprint. Interdisciplinary design should be constantly available as a classroom option. It should not be ideologically singled out as inherently better for its own sake. Curriculum planning is served by a riveting look at the consequences of our designs cumulatively across K–16. The outcomes for better or worse are seen in the work and lives of our students long after they leave our classrooms.

Recommended Readings

- Robert Lynn Canady and Michael D. Rettig. 1996. *Teaching in the Block: Strategies for Engaging Active Learners*. Larchmont, N.Y.: Eye on Education. Canady and Rettig provide a thorough research base for their look at different ways to configure curriculum within larger blocks of time. Many interdisciplinary programs have emerged because a scheduling opportunity has arisen in a school setting. Laced with multiple examples, *Teaching in the Block* describes different ways teachers can set up their classrooms and rework their instructional methods to enliven learning. This book is an absolute must for planners wishing to give students maximum benefit from supportive work conditions.

- H. Lynn Erickson. 1998. *Concept-Based Curriculum*. Thousand Oaks, Calif.: Corwin Press. This is one of the most straightforward and focused guides available to help educators write curriculum based on concept building in the field. Erickson assists planners in the nuts and bolts of working with concepts in cross-disciplinary units and courses. She is practical and clear on the different techniques curriculum developers can use when writing programs. The book includes an excellent review of the literature of K–12 integrated approaches to the field.

- Julie Thompson Klein. 1996. *Crossing Boundaries: Knowledge, Disciplinarities, and Interdisciplinarities*. Charlottesville, Va.: University Press of Virginia. A refined and intricate examination of the nature of the disciplines and their relationships pervades this book. Klein sets up an intelligent perspective for an epistemology to guide educators into the next century. There is a rich historical context to Klein's interpretation of why knowledge has been structured in the ways that it has. Organizations attempting to give serious thought to major departmental changes would do well to consider *Crossing Boundaries*. Scholars and graduate students will find this book a staple for their reference materials on epistemology.

- Grant Wiggins. 1998. *Educative Assessment*. San Francisco, Calif.: Jossey-Bass. A provocative and useful set of design templates, guidelines, and tasks are provided to enlarge the curriculum designer's repertoire of choices. Assessment is cast in the most central way as a means to help students learn how to improve their own performance. We are challenged by Wiggins to adjust our own teaching approaches to help learners become self-assessors. This substantive volume is a necessity for all interdisciplinary planners seeking rigor and results. Of particular value are the numerous examples of lessons, assessment plans, and rubrics. *Educative Assessment* is a sensible, stimulating, and powerful book based on our highest aspirations for K–16 learners.

- Hilda Taba. 1962. *Curriculum Development: Theory and Practice*. New York: Harcourt Brace Jovanovich. Professionals in any field should read classic works. In curriculum planning, Taba's *Curriculum Development* is an absolute foundation for aspiring instructional designers. She was a strikingly effective staff developer who wrote eloquently and practically for teachers. She asks us to simultaneously take into account how the mind processes information and the context for active curricular response. A stage theorist, Taba weaves together innovative and engaging strategies to enable learners to become more capable and sophisticated thinkers and doers. Taba sets up a new platform for considering curriculum as a set of elements to be manipulated by educators in the classroom.

2

Introduction to *Interdisciplinary Teamed Instruction*

One of the most effective professional development tools appeared in 1995, when the Appalachia Educational Laboratory (AEL) published *Dissolving the Boundaries: Planning for Curriculum Integration in Middle and Secondary Schools*. Written by Rebecca Crawford Burns, and reissued in 1999, the book is aimed at school-improvement councils, district committees, teacher-education classes, and individual schools. It covers the topics of understanding curriculum integration, assessing readiness for change and preparing teams. Frequent checklists of key questions and reflection boxes provide focusing points for group dialogue. The book is available separately or packaged in a three-ring binder with a *Facilitator's Guide*. Cowritten with Beth D. Sattes, the Guide contains a timeline for interdisciplinary teamed instruction, step-by-step directions for administrators and facilitators, interactive group activities, guidelines for meetings, and accompanying handouts and copy for overhead transparencies.

Dissolving the Boundaries was an outgrowth of a two-year research and development project on the model of Interdisciplinary Teamed Instruction (ITI) in four Virginia secondary schools. The project was a response to the Virginia Department of Education's request for help in preparing educators capable of developing interdisciplinary approaches to the state's emerging Common Core of Learning. The Common Core was intended to minimize subject boundaries and to emphasize relationships among disciplines and life beyond school. It centered on issues, themes, problems, and decisions. Burns has continued to work with schools in Virginia and around the country, helping them use the ITI model to develop standards-based curriculum while integrating academic and occupational programs and creating student-centered learning.

In Chapter 2, Burns describes the organizational patterns, research base, and philosophical premise of the ITI model. She also offers solutions to common problems and presents new data on effects. The centerpiece of her chapter is her five-part continuum of the "Evolutionary Stages of Curriculum Integration." The continuum is a framework for evaluating where a curriculum is at and how it might evolve. Burns goes beyond other continua by delineating changes in four key variables: curriculum, instruction, assessment, and classroom culture. Change in any one variable precipitates change in the others. Moreover, planners and teams do not necessarily move strictly from one stage to another. In any given school, the process of collaboration, integration, and teamwork will be influenced by the philosophical beliefs of participants and the pragmatic realities of organizational support. Like Heidi Jacobs, Burns finds that "integration" has a more plural meaning today and that integrative learning is not necessarily at odds with the standards movement. A results-oriented approach to instruction need not conflict with integrated approaches if learning is emphasized, not just teaching. Teaming—the particular focus of this chapter, brought to life in Burns's array of new examples from classrooms—is a powerful way of focusing curriculum design on knowledge and skills in disciplines while making connections across subjects.

Interdisciplinary Teamed Instruction

Rebecca Crawford Burns

Interdisciplinary Teamed Instruction is a complex process that requires fundamental changes in beliefs about teaching and learning. Some educators have already made shifts in beliefs and the path is clear, but for many this is new territory. When I wrote *Dissolving the Boundaries* I had just completed two years of research in four secondary schools where teams of teachers and administrators were embarking on the journey toward curriculum integration. These schools entered the research project voluntarily but with varying degrees of readiness for change. They also completed the project with varying degrees of success.

Invariably, readiness for change was the determining factor for success. Readiness is enhanced by a culture of collaboration within a school and a shared vision or compatible core beliefs about the nature and purpose of schooling. Building collaboration and shared vision requires time for dialogue to clarify one's beliefs and to explore them with others. Educators also need time to discuss and understand models of integration and to determine which are most appropriate to their school's vision for learning. Supports for change, such as leadership and professional development, and facilitating structures, such as time and monetary resources, must be in place if this dialogue is to occur.

Most schools do not give these conditions the appropriate attention. Therefore, many efforts to implement Interdisciplinary Teamed Instruction fail, or do not go beyond initial stages. Sadly, this problem is evident throughout the history of curriculum integration in this century. Further, change seldom occurs unless there is dissatisfaction with the status quo. In this chapter I offer observations, examples, and insights from my continuing work with schools that I hope will raise questions, clarify issues, critique the status quo of traditional teaching, and promote wider use of interdisciplinary structures.

Introduction

In the last decade there has been renewed interest in integrating curricular content with students' life experiences. The call for relevance in education, new evidence that the brain constructs meaning by searching for patterns and interconnections (Caine and Caine 1991), and reform movements—such as middle schools and school-to-career initiatives, the standards movement, and incorporation of performance-based assessment in state-mandated testing programs—have all garnered renewed commitment to interdisciplinary curriculum organization. Described by Martin-Kniep, Feige, and Soodak (1995) as "an intricately woven tapestry or a beautifully choreographed dance" (227), integrated curriculum helps students make connections between and across disciplines of knowledge and between knowledge and its applications.

Curriculum integration makes sense at all levels of education. However, at middle and high school levels, where many students are lost in the increasing volume, complexity, and fragmentation of knowledge, and where many see little relationship between what they do in school and life beyond school, Interdisciplinary Teamed Instruction (ITI) is a necessary organizational structure. For teachers, who must deal with the inherent complexity of the world and rapidly increasing knowledge base, not to mention new expectations from parents and community and curricular mandates from policymakers, ITI offers greater curricular and pedagogical efficiency. The goal is to build learning communities in schools by dissolving boundaries between disciplines, between teachers and students, and between schools and their communities.

The ITI model began with a research project conducted by the Appalachia Educational Laboratory from 1992 to 1994 in four Virginia middle and secondary schools. Initially, the project was designed to meet a need expressed by the Virginia Department of Education to prepare a cadre of educators who could assist others in developing interdisciplinary approaches to delivering the state's emerging Common Core of Learning. Centered on issues, themes, problems, and decisions, the Common Core was designed to minimize subject boundaries, emphasize interrelationships among disciplines, and support learning in new ways that reflect the world beyond school. It incorporated a holistic view of curriculum, instruction, and assessment.

The Department of Education recognized several potentials in the model: to combine content and reduce an overwhelming amount of information and duplication; to promote mastery of fundamental knowledge and skills; to deepen understanding and enhance connection-making across the curriculum; and to increase students' motivation as they become more active, engaged learners (Burns 1994). Political circumstances in Virginia prevented implementation of the Common Core statewide, but the project was successfully completed. Since 1994, Virginia educators have developed Standards of Learning, K–12 frameworks for core academic disciplines and technology. Several Virginia school divisions, plus schools and districts across the country, are now using ITI models and processes to develop and deliver standards-based curriculum, to integrate academic and occupational programs, and to design more student-centered learning.

Organizational Patterns and Design Continuum

The ITI model uses a total staff approach and interdisciplinary teams. Its conceptual framework is also applicable in self-contained, blocktime structures. The total staff approach, used effectively in primary through high school, works best when broad themes or topics that can integrate all the disciplines are selected. These topics provide possibilities for appropriate learning activities across disciplines and grade levels. For instance, the faculty in a combined middle and high school (grades 6–12) in southwest Virginia used a total staff approach to design a six-week unit on the presidential election. In an Iowa primary school (grades K–3), teachers designed instruction around the yearlong theme of Building a Caring Community. A cadre of teachers from preschool through grade 5 used the human-animal bond in a thematic unit on Pets and Me.

In the interdisciplinary team approach, teachers of different disciplines in middle school through college identify curricular priorities in each discipline and find overlapping skills, concepts, and attitudes. Using this approach, a rural Virginia high school team composed of an English teacher, a social studies teacher, and a chemistry/biology teacher developed a series of units. For a unit on global awareness and interdependence, the team identified problem solving, critical thinking, communicating, and decision making as focus skills. Students looked at various world cultures through the lenses of these disciplines to increase their understanding of diversity and to reduce prejudice. The culminating activity was a mock United Nations General Assembly. Focusing on overlapping skills and concepts in science, history, and geography, an Iowa middle school team designed a unit on natural disasters, beginning with a recent local event—a tornado that caused serious damage to the community.

Sometimes the interdisciplinary team approach is combined with the total staff approach. At a Virginia middle school, the entire faculty participated in a six-week interdisciplinary unit called Survival in a Changing World. Each of the school's five instructional teams designed a unit plan to develop this theme through focused study of one of the following topics: the environment, multiculturalism, technology, social/economic issues, or job skills.

The blocktime strategy is often employed in elementary schools, particularly in whole language classrooms where literature-based themes are the organizing center and cross-disciplinary content is correlated with the theme. Blocktime is also used in special and alternative education programs at all instructional levels. Some two-member teams have emerged from the blocktime core strategy. For instance, a two-person middle school team in Spotsylvania County, Virginia, coordinates language arts/social studies and math/science instruction in two two-period blocks.

Developing a schoolwide philosophy and implementation of Interdisciplinary Teamed Instruction requires understanding a variety of team design options as well as a sound curriculum planning process. A number of writers describe the process (e.g., Beane 1993; Brazee and Capelluti 1995; Freeman and Sokoloff 1995; Lounsbury 1992; Stevenson and Carr 1993; Vars 1993). Others offer a continuum of design options (e.g., Brazee and Capelluti 1994; Burns 1995; Fogarty 1991; Jacobs 1989). A continuum enables teachers to define where they are in terms of interdisciplinarity and where they would like to be. A planning process provides guidelines for writing rich, rigorous, and relevant curriculum. Figure 1 is a continuum of five organizational designs that depicts structures for teams, options for organizing curriculum, and approaches to instruction and assessment.

Figure 1. Evolutionary Stages of Curriculum Integration

Used with permission of Rebecca C. Burns, Appalachia Educational Laboratory, Charleston, WV.

VARIABLE/COMPONENTS	EVOLUTIONARY STAGES OF CURRICULUM INTEGRATION				
	Parallel Disciplines	**Multidisciplinary**	**Interdisciplinary**	**Integrated**	**Transdisciplinary**
I. Curriculum					
A. Focus	Content and procedures of separate disciplines		Generic and metacognitive concepts and skills	Real-life skills, issues, concerns, and questions	Students' social-personal concerns and questions
B. Decision maker (architect)	Individual teacher	Individual teacher	Teaching team	Teaching team with student input	Students with teacher input
C. Deviation from traditional curriculum	Resequenced content	Revised content to fit a theme	Blended content that emerges from disciplines	Discipline boundaries dissolved; essential-concept orientation	Subject-transcendent, student-identified topics
D. Degree of implementation	Sporadic-convenient	Periodic "add on"	Regularly planned instructional blocks	Full core curriculum (usually half day)	Total curriculum
II. Instruction					
A. Teacher role	Specialist	Specialist	Generalist	Generalist	Generalist
B. Teaching style	Director	Director	Facilitator-director	Facilitator	Mentor
C. Learning activities	Mimetic	Mimetic-constructivist	Constructivist-mimetic	Contructivist	Constructivist-experiential
D. Learning environment	School	School	School	School and community	Community and school
III. Assessment					
A. Purpose	Summative	Summative	Formative and summative	Formative and summative	Formative and summative
B. Methods	Standardized, product-oriented	Standardized plus alternatives	Performance-based; emphasis on process	Performance-based and portfolios	Portfolios and exhibitions of mastery
C. Evaluator	Teacher	Teacher	Teacher, peer, self	Peer, self, teacher	Self, peer, others, teacher
IV. Classroom Culture					
A. Climate	Competitive	Competitive-cooperative	Cooperative-collaborative	Collaborative	Collaborative
B. Student role	Passive	Passive-active	Active	Active	Active-reflective
C. Student-teacher relationship	Dependency	Dependency	Dependency/self-direction	Self-direction	Self-direction

The Design Continuum for ITI

Although stages of the continuum are evolutionary and incremental, faculties or teams do not necessarily move through them in a linear way. The degree of intensity of collaboration, integration, and teamwork are influenced by philosophical beliefs and organizational supports. The continuum in Figure 1 illustrates evolutionary stages between the traditional subject-centered, single-teacher approach and a fully integrated curriculum that requires high levels of collaboration. It provides a framework for assessing readiness for integration and teaming and for choosing the most appropriate design for a school. It differs from those of Jacobs and others in that the five stages—parallel, multidisciplinary, interdisciplinary, integrated, and transdisciplinary—are delineated by changes in four variables: curriculum, instruction, assessment, and classroom culture.

The selection of these four variables is based on three beliefs:

1. Philosophically, curriculum, instruction, and assessment are not separate entities but are inextricably linked and interdependent, comprising the integrated whole of teaching;
2. What we teach, how we teach, and how we evaluate student learning affect classroom culture;
3. Change in any of the variables precipitates change in the others.

Within these four variables and across the continuum, the focus changes from subject-centered to student-centered; instruction moves from school-based, teacher- and textbook-dominated to become more constructivist and community-based; and classroom culture becomes less passive and competitive and more collaborative, active, and self-directed (Burns 1995).

Generally, if teachers experience success with less intense stages of integration—Stage 1 (parallel: sequencing curriculum in two disciplines, as in American studies or world studies courses) or Stage 2 (multidisciplinary: a topic or theme woven through several disciplines, as when the Renaissance is studied through literature, history, and the arts)—they are more willing to increase the degree of collaboration and integration reflected in other stages on the continuum. It is fairly common to see middle school interdisciplinary teams using the multidisciplinary approach for both schoolwide and interdisciplinary team approaches, because it is a familiar, straightforward model that allows individual disciplines to maintain their autonomy. Likewise, parallel disciplines is a common model in high schools, mainly because it is fairly easy to implement in terms of scheduling and requires little change in instructional methodology on the part of individual teachers. For these teams to move beyond less intense stages of collaboration and integration, as two teams from the ITI project were able to do, requires change in all four variables of the continuum and the presence of supportive conditions within a school.

A unit on Thoreau's *On Walden Pond* described in my earlier work evolved from a parallel structure to an interdisciplinary one. Rather than merely sequencing curriculum, the two teachers selected common unit outcomes and shared learning activities and assessments; they developed common performance tasks in addition to traditional teacher-made tests; and they engaged students in more active learning such as field experiences, creating a more collaborative, active, self-directed classroom culture (Burns 1995, 75). Similarly, a middle school faculty moved beyond the multidisciplinary stage to interdisciplinary collaboration and integration by organizing units on Survival around generic skills of problem solving, decision making, and communicating through focused study of the environment, technology, multiculturalism, social/political issues, and job skills across the curriculum (Burns 1995, 78). In both schools there was a collaborative culture and staff shared beliefs about teaching and learning—the result of ongoing conversations and professional development that fostered a learning community. Both faculties also reported a strong sense of administrative leadership and support (Burns 1994).

The experiences of schools that have used interdisciplinary teaming for several years support these beliefs. The schools have changed not only what is taught but also how it is taught and how learning is assessed. In schools that have shared experiences online using the Interdisciplinary Teamed Instruction listserv (iti@ael.org), teachers have designed curriculum around student-generated topics and questions while maintaining a focus on standards. They have engaged students in individual and group projects within and beyond the classroom, and they have used performances and products to measure student mastery of standards and learning goals.

Issues related to the environment are rich sources for student-centered integrated and transdisciplinary curriculum in Stages 4 and 5 of the continuum. Teachers representing various grade levels in Minnesota, Indiana, Illinois, and Tennessee have designed curriculum around the topic of Water. Several have described curriculum connected to online projects, such as Rivers of Life focused on the Mississippi River and local watersheds. This project and others like it also exemplify K–16 dialogue. They are supported by university staff who provide teaching materials and other online resources. Students collect water samples, analyze data, and report their findings, which are collected and posted on a Web site. They also participate in e-mail conversations with peers in other parts of the country. As students conduct experiments related to water, its quality, conservation, and similar topics, they read and write about the river or other bodies of water that have a direct impact on their lives and engage in related activities in the school and community. A Tennessee middle school team designed a unit on water quality in which students tested water quality in their school and community, analyzed data from samples, and reported their findings in a presentation to the Tennessee Valley Authority.

Other students concerned with environmental issues have followed the migration of the monarch butterfly, a yearlong study that integrates geography, history, science, literature, and the arts. This example is appropriate for elementary through high school, depending on materials and activities. Similarly, students in a Washington elementary school study migration of salmon. And a first-grade teacher in Indiana described online her yearlong theme Out on a Limb, which was conceptually about growth and change and used trees as the vehicle to teach key concepts and skills. The curriculum integrated science, social studies, and language arts. It included in-depth study of three animals that use trees for homes, a study of products made from trees, and discussion of the human role in conservation. Describing how she integrated literature, the teacher wrote: "Once I started looking at literature with regard to a big, conceptual idea, I found it so much easier to help children make the connections." Her statement captures the essence of what individuals and teams need to do in order to design integrated curriculum.

Another popular organizer is a historical event. Teachers from Virginia to Utah use presidential elections, the Holocaust, and the American Civil War. Taking the Civil War as an example, it is possible to see three stages of integration. At the simplest stage—parallel design—a high school English teacher resequences an American literature curriculum to align study of the novel *The Red Badge of Courage* with the American history teacher's study of the Civil War. In contrast, in the sixth grade at a northern Virginia middle school, a team of teachers organizes a transdisciplinary Civil War unit on the topic Voices from the Past. After discussion of the times and situation, students examine the event from the perspectives of real or fictional characters from the era of their own selection or creation. They are engaged in what Kovalik (1997) calls an immersion experience and Jacobs (1989) labels an integrated day, as they write journals, organize field drills, design clothing, create models, sing and write music, research the development of photography, and assemble soldiers' packs. Teachers describe their role as "facilitators and cheerleaders." Another team introduces a Civil War unit by helping students frame meaningful questions about the topic, such as, How were lives of people affected by the Civil War? More specifically, how were lives of slaves, poor white farmers, or people in Washington, D.C., affected? What was culture like in various parts of the country during the Civil War? How were power and authority used? These questions guide the choice of materials, learning activities, and assessments for the unit.

Teachers who offered these and similar curricula report improved student performance. A growing body of evidence, in fact, affirms the use of curriculum integration and provides greater understanding of changes in instructional practice that ensure its effectiveness.

Effects and Results

During our initial research from 1992 to 1994, teams of teachers and administrators ranging in number from five to 12 designed integrated curricula, taught them in their schools, evaluated their effects on students, and redesigned integrated curricula based on their findings. They were supported by a professional development program that included two week-long summer institutes centered on curriculum development and team building, four yearly on-site workshops that addressed instructional strategies and alternative forms of student assessment, as well as collaborative-action research conducted at each site on the effects of ITI (Burns 1994).

Researchers found that ITI had positive effects on learning and teaching at all four sites. Most teachers and administrators reported improved student performance, particularly for low achievers. Students showed greater enthusiasm for learning and increased engagement in learning activities, demonstrated better grasp of concepts and skills, made connections across disciplines, had fewer behavior problems, and improved attendance. Teachers benefited as well, particularly in terms of professional growth, reflective practice, and collegial interaction. They also reported personal feelings of increased efficacy, empowerment, and enthusiasm for teaching; learning from colleagues; increased creativity, and professional renewal (Burns 1994). Continuing research between 1996 and 1998 on the effects of the model on school culture reveals positive gains on five of Cavanagh and Dellar's (1996) six traits—teacher efficacy, emphasis on learning, collegiality, transformational leadership, and shared planning—and statistically significant improvement on teacher collaboration (Burns 1998).

Educators who have used ITI continue to report positive effects. Most often, teachers cite higher degrees of engagement in learning, improved performance on teacher-designed assessments, greater self-direction and motivation, increased ability to make connections between concepts and skills that cross disciplines, and improved skill in applying school-based learning in workplace experiences or other community-based activities. Recently, three schools that have been using the model for two or more years reported overall upward trends in standardized test scores. Data analyses of district testing reports indicate stronger student performance in two of these schools when compared with national and district averages. Furthermore, in these same two schools, students in teamed environments performed better than students in traditional classrooms on certain standardized measures (Burns 1998). These findings affirm prior claims and add new understandings to previous studies, including those reported by the National Association for Core Curriculum (1991), on the effectiveness of integrated programs.

Research on teaming prior to 1985 was somewhat limited and inconclusive, though some claims of academic gains resulting from teamed instruction were reported (Arhar, Johnston, and Markle, cited in Lounsbury 1992). More recent studies report that teaming produces higher achievement. A study conducted in 100 particularly effective middle schools indicates that 62 percent of respondents described consistent academic improvement resulting from interdisciplinary teaming. An additional 28 percent of respondents reported increased scores on standardized tests. Eighty-five percent observed that teacher confidence in students' abilities had increased (George and Oldaker 1985).

After comparing math and reading achievement of seventh-grade students in interdisciplinary teams and traditional departments, Bradley (1988) concluded that the team arrangement was more effective in fostering math achievement. Both arrangements were equally effective in promoting reading achievement. George and Oldaker also reported improvement in school discipline and personal development as a result of enrollment in middle schools where team teaching was used: "Approximately 80 percent of the sample noted significant reduction in office referrals and suspensions, while close to 60 percent expelled fewer students after the transition. Almost 90 percent observed that teacher and staff confidence in managing disruptive students increased, diminishing administrative involvement in discipline in many schools" (1985, 31).

Other emerging research findings do support the use of integrated curricula. One such source is Cotton's (1995) update on effective schools research. Cotton identified the following items in a long list of attributes of effective schools:

- Teachers provide instruction that integrates traditional school subjects, as appropriate.
- Teachers integrate workplace readiness skills into content-area instruction.
- Administrators and teachers integrate the curriculum, as appropriate.

Another body of research that supports curriculum integration and interdisciplinary teaming is emerging from the high school restructuring movement. In a study of 820 secondary schools, Lee and Smith (1994a, 1994b) concluded that the consistent pattern of findings allowed them to make quite unequivocal statements about the organizational structure of high schools, including "students learn more in schools which are restructured" (23). About 25 percent of these restructured schools were using interdisciplinary teams.

Some teachers' reluctance to use available research is a hindrance to implementing curriculum integration. Many are skeptical about educational research. Others say it is not accessible or "user-friendly." Most are more easily convinced by reports of practitioners than articles and books written by researchers. Both researchers and teacher educators need to do a better job of communicating positive results at conferences and in publications for a K–16 audience, through listservs and Internet sites, and in preservice and inservice teacher education. Furthermore, K–12 educators should be encouraged and supported in efforts to conduct research on their own or in K–16 collaborations.

Purpose and Assessment

If the goal of interdisciplinary teaching is to deepen students' understanding of themselves and their world, then teachers need to keep the focus of interdisciplinary planning on students—their questions, needs, and interests. Furthermore, they should determine what is *really* important for students to know and be able to do in each of their disciplines while collaborating to find natural connections around which to design an integrated curriculum. Finally, teachers should consider how their students learn best.

A Virginia school provides a perspective on successful teamed instruction:

> We took a serious look at interdisciplinary teamed instruction as a means to improve student understanding and enhance learning. This led to development of a schoolwide coordination and philosophy of integrated study that permeates much of what we do. It is not uncommon to find students working on research projects that draw from literature, history, and science classes.   (Jervis, Bull, Sauter, and Turner 1997)

The philosophical framework for ITI and most reforms it parallels (e.g., the standards movement, performance-based assessment, school-to-career initiative) is grounded in the need to change both *what* is taught and *how* it is taught. The knowledge explosion and plethora of state- and district-mandated requirements have pushed the school day to its limits; it is impossible to keep adding courses and periods. The detrimental effects of proliferation are evident in increased numbers of Carnegie credit units required for high school graduation and a fragmented, overcrowded curriculum, especially at the secondary level.

Proliferation encompasses more than adding on course requirements; it requires decision making about how to deal with the ever-increasing body of knowledge in all disciplines. Teachers can overcome fragmentation by integrating new requirements into existing programs and replacing the add-on approach with frameworks that connect learning. Middle school comprehensive health education can be integrated into social studies and science programs. High school fine arts requirements can be met through a team approach to humanities that integrates literature, writing, the arts, and history in a thematic study (Burns 1995). Reading, writing, critical thinking, career exploration, and technology activities should be incorporated in all instructional units, not taught in separate classes or as peripheral activities.

Closely related to the issue of proliferation is the issue of relevance. The trend toward creating curriculum by simply adding more has produced curricula that are overcrowded, incoherent, and lack an informing sense of the large questions, issues, and problems that drive learning in the world (Beane 1995; Boston 1996; Jacobs 1989). When teachers integrate curriculum around problems or projects that require students to apply knowledge and skills to real-world problem solving and decision making, they are increasing relevance. When students explore water quality or participate in a community project like Save our Stream—as students in a West Virginia high school did to receive credit in biology, environmental studies, civics, and English—they begin to understand the interactions, interrelatedness, and interdependencies of disciplines and their applications in the world. When students participate in workplace learning experiences (job shadowing, mentorships), they gain a context for applying knowledge and skills.

As teachers use more student-centered designs, subject matter is not discarded. It is honed, repositioned, and focused on essential concepts, skills, and attitudes. When fully integrated, curriculum reflects the cultural and social makeup of the community, the rhythm of the school day and year, the strengths of teachers, the questions that students have about their world, and essential content across disciplines (Burns 1995). At a Utah middle school, a traditional history unit on World War II was honed and repositioned into a new unit on Survival of the Human Spirit that included literature, writing, art, music, technology, and history. Students generated essential questions about the topic and teachers designed learning activities to help them find answers, including e-mail interviews with Holocaust survivors. The culminating exhibition was a student-designed Web site that included writing and artwork depicting the theme.

Psychologists, philosophers, researchers, and educators agree that effective learning means thoughtful learning that enables students to construct a range of "understanding performances" around a topic (Gardner 1991; Perkins 1991). Understanding performances require students to demonstrate and use what they know by applying it in a real-world context. Interdisciplinary teams have designed a rich variety of assessments: preparing a brochure about a community event or problem, writing a children's book or creating a puppet show and presenting it to a group of younger students, producing a video about the community to promote economic growth, constructing a model of a mousetrap-powered vehicle, designing a Web site to communicate findings and conclusions from an investigation, and developing a public presentation or exhibit.

Today, business, industry, and higher education pronounce many high school (and college) graduates incapable of applying knowledge, thinking critically and creatively, solving problems, making wise decisions, and working with others. These deficiencies are related to how we teach, too often with teacher-dominated instruction that requires students to read, listen, memorize facts and information, and reproduce them in mimetic fashion on traditional paper-and-pencil tests or standardized tests. Interdisciplinary teams combat this problem by engaging students in project- and problem-based learning. A group of Virginia ninth-grade students researched environmental and social issues in their town and made a presentation with recommendations to the Board of Supervisors. A fifth-grade class in Tennessee researched their town's history, then wrote and performed an original play for the community. Teachers in rural southwestern Iowa and in Puerto Rico designed curriculum around community history, issues, and events to increase students' awareness, understanding, and appreciation of their culture and history.

For some educators, the standards movement represents a threat to integration and to thoughtful teaching. This need not be the case if natural connections are made across content standards and they are placed within an interdisciplinary design that focuses on real-life problems and concerns. A team of health science, biology, and social studies teachers who found natural overlaps in content standards designed a unit on world health and communicable diseases. For their assessments, which received credit in two or more content areas, students designed informational brochures on various diseases and participated in a mock World Health Organization meeting.

The standards movement may actually facilitate integration. Teams of teachers are beginning to focus curriculum design on essential knowledge and skills in each discipline while finding natural connections across the curriculum. Many teachers, too, are using a more results-oriented approach to instruction—placing emphasis on learning more than on teaching—as they evaluate student progress through a variety of assessment methods and arrive at instructional decisions based on student needs and assessment data. In some schools, teachers report a more collaborative, reflective, student-centered environment:

The conscious efforts to look at what we are doing, its impact on our students, how we use resources, how we can enhance and reinforce content and process development, how we can connect what is in school to the larger global environment are a few of the changes we've made. The successes of students will assure that our movement toward a fully integrated program continues.

(Jervis, Bull, Sauter, and Turner 1997)

Educators in the progressive era and today agree that teacher-dominated mimetic instructional methods, a curriculum limited to facts and information, segregation of disciplines, and separation of school-based learning from application in the world beyond school do not result in real learning. When the Virginia teachers who designed the unit on Thoreau's *On Walden Pond* engaged students in observation and investigations at a local pond, they were unifying their experiences with Thoreau's. This experience recalls Bruner's (1986) observation that students need to be engaged in learning that is deeply intellectual and connected with moral purpose. When the Utah team invited students to generate significant questions about the Holocaust and use e-mail interviews with Holocaust survivors to find answers, they created a powerful intellectual experience with moral purpose. Student engagement is important in developing curriculum that is rich, rigorous, and relevant; at the highest stages—integrated and transdisciplinary design—it is where instructional design begins. Other activities that reflect Bruner's high moral purpose include experiential learning activities such as community study and service learning.

Curriculum integration has reemerged to help students make sense of, reflect on, and apply what is learned. In more intense student-centered stages, teachers assume the role of facilitators, not dispensers of knowledge. Students, in turn, engage in meaningful exploration as they participate in constructivist and experiential learning activities in both school and community. They demonstrate their learning through behaviors that require thinking, feeling, and acting. They produce products, develop portfolios, and participate in real-world experiences and applications that provide evidence of understanding knowledge across disciplines. And, these understanding performances are reviewed by an expanding group of evaluators, including mentors, peers, and students themselves.

When teacher-dominated learning and subject-centered curriculum give way to integrated, student-centered curriculum, instruction, and assessment, the learning environment becomes more collaborative, active, reflective, and self-directed—mirroring the real world and helping students to attain Bruner's "higher ground."

Quality Issues in Teaming and Curriculum Design

In view of the volume of evidence on positive effects of teaming, it is surprising that a majority of schools do not use teams. Data from a study conducted by Epstein and MacIver for the National Middle School Association (1990) indicated that most schools did not use interdisciplinary teams, including about 60 percent of middle schools and 75 percent of elementary and high schools. Furthermore, while teams exist in many middle and secondary schools, few have moved beyond the subject-centered curriculum. The discipline-based paradigm is difficult to change, and the standards movement has intensified many teachers' concerns about content coverage. One recently stated: "I am not sure we have time for another interdisciplinary unit this year. We have so much to cover before the state test is given."

If conditions that support teaming are in place, the problem of moving from teams to interdisciplinary teamed instruction may be attributed to three causes: (1) lack of understanding of the nature, purpose, and function of teams; (2) different interpretations or philosophies regarding the meaning of "interdisciplinary" (Black 1997); and (3) inadequate understanding of the curriculum design process.

Barriers to Teaming

Although teaming is a key strategy for integration, many teachers resist or struggle with implementing interdisciplinary instruction for several reasons. First, many secondary teachers identify not just as teachers but as teachers of particular subjects (e.g., an English teacher or a math teacher). Furthermore, subject identities may have larger meanings for status differentiation: academic subjects may be valued over occupational, for instance, or math and science may be admired as most rigorous. These identities and status systems may become tied to particular classrooms, scheduling priorities, or grouping patterns (Beane 1993). To be successful with ITI, a faculty must commit to school reorganization in teams, subordinating the traditional departmental organization and hierarchy. Changing identities, though, becoming more generalist than specialist, is not an easy move for most secondary teachers. Beane describes the necessity and difficulty of this change:

> Since knowledge and skill are not identified along subject lines, teachers who have seen themselves as specialists are asked to literally leave their teaching certificates at the classroom doors and enter instead as "teachers" in a generic sense, whose work is to help young people "search for self and social meaning." (Beane 1993, 21)

Some teams never get an interdisciplinary program launched or experience conflict because they suffer from the *polarity problem*. They view discipline-based and interdisciplinary as an either/or proposition. Because many teachers are territorial about their subjects, they feel threatened by new views of their field. A classic statement of the polarity problem was voiced by a Virginia high school English teacher. While her team was designing a unit on Conflict, she loudly declared: "I will never give up teaching *Romeo and Juliet!*" Her teammates helped her realize she would still be teaching *Romeo and Juliet*, but in a different context and perhaps with some different learning strategies.

At another high school, a biology teacher and an English teacher avoid the polarity problem by using selections from Thoreau's *On Walden Pond* and other appropriate writing as common ground for presenting historical, aesthetic, and scientific contexts of literature and the ecosystem of the pond. These teachers and their students also share a field trip experience at a local pond or lake and complete scientific and aesthetic tasks comparable to those described in *Walden* and other literature. Students later present an individual or small group culminating performance (e.g., forum, collection of essays, presentation to a civic group) to demonstrate the findings from their study of a local environmental problem, for which they receive dual credit in English and biology (Burns 1995, 75).

Success Factors

For ITI to be successful, each teacher on the team must view him/herself as part of a strategic whole, as the team from Virginia eloquently described in the previous section. Integration of team members begins to happen when teachers talk, plan curriculum together, evaluate its effectiveness, and become aware of their roles and the insights and expertise they can contribute. This process often takes time and must be facilitated by administrative leadership and supports such as scheduling for common planning time; autonomy for teams to create their own policies, schedules, curriculum, and systems for monitoring student progress; and professional development (Burns 1995).

Another factor that affects the success of teams is the way in which they are selected. The consensus among most principals and teachers who have implemented ITI is that volunteerism is the best approach. To identify prospective teams, teachers may be asked to name others with whom they would most like to work. Most administrators in the original research on ITI indicated that commitment to interdisciplinary instruction, flexibility, open-mindedness, effective communication, and compatibility of personalities and core beliefs about teaching and learning were keys to successful teams (Burns 1994).

Teachers and principals should also determine which team structure(s) will be most appropriate in their particular schools. Middle school and high school teams generally range in size from two to five members and represent core academic areas at a particular grade level. However, some high schools are using career clusters, or the Academy Model (Grubb 1991), to integrate academic and occupational programs. Academies may operate as schools-within-schools and usually consist of four teachers—one in math, one in science, one in English, and one in the occupational area that is the core of the academy (e.g., engineering/technology, health sciences). One of the most successful team structures in high schools today is an approach to English and history described as American studies, global studies, or humanities. In a three-year humanities curriculum in a West Virginia high school, world history is the driving force, but literature, writing, the arts, and sometimes science are integrated. History is usually studied through primary sources and other literary and artistic genres.

Once teams are selected, leadership and organization are vital. All successful teams have a leader who is able to work well with both teachers and administrators. The leader facilitates team meetings and serves as liaison between the team and principal or others. A good team leader is well liked, trusted, efficient, and task-centered (Burns 1995). Equally important is the need for each team member to have a specific role: everyone should be responsible for something. Other roles that contribute to team effectiveness include recorder, who keeps written records of team planning, decisions, and agenda; timekeeper, who helps the team to stay on task; intelligence officer, who conducts research and collects and stores materials for team use; and external communicator, who communicates team needs and decisions to consultants and others working with the team.

Without leadership and organization, teams flounder. Examples from the original research on ITI are illustrative of teams across the country. During the project's first year, two of the four teams organized themselves in terms of leadership and task roles. They made greater progress toward integrated curriculum design and implementation than the others, demonstrated more regular communication with the researcher, and reported fewer problems with finding time to accomplish their goals. The two less successful teams struggled with completing project tasks, such as designing and teaching an integrated unit and submitting plans for on-site workshops. They also experienced more frequent misunderstandings and conflicts. At the beginning of the second year, one of these teams set as its initial goal to organize the team! From that point on they employed team roles and responsibilities in all their work, increasing their efficiency, collaboration, and success. Unfortunately, the fourth team never really got organized. Consequently, their efforts were fraught with conflict and their course floundered (Burns 1994).

Even when teams are organized and ready to work, some find the process hindered by the absence of conditions that support teaming and the changes it requires. These conditions are discussed in *Dissolving the Boundaries* and reported in other studies. They include a collaborative school culture; compatible beliefs about teaching and learning; readiness for change; a work environment that nurtures change and supports risk-taking; administrative leadership; ongoing professional development; and facilitating structures such as common planning time, block-of-time scheduling, flexible instructional space, and an adequate budget for resources and supports (Ackerman 1989; Brazee and Capelluti 1995; Burns 1995; Maeroff 1993; Merenbloom 1991).

Providing these supports in small schools can be especially difficult. To provide common planning time for a schoolwide instructional leadership team whose members taught at different grade levels, one principal scheduled team members for the same lunch period in a split-lunch timetable. They also found time to meet before and after school and dedicated district "work" days to interdisciplinary planning. Another principal shortened the instructional day once a week, lengthening it the other four days, to provide two hours of team planning time. To create flexible team space, another principal had the common wall between two large classrooms removed and a flexible sliding door installed to allow large- and small-group teamed instruction. In another school, all professional development and district planning days were dedicated to interdisciplinary planning, and the school's professional development budget limited to activities supporting teaming and integration, such as consultant workshops and visits to other schools using ITI.

Many administrators and faculties fail to realize that implementing ITI affects all key components of schooling: organization and management, curriculum, instruction, assessment, and culture. Therefore, whether or not an entire faculty will be involved in teaming, they all must be aware of changes that will affect them. Some may be asked to change classrooms so a team can have shared or proximal teaching space. There may be schedule changes to accommodate longer blocks of time for interdisciplinary teaching and common planning time. Student grouping and teaching assignments may change. Instructional budgets and resources will probably shift from departmental to team control. For many, these are "sacred cows" that won't easily be relinquished. Overcoming barriers that are deeply rooted in assumptions about teaching and learning requires time and discussion. Through inquiry and investigation a school staff can build commitment to working together and determine ways to promote understanding and acceptance of inevitable changes that accompany the move to interdisciplinary teaching (Burns 1995).

Faculties that are successful with integration also take time to explore a continuum of interdisciplinary designs and team structures and to assess their readiness for change. A Utah middle school's first-year experience serves as a reminder of this lesson:

> Implementation of ITI should have begun only after the faculty had been given an opportunity to develop a more unified culture, skills for working cooperatively, and shared vision of the school's educational mission.
>
> (Allison, Beecher, and Jemmett 1998, 60)

Overcoming barriers is part of the journey to success. Susan Drake compares the "Journey of the Hero" to five stages of developing integrated curricula.

> The heroes as curriculum writers hear a *call to adventure*. They leave behind traditional methods of curriculum development and experience *endings* accompanied by loss. This is followed by a *struggle* as they encounter anxiety, conflict and the excitement of stepping into the unknown. Finally, they reach the *reward* and personal satisfaction of understanding how to integrate curriculum. The last stage is *service* where the heroes, feeling fulfilled, share what they have learned with other interested educators.   (Drake 1993, 6–7)

Once teams are organized and ready to write curriculum, they must develop a common understanding of what *interdisciplinary* means. As they develop integrated units, they should follow certain guidelines: the whole must have a character and significance different from the sum of its parts, and there should be a principle of unity that is founded in a compelling purpose or interest (Martin-Kniep, Feige, and Soodak 1995). Integrating disciplines around exploration of problems and issues of life is clearly an interdisciplinary approach and a natural, purposeful teaching strategy. However, integrating facts and information from several *subjects* is contrived and produces a superficial, narrow study, a criticism of interdisciplinary curriculum in some schools (Black 1997, Freeman and Sokoloff 1995). The *potpourri problem* of sampling knowledge from each discipline is illustrated in a West Virginia high school team's conversation about a unit on Appalachian Culture.

"I'll get some artists to demonstrate crafts, quilting, etc."

"Oh, okay, we can do tessellations in geometry."

"How about getting some parents to cook Appalachian specialties and we'll have a tasting party?"

"We can play blue grass music in the background."

"Let's read some Appalachian folk tales, too."

"And we can take the students over to Tamarack to see some art exhibits."

To alleviate the potpourri problem, interdisciplinary teams should insure that the theme is neither too broad nor too narrow and that it demands the best from each discipline, is engaging for students, and doesn't force but naturally supports integration. Furthermore, a team must determine specific outcomes (guiding questions, standards, performance tasks) and be careful to make connections between intended outcomes and learning activities and assessments. Instead of beginning planning by generating activities or specific content, as the Appalachian Culture team did, teams should begin by focusing on what students should know and be able to do—knowledge and skills to be gained.

Some writers suggest that the organizing center of an interdisciplinary unit should be essential questions or generative issues. They are rich and engaging topics that hold interest and invite multiple ways of knowing (Beane 1993; Freeman and Sokoloff 1995; Gardner and Boix-Mansilla 1994). In a Community Connections program, two Washington high school teachers integrate instruction in math, science, English, and history for approximately 50 students. They organize curriculum in eight yearly units around universal human issues such as power, vision, and truth. Another team organizes curriculum around essential questions such as "What is justice?" Others topics related to current issues are fruitful. The faculty of a West Virginia high school that was moving to a new building selected the theme of Change for the first six weeks of the school year. A California high school uses Patterns to integrate science and humanities curricula in a yearlong theme. This program illustrates integration both within and across disciplines. The science program integrates concepts from earth science, chemistry, physics, and life science through the theme Patterns and Evolutionary Change, while the humanities course integrates literature, history, and arts through the theme of Patterns and Cultures.

Conversely, when teams select organizing centers that are too narrow and content-specific, they experience difficulty creating an integrated curriculum that is greater than the sum of its parts. When a Virginia team composed of English, science, math, and history teachers designed a two-year core program for ninth-grade students around the theme Great Cultures Past and Present, they found it impossible to apply it successfully to study of science and math. The problem was due in part to a chronological approach, though the topic itself was not applicable to science and math content.

Perkins (1989) addresses this problem when he defines a "fertile" theme as a lens through which to study different subject matter. A "good" lens applies broadly to a wide range of topics and pervasively throughout a topic. It discloses patterns across subjects as well as similarities and contrasts within and across disciplines. And it fascinates students and teachers, provoking curiosity and inquiry. Unfortunately, Great Cultures Past and Present did not meet these criteria. In contrast, a theme used in another school, Survival in a Changing World, did. It was easily applied across disciplines, yet allowed in-depth study in a field (e.g., global interdependence, environmental stewardship). Teachers were able to design lessons enabling students to see similarities among disciplines through focused study of certain pervasive concepts and life skills, particularly problem solving, decision making, and communicating. Since students conducted research within the community on a chosen career and other issues of personal interest, they were engaged in relevant activities, such as job interviewing, that piqued their curiosity.

Once an appropriate organizing center is chosen, a team continues to design curriculum by identifying learning goals, activities, and assessments. Teams often find this process challenging, particularly defining learning goals for students and aligning activities with goals. Ackerman (1989) identifies four intellectual criteria for quality in integrated curriculum: (1) importance of concepts in each discipline; (2) an interdisciplinary design that enhances discipline-based concepts; (3) learning that transcends concepts and creates a metaconceptual bonus; (4) activities that contribute to development of desirable intellectual and personal dispositions. Likewise, Martin-Kniep, Feige, and Soodak (1995) identify *significance, coherence, and relevance* as criteria for assessing the conceptual integrity of integration. *Significant* units address content that demands the best from each discipline in the integration. *Coherence* pertains to the way in which learning goals, activities, and assessments are integrated. *Relevance* pertains to how well the curriculum personalizes content and connects to students' experience.

We can apply these criteria to sample units. When a Virginia team created a weeklong unit on hurricanes, they combined facts and information from science, geography, and English. The science teacher taught hurricane development and tracking, while the geography teacher taught latitude and longitude. Concurrently, the English teacher introduced haiku poetry by having students write about hurricanes. The science and geography concepts had validity and significance within their disciplines, but most would question the significance of writing haiku poetry in a ninth-grade class. Furthermore, the interdisciplinary design did not enhance learning of discipline-based concepts, nor were activities necessarily engaging for students or related to learning goals. Finally, there was little transcendence of concepts or connection to students' experience. Had the unit been taught during hurricane season, when students could experience tracking a hurricane firsthand, writing daily weather and news reports and charting its progress, there would have been greater relevance and engagement. Had the English teacher chosen to use articles and stories about the impact of hurricanes on people's lives and have students conduct interviews with meteorologists and persons who experienced hurricane destruction, there would have been greater significance. This unit is a good example of the "separate but equal" syndrome—teachers sequence instruction but fail to purposefully combine knowledge, skills, and understanding from various disciplines to help students learn and apply what they learn. The study of hurricanes may have included some interesting activities but no real connections between or among disciplines, and the topic was too narrow to be a fertile theme for integration. It also illustrates the fact that not all concepts are necessarily taught best in an interdisciplinary approach. Significant, coherent, relevant learning can occur in discipline-based settings.

In a New York school, English and social studies teachers developed an eight-week unit on human-environment interaction and tradition and change. Activities included reading selections such as Richard Connell's "The Most Dangerous Game," set in Latin America, and geography-related activities that encouraged exploring the ways individuals and cultures interact with the environment, maintain their cultures and traditions, and make changes based upon needs and circumstances. After students identified salient features of Latin America and the Caribbean and examined relationships between humans and their environment, they participated in a simulation entitled "How Do We Get to Rio?" Students worked in teams to chart a course from New York to Rio. After a simulated plane crash, they had to find a way out of a specific Latin American location (Martin-Kniep, Feige, and Soodak 1995, 235–38). One can see the germane content of this unit. Explicit connections between English and social studies concepts and skills and activities requiring students to apply what they learned illustrate its coherence. Having students apply concepts from literature to their own lives and plan a trip from home to Rio are relevant, authentic activities that personalize and connect learning to their experiences.

To conclude, curriculum integration can create schools where boundaries are dissolved. It can bring order to proliferation in secondary schools and transform them into more humane and empowering institutions. To design quality curriculum, interdisciplinary teams should consider the needs and interests of students as well as the essential content and processes in each discipline and their application to authentic tasks. The exemplary programs described here, in the rest of this book, and in my recommended readings and the bibliography share a vision of learning that is more humane and empowering than the traditional curriculum. However, to create this vision and employ effective teaming practices that foster growth of the school as a learning community, teachers need time together to learn, to plan, to teach, to reflect on and evaluate their work and the work of students, and to redesign their efforts. This can happen only if professional roles, rules, and relationships are redefined and necessary supports for change are in place.

Recommended Readings

The last decade has seen an increasing volume of literature on curriculum integration. The following five selections are particularly enlightening and helpful. The first two, in particular, may be considered seminal pieces.

- Heidi Hayes Jacobs, ed. 1989. *Interdisciplinary Curriculum: Design and Implementation*. Alexandria, Va.: Association for Supervision and Curriculum Development. This is the definitive volume on interdisciplinary curriculum K–12. It provides an explanation of the need for curriculum integration and presents models and processes for achieving successful integration in a variety of school settings.

- Julie Thompson Klein. 1990. *Interdisciplinarity: History, Theory, and Practice*. Detroit, MI: Wayne State University Press. Klein's volume defines interdisciplinarity in the broad sense and provides the first comprehensive bibliography of interdisciplinary literature. The book is a guide to understanding interdisciplinary research and to understanding the gap between interdisciplinary theory and practice.

- J. Brooks and M. Brooks. 1993. *In Search of Understanding: The Case for Constructivist Classrooms*. Alexandria, VA: Association for Supervision and Curriculum Development. The insight that *how* we teach is as important as *what* we teach is the premise of this volume. It offers several comprehensive case studies of classrooms and provides the reader with a clear understanding of the whys and how-tos of student-centered instruction.

- James A. Beane. 1995. "Curriculum Integration and the Disciplines of Knowledge." *Phi Delta Kappan* 76 (8): 616–22. This article gives a clear and concise explanation of curriculum integration and carefully clarifies the role of the disciplines in effective integrated studies. Beane points to the distinction between disciplines of knowledge and subjects as he describes how knowledge should be organized and used in an integrated curriculum.

- William G. Wraga. 1997. "Patterns of Interdisciplinary Curriculum Organization and Professional Knowledge of the Curriculum Field." *Journal of Curriculum and Supervision* 12 (2): 98–117. For those who want a brief overview of the history of interdisciplinary curriculum, Wraga's article offers a survey of the efforts throughout the twentieth century and a commentary on their successes and failures. He provides a comprehensive perspective on the major trends and issues in the curriculum field.

3

Introduction to *Politics and Possibilities Beyond the Separate Subjects*

Heidi Jacobs and Rebecca Burns conceptualized integrative education as choices along a continuum of design models. James Beane's model of a democratic general education hearkens back to the work of progressive educators in the 1920s and 1930s. A full-scale version appears in his book, *A Middle School Curriculum: From Rhetoric to Reality* (1990/1993). Published by the National Middle School Association, the book describes the progressivists' vision and model of education. The model is rooted in a holistic interrelationship of three elements—themes emerging from intersections of personal and social concerns, pertinent skills, and informing concepts. The intersection of personal concerns and social issues generates curriculum themes and related skills of reflective thinking, critical ethics, problem solving, valuing, self-concepting and self-esteeming, social action, and searching for completeness and meaning. Traditional content and skills are not abandoned. They are repositioned in the context of themes and questions. The informing concepts are enduring ideals of education—democracy, human dignity, and cultural diversity. When students are engaged in planning their own learning and constructing knowledge, classrooms become genuinely democratic communities.

When the term "curriculum integration" reemerged in the literature and conference programs during the late 1980s, Beane was struck by its generic alliance with thematic studies and correlation of content and skills from various subject areas. In his 1997 book, *Curriculum Integration: Designing the Core of Democratic Education*, he sought to inform the current movement with a theoretical account of curriculum integration, its place in general education, and practical lessons learned from 30 years of working with the model. His historical sketch spans the Herbartian movement of the late nineteenth century, the work of early progressivists in the 1920s, and subsequent efforts to create a "core curriculum." In Chapter 3, he brings that perspective to bear on the curriculum, students, and the standards movement of today.

Historical perspective underscores the importance of definition. The "multidisciplinary" or "multisubject" approach that is currently popular builds on the traditional separate-subject approach. The historical model of "curriculum integration," which still has advocates today, moves beyond disciplines as organizing centers to focus on student concerns. In contrast to Jacobs and Burns, Beane sees the standards movement as a threat to curriculum integration. Inclusion of interdisciplinary frameworks in the Goals 2000 standards project is often cited as proof of substantive change. Yet activities do not typically depart from or threaten to replace existing subject-matter divisions. Optimism about the current resurgence of interest is also checked by concerns about achievement on standardized tests and a cultural politics that pits innovation against convention. In the future, Beane predicts, "multidisciplinary" approaches are likely to continue expanding. They offer a compromise for subject loyalists and a solution to repetitive subject coverage requirements. He is less optimistic about the future of "curriculum integration." The deeper meaning of "curriculum integration," he suggests, will continue to be marginalized when "integration" is understood only in terms of "multidisciplinary" approaches.

Politics and Possibilities Beyond the Separate Subjects

James A. Beane

As a young teacher more than 30 years ago, I struggled with the disconnections I sensed between the curriculum I was supposed to teach and the minds and hearts of the young people who stared back at me across their desks. They were not rude or unkind to me. Our pre-class banter was friendly and interesting. But when the bell rang and the books came out, a desultory mood set in. It was a mood that group discussion, dramatization, and even inquiry projects could not alter. Oddly enough, I was, and probably still am, one of the few teachers who was ever "saved" by graduate school, for it was there that I first encountered the literature of that loosely defined movement known as "progressive education." While the methods described in that literature, like teacher-student planning, proved helpful, the idea that most profoundly changed my classroom, and my career, was this: There are ways of designing and organizing the curriculum other than the separate-subject approach.

Although the curriculum field increasingly turned its attention toward cultural politics in the 1970s and 1980s, I continued working on curriculum design theory, especially with middle schools since educators at that level seemed more receptive to alternatives than those in the high schools. Using concepts associated with "curriculum integration" and dating back to the 1920s, I developed the design described in *A Middle School Curriculum: From Rhetoric to Reality* (1990/1993). Explaining that design to educators caught up in emerging discussions about curriculum approaches beyond the separate subject led me to see a number of problems in those discussions: their lack of historical grounding, their disconnection from curriculum theory, their misuse of terminology, and their failure to push beyond merely correlating subjects. A grand idea with a long history of progressive struggle was being trivialized in the popular culture of the 1990s education scene.

Working alongside teachers who were trying to push beyond the mainstream conversation and researching the content of *Curriculum Integration: Designing the Core of Democratic Education* (1997), I began to see more clearly the complicated politics in pressing for progressive ideas in a decidedly conservative time. I realized that this apparent contradiction is no contradiction at all. It simply depends upon which approach one is talking about. As I explain in this chapter, some approaches require relatively little serious curriculum reform. Those that do, however, require not only complex teaching skills, but risky political commitments.

Politics and Possibilities

The 1990s have been marked by a renewed interest in curriculum arrangements beyond what is called the "separate-subject approach" in K–12. A number of factors have converged to give that interest some serious momentum. First, there is growing support for curriculum arrangements that involve application of knowledge rather than mere memorization and accumulation. Second, according to widely reported research, the brain processes information through patterns and connections with an emphasis on coherence rather than fragmentation (Caine and Caine 1991; Macdonald 1971; Sylwester 1995). Third, postmodern and poststructural fascination with multiple meanings of language and action, and with the idea that knowledge is socially constructed, has contributed to an emerging sense that knowledge is neither as fixed nor as universal as classical subject-area advocates have often implied. Fourth, a growing number of scholars point out that problems of real significance cannot be solved using only a single discipline of knowledge and, therefore, it is increasingly necessary to look at the world across disciplines (Klein 1990).

An added factor should be recognized as well. Despite the decidedly conservative direction of educational thinking in general, many educators maintain a serious interest in progressive educational ideas, including curriculum design beyond the separate subjects. This group includes advocates of "whole learning" arrangements such as whole language, unit teaching, thematic curriculum, and problem- and project-centered methods. It would also include those who argue for a social problem focus and instrumental uses of knowledge in the context of those problems as an aspect of democratic education (Apple and Beane 1995).

And, too, it would include representatives of subject-area associations and projects, including those in mathematics and science, who have called for ending fragmentation within their areas and connecting them to larger problems and issues.

Despite the apparent breadth of that support, the future of non-subject-centered curriculum approaches is by no means assured. In this chapter I explore the prospects for such approaches given the present state of curriculum and cultural politics. As we shall see, the future is complicated. Given that there is more than one such approach, the choice among them becomes crucial. Historically speaking, such approaches have had many names—broad-fields, activity, experience, fusion, democratic core, integration, common learnings, unified studies, interdisciplinary, holistic, areas-of-living, problems, emerging needs, and more—and the differences among them are more than just semantic. The future of curriculum approaches beyond the separate subjects is further complicated by the question of whether advocates of these approaches are prepared to take on important theoretical and practical issues that have surrounded them for almost a century.

Multidisciplinary Approaches and Curriculum Integration

One does not need to be a curriculum theorist to know that the history of the school curriculum has been dominated by the separate-subject approach. So dominant has it been that many people, most educators included, find it almost impossible to imagine other models. Yet this story is not the only one. For more than one hundred years, work has continued around two other approaches. One, which I will call "multidisciplinary" or "multisubject," builds upon the separate-subject approach while seeking to assuage some of its shortcomings. The other, which I will call "curriculum integration," breaks altogether from the subject-area tradition in search of very different purposes.

The historical sketch that follows, brief as it is, contains important messages for those who seek to work beyond separate subjects today. Contrary to some popular belief, this work did not originate in the late 1980s, or even in the last two or three decades. Rather it has a long and rich tradition over more than a century in both the curriculum field and in the schools. Furthermore, not all work is the same. The multidisciplinary/multisubject approach and the curriculum integration approach represent different views on matters such as the purposes of the curriculum, the uses of knowledge, and the place of the disciplines in the curriculum.

One line of work began in the late 1900s with a group known as the Herbartians. Led by Charles DeGarmo (1895), the Herbartians advocated a curriculum organization based upon two concepts: concentration and correlation.

The first of these, concentration, involved focusing the curriculum on a theme or problem; the second correlation involved using themes as vehicles for revealing or creating correlations across otherwise disconnected and fragmented subject areas. The themes themselves were most often chronologically ordered "cultural epochs" following the Herbartian tenet that ontogeny (individual human development) recapitulates phylogeny (development of "civilization"). In this way, the Herbartians believed, the curriculum could match the development of the child and thus be more accessible and meaningful.

Though the tenuous theories of Herbartianism, such as the ontogeny-phylogeny connection, were criticized by John Dewey, Francis Parker, and other early progressives, the Herbartian movement represents an extremely important moment with regard to curriculum organization beyond separate subjects. For it is here that we find the roots of the many multidisciplinary and multisubject curriculum arrangements that have gained increasing popularity in our own times (e.g., Clarke and Agne 1997; Jacobs 1989; Krogh 1990). It is true that these arrangements remain true to the primary goal of mastering separate subjects, but they nonetheless break away from the notion that disciplines of knowledge and school subjects are so differentiated as to be beyond correlation.

A second line of work emerged in the 1920s out of a combination of child-centered and democratic interests. Eager to reject the mechanistic, stimulus-response theory of mental discipline that had dominated learning psychology, many progressives embraced the new theories of organismic and Gestalt psychology that described learning as a continuous process of growth resulting from an interactive relationship between people and their environments—a process that organismic psychologists called *integration* (Hopkins 1937; Meriam 1920; Smith 1921, 1927). At the same time, a push began to frame a concept of general education that was more appropriate for a democratic society than the discipline-based Classical curriculum recommended by groups such as the Committees of Ten (National Education Association 1893) and Fifteen (National Education Association 1895)—a general education that would revitalize the role of the school in what was called *social integration* (Hopkins 1937, 1941; Rugg 1936).

While the Herbartians and other multidisciplinarians sought an improved curriculum design for bringing subject-centered knowledge to young people, advocates of integration theories were interested in a much broader purpose. In short, they sought a curriculum design that would enhance the possibilities for personal and social integration. To do this, they looked beyond the disciplines of knowledge for organizing centers or themes and focused on the significant needs, problems, interests, and concerns expressed by young people and those that were evident in the society at large. These themes were to be approached without regard for subject-area lines and, more specifically, through the organic integration of knowledge. Moreover, so as to promote the integration of experiences through meaningful learning contexts, advocates of integration insisted that young people have an opportunity to directly voice their personal concerns through teacher-pupil planning of the curriculum.

From the 1930s on, progressive educators increasingly used the popular term "core curriculum" in reference to their vision of general education (e.g., Faunce and Bossing 1951; Hopkins 1941; Vars 1969, 1987; Wright 1958). Rejecting the view of general education as a collection of required subjects, they instead framed a new type of "core" program whose curriculum design was based on integration theories and specifically on what had come to be called *curriculum integration*. It was these programs that would come to play a central role in the progressive educational platform and in the long line of research that would support them. And it is here that we find the roots of a small but growing number of current curriculum integration projects (e.g., Alexander 1995; Beane 1993, 1997; Brazee and Capelluti 1995; Brodhagen 1995; Nagel 1996; Pate, Homestead, and McGinnis 1996; Siu-Runyan and Faircloth 1995; Stevenson and Carr 1993; Wisconsin Department of Public Instruction 1996).

Because the differences between the multidisciplinary and curriculum integration approaches figure largely in thinking about the future of non-separate-subject curriculum approaches, I want to define them a bit more sharply before moving on. One way to begin illustrating the differences is to contrast the ways in which they are planned (see Figures 2 and 3). In curriculum integration, planning begins with a central theme and proceeds outward through identification of big ideas or concepts related to the theme and activities that might be used to explore them. This planning is done without regard for subject-area lines since the overriding purpose is to explore the theme itself. In a multidisciplinary or multisubject approach, planning begins with recognition of the identities of various subjects as well as important content and skills that are to be mastered within them. A theme is then identified (often from within one or another subject) and approached through the question, "What can each subject contribute to the theme?" In this way, the identities of the separate subjects are retained in the selection of content to be used (Young 1991/1992). And, as multidisciplinary units are carried out, students still experience a daily round of separate subjects in which the teacher(s) more or less attempt to relate subject areas to the organizing center. This arrangement is very different from curriculum integration in which students move from one activity or project to another, each one involving knowledge from multiple sources.

Figure 1. Schematic Web for Curriculum Integration

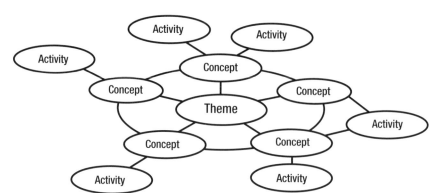

Figure 2. Schematic Web for Multidisciplinary/Multisubject Approach

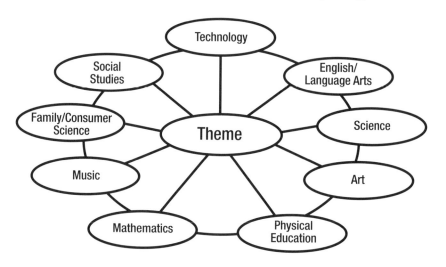

But more than this, the two approaches, multidisciplinary and integration, have deeper, virtually paradigmatic differences. Like the separate-subject approach, the multidisciplinary one still begins and ends with subject-based content and skills while curriculum integration begins and ends with problem- and issue-centered organizing centers (Bellack and Kliebard 1971). Along the way, these organizing centers also contextualize knowledge and give it significant purpose. Because the multidisciplinary approach begins with content and skills, knowledge is still regarded as fixed in predetermined categories and sequences, while integration recognizes external knowledge but sequences it by relevance to the problem at hand.

Political Intrigue Beyond the Separate-Subject Approach

Working beyond separate subjects is never easy, even for those who do so enthusiastically. Practically everything in the educational system is set up for the separate subjects, from schedules to textbooks to room arrangements. Virtually every educator who tries to push beyond this approach must contend with these logistical obstacles. Inhibiting as they may be, however, those obstacles pale in comparison to other sources of conflict that emerge from curriculum and cultural politics.

For one thing, educators who move beyond separate subjects often find themselves the object of criticism from colleagues. While there may be many reasons for such criticism, they are only compounded by the nondisciplinary nature of such work. Teachers can hide behind the symbolic walls that surround each subject and claim immunity from pedagogical scrutiny on the basis of their subject's "uniqueness." Those teachers who move outside subject boundaries question the "unique" status of individual subjects and thus cannot claim such immunity. As Bernstein has pointed out:

> Whereas the teaching process under collection [separate-subject approaches] is likely to be invisible to other teachers, unless special conditions prevail, it is likely that the teaching process regulated through integrated codes may well become visible as a result of development in the pedagogy in the direction of flexibility in the structure of teaching groups.
> (Bernstein 1975, 107)

Even as they respond to the concerns of critical colleagues, those who use non-subject-centered approaches face even greater danger beyond the school walls. For example, no matter how persuasive argument and evidence for their work may otherwise be, subject-centered approaches are protected by the interests of a powerful network of educational "elites" whose symbiotic relationships are based upon the dominance of subjects in curriculum organization. That network includes such groups as high-culture academics who define the "good life" in terms of their intellectual interests, state and federal bureaucrats whose jobs are defined by particular subject areas, text and test publishers whose multibillion-dollar self-interests rest on the separate-subject curriculum, and others. It is these groups, in concert, who hold political sway in defining both the content and organization of the curriculum. As Michael Apple noted, "one major reason that the subject-centered curricula dominate most schools, that integrated curricula are found in relatively few schools, is at least partly the result of the place of the school in maximizing the production of high status knowledge" (1990, 38).

While it is hard to exaggerate the power of this network of educational "elites," I do not want to imply that it is completely monolithic. Other, equally powerful, forces also have interests and can lead to certain kinds of compromises. For example, when business and industry, in league with government agencies, call for skills and predispositions beyond those usually encouraged by a subject-centered curriculum (SCANS 1992), parties in the network may throw some support behind multidisciplinary approaches that appear to promote complex learning while leaving subject identities intact. Such flexibility is necessary for subject-centered interests to avoid crises in their legitimization, just as advocates of alternative models must often show how important subject interests are addressed in their approaches.

I also want to be clear that when speaking of the network of educational "elites," I am referring to the interests of groups. Not all individuals within one or another of the parties to the network necessarily support its loyalty to subject-centered curriculum and related structures. For example, some disciplinary scholars might well support a high degree of curriculum integration in K–12 schools, regarding serious subject-centered study to be appropriate when students reach colleges and universities. In general, though, the positions of groups just reviewed are supported by individuals within them. After all, their self-interests are at stake here. The struggles to form, institutionalize, and defend the subject areas have not been easy ones, and neither the subject areas nor the job titles that go with them are going to be given up easily no matter how persuasive the educational arguments to do so (Goodson 1985; Kliebard 1986; Popkewitz 1987).

Another source of scrutiny is the parents of students. There are many parents who are tremendously supportive of non-separate-subject approaches and, in fact, seek to have their children placed in programs where they are used, at least partly because they seem to be more challenging and engaging than traditional subject-centered arrangements. After all, it is not true that all parents and other adults had wonderful school experiences or found the subject-centered curriculum to be thoroughly engaging or challenging. And we must not forget that in some places programs based upon non-separate-subject approaches are in place with explicit approval of the community, including school boards.

However, not all parents are so approving. For many reasons—contextual learning, nonfragmentation, flexible uses of knowledge, and so on—the multi-disciplinary and integration approaches seem to offer greater access to knowledge for more young people. Moreover, because they often encourage multiple routes to knowledge and multiple ways of demonstrating it, young people who have traditionally monopolized "success" in the classroom are likely to find themselves joined in success by more of their peers. While this may be a surprise to them, it is often profoundly upsetting to some of their parents whose ambitions for their children include being at the top of the class in school and getting into elite colleges. From these parents, questions about achievement test results are not a concern about their own children's continued success but about the possibility that their monopoly on success will be threatened (Brantlinger et al. 1996).

Other parents criticize alternative approaches, especially curriculum integration, on different grounds. It is no secret that we are living in a very conservative era in which historically dominant political and economic groups are noisily reclaiming grounds and goods they believe have been taken away from them by progressives (Apple 1993). Most of the social road signs advise, "merge right." In the midst of this conservative restoration comes a call for moving beyond separate subjects toward approaches such as curriculum integration that are partly rooted in the progressive philosophy of social reconstruction. Unlike many educators who think that curriculum integration is simply about rearranging lesson plans, conservative critics (e.g., Citizens for Excellence in Education 1992) have figured out that it involves something much larger and they don't like it.

Finally, the use of non-separate-subject approaches is also often caught up in cultural politics. In this case, such approaches are correctly identified as part of a long line of largely (but not entirely) white, upper-middle-class educational innovations that often worked from a tacit assumption that the skills upon which school success depended were reinforced by the culture in which the children lived. True, the kind of progressive pedagogy I am describing was also proposed by African-American educators for schools attended by African-American children (Daniel, 1932, 1940; Bond 1935; Wesley 1941). But, given whose knowledge is taught and tested in most schools and on standardized tests, the assumption of cultural reinforcement was certainly a reasonably safe one for the white upper-middle class. However, it is argued, the same assumption cannot be made for children whose cultures are not of that type, namely those children who are of different racial, ethnic, and economic backgrounds (e.g., Delpit 1995). It is these children who have historically been treated most harshly by the "sort and select" mechanisms of the schools. And now, just as their scores on standardized tests seem to be rising, progressive educators introduce non-separate-subject approaches in which test-based skills are neither as visible as they are in the typical subject-centered curriculum nor as relentlessly emphasized.

For this reason, such approaches seem to move the target of school success and to ignore the fact that children from nonprivileged homes simply may not bring to school with them the cultural codes and skills that are involved in that success. This concern, especially as it is understood by teachers who themselves come from nonprivileged backgrounds, goes a long way toward explaining why multidisciplinary and integration approaches are often resisted in large urban school districts by educators and noneducators alike. And this concern is likely intensified by the probability that educators from nonprivileged backgrounds may never have seen anything like these approaches in their own schooling.

Even if all of these issues were suddenly resolved, there is one more that looms large enough that it threatens virtually all non-separate-subject work, namely the political juggernaut known as the national and state standards movement. There are, of course, many arguments offered in favor of setting and testing for such standards (Apple 1997). In relation to curriculum design theory, however, the current interest in standards is one of those moments when humanists committed to classical subject- and discipline-based approaches manage to reassert, in the debate over what ought to constitute a general education program for all young people, their claims for a curriculum centered on Western heritage and traditions. In many ways, the rush to elevate often obscure pieces of information to the status of universally important knowledge is even more frenzied, and the pieces more detailed, than the similar work of the Committees of Ten and Fifteen in the 1890s (National Education Association 1893, 1895).

While alternative approaches, even curriculum integration, have never abandoned the disciplines of knowledge (Beane 1995), there can hardly be a doubt that almost everyone from politicians to parents to most teachers expects that the bits and pieces of the standards will be named and taught along exactly the same separate-subject lines into which they are divided in their collective statements. This expectation, reinforced by test makers, text developers, media pundits, and real estate agents eager to say they sell in a "standards-driven" district, will undoubtedly cast a chill over non-separate-subject initiatives in many places.

Such realities also take the optimistic edge off apparent possibilities such as the fact that funding for Goals 2000 projects included allotments for "interdisciplinary frameworks." History tells us that even the most broadly stated self and social purposes may simply be parceled out to various disciplines or subjects, as was the case with both the 1918 *Cardinal Principles of Secondary Education*

(Commission on Reorganization of Secondary Education) and the 1945 *General Education in a Free Society* (Report of Harvard Committee). In other words, there seems to be no end to the number of curriculum critics these days, and their ire is almost certain to be aimed at the substance of the separate-subject version rather than its fundamental form.

Given the complicated curriculum and cultural politics involved in working beyond separate subjects, it is hard to imagine that there would be any future for multidisciplinary and integration approaches. Yet, as we have seen, such approaches have been a part of the curriculum scene for over a century. That they survive in the face of seemingly insurmountable obstacles suggests that the reasoning behind them is attractive and, as a long line of research suggests, claims for them are warranted (Aikin 1942; Alberty 1960; Informal Committee of the Progressive Education Association 1941; Jenkins 1947; Mickelson 1957; Oberholtzer 1937; Vars 1996; Wright 1958, 1963; Wrightstone 1935, 1936, 1938). Were it not so, such approaches would surely have disappeared by now. On the other hand, multidisciplinary and integration approaches seem no better off today, with regard to status or understanding, than they were during the earlier round of activity from the 1920s to the 1950s. Given what these approaches have to offer, however, mere survival is hardly a satisfactory condition. Instead they ought to be expanding both in use and understanding.

Polishing the Multidisciplinary Approach

For several reasons the multidisciplinary approach is likely not only to survive but also to receive even more attention in the future. The idea of using multiple disciplines to approach particular topics and issues has become more widespread and more visible in higher education and in business and industry. Thus, the use of multidisciplinary approaches in schools is likely to be encouraged more and criticized less, especially if its advocates do more to explain how they match developments in those other arenas.

The fact that the identity of subjects need not be given up in multidisciplinary arrangements means that the approach will offer a reasonable compromise for subject loyalists even as educators are encouraged to work beyond their separate subjects. This possibility for compromise will become increasingly important in the near future as the discipline-based standards movement runs its course. Moreover, as the number of skill and content requirements increases, the potential for this approach to reduce repetitive coverage caused by subject isolation will make it more attractive to educators who feel overwhelmed by growing demands. In the long term, however, needed expansion of multidisciplinary curriculum arrangements will not occur unless its advocates address certain problems that have arisen as the approach has been used in recent years.

For example, apprehensive as some parents and colleagues are about thematic units, they are particularly put off by themes that seem trivial. Unfortunately, their apprehensions are too often reinforced by themes such as Apples, Teddy Bears, Chocolate, and other apparently appealing topics. In questioning the educational value of such themes, they open the whole multidisciplinary approach to question on the mistaken grounds that it ignores significant knowledge.

Likewise, a problem emerges with regard to justifying selection of one particular theme from a pool of similar possibilities. For example, a popular unit theme among middle and high school teams these days is the 1960s. The use of a historical period is common in multidisciplinary arrangements, ironically just as it was in the Herbartian movement, and may well be defended on grounds that social studies (or history) involves broad ideas and concepts to which skill areas such as mathematics, language arts, art, and so on might be applied. But why choose the 1960s as an era for concentration? We might well ask why not the 1950s or the 1980s or, for that matter, the 1670s. In the case of the popular 1960s theme, of course, the selection most likely has to do with the fact that many teachers were in school and college at that time and have fond memories of it. But this is exactly the point, just as it was in the case of the "appealing" topics above: the criterion of teacher interest alone will not suffice in the long run as a justification for selecting one or another theme.

Other criteria that speak to the educational significance and potential of the theme will be needed to safeguard the multidisciplinary approach from unwarranted criticism. These might include such factors as the theme's apparent promise for drawing on a variety of disciplines of knowledge, for reaching beyond the surface of those disciplines, for engaging substantive resources, and, perhaps most importantly, for tapping the major concepts in various disciplines. In this sense, topics like Ancient Egypt, Metrics, Aviation, Oceans, and The Middle Ages are likely to pass muster while those mentioned earlier are almost certain not to.

Advocates of the multidisciplinary approach must also address the matter of how decisions are made regarding the involvement of various subject areas in particular units and projects. Anyone who has worked with teachers beyond the separate-subject approach for very long has surely encountered the question, "But how does mathematics fit in?" And, of course, multisubject teaching teams around the country have been paralyzed by that question (or the same question with a different subject area named). In my own experience, that question is usually offered by those who view subject areas as distinct and differentiated entities with internal consistency and logic so unique that no one of them can be related to the others (especially if the correlation involves some additional planning or creative teaching).

In considering the future for multidisciplinary curriculum arrangements, however, my concern is not so much with those who raise such questions as it is with those who desire to initiate or become more involved with multidisciplinary work. In support of their desire, then, the issue at hand is this: What are the criteria to be used in deciding which subject areas are to be included in multidisciplinary units and projects? Related to this question are others: Do the criteria vary according to certain types of themes? Do certain types of themes or projects suggest differing degrees of inclusion for various subject areas? In responding to these questions, advocates of the multidisciplinary approach must also speak more firmly to the issue of involving subject areas in ways that use significant concepts and skills from subjects rather than frivolous or superficial skills.

In relation to that same issue, advocates of multidisciplinary curriculum arrangements must more seriously consider the involvement of those subject areas outside the so-called academic subjects of English/language arts, mathematics, science, and social studies/history. While multidisciplinary projects frequently emerge on a nonformal basis across a variety of subject areas, needed expansion of the multidisciplinary concept will depend upon securing a place for it in the formal, ongoing program of the school. A most reliable way of doing so is to involve as many subjects as possible to ensure the richest curriculum experience and the commitment of the greatest number of faculty in a school. For this reason, advocates of a multidisciplinary approach must enter into attempts to bring "other" subjects—the arts, technologies, health and physical education, and so on—in from the fringes of the school program.

Suggestions to involve those subjects in multidisciplinary units along with the "big four" academic subjects are usually met with the objection that such arrangements cannot be scheduled. But the fact is that this issue is not a problem with scheduling but with curriculum status. As long as the arts, technologies, health, and other subjects are considered to be outside the central program, they simply will not be included in most formal multidisciplinary arrangements. For that reason, advocates of the multidisciplinary approach must speak out in favor of a broader definition of subject significance. At the same time, they must consider ways of reconfiguring multisubject teaching teams to include variations other than the "big four," such as Humanities or Technologies teams as well as teams of only two or three teachers using various subject combinations appropriate for working with particular themes or topics.

Standing Up for Curriculum Integration?

About the future of the curriculum integration approach I must admit to being somewhat less optimistic than I am about the multidisciplinary/multisubject approach. Again, that approach remains close to the separate-subject approach in purpose while offering a form that has the potential for some coherence to counter the fragmentation of the subject approach. Curriculum integration, on the other hand, is a distinctly different approach with quite different priorities and commitments (Beane 1997).

Curriculum integration was conceived as a curriculum design for a general education that would promote self and social integration as aspects of the democratic way of life. In practice it focused on themes drawn from significant self and social issues, collaboratively planned by teachers and students without regard for subject area lines. As such, it was meant to bring young people of diverse backgrounds together in a common setting to experience the collaborative, thoughtful problem solving that is a hallmark of democracy. And while knowledge was to be drawn from many sources, including the traditional disciplines and "everyday" knowledge, that knowledge (along with the disciplines) was considered instrumental in the problem context rather than an end in itself.

Clearly, that kind of general education, as well as the rhetoric and practice associated with it, is hardly in fashion today. The fact is that we are living in an era in which conservative ideas are being reasserted in almost every aspect of life, education included. The retrenchment of "worthwhile" knowledge along traditional disciplinary lines is but one example of this. Another is marketization of educational programs in which the consumer-public is to choose among alternatives according to personal desire without regard for the common good. Children and youth are not young citizens in a democratic state, but rather potential workers in the worldwide corporate marketplace. Theirs is to learn the skills to enter the labor pool, not the democratic forum. And the parents understand this well, as well as they often seem to understand that it is not so much what one knows as whom one gets to know it with that counts.

History tells us that this is a very dangerous kind of world for the curriculum integration approach and its advocates. Mainstream curriculum historians usually ascribe the previous "death" of progressive approaches like curriculum integration to the launching of Sputnik in 1957 and the structure of the disciplines movement that followed. However, such approaches were buried some years before in conservative attacks on progressive education by Robert Hutchins, William Randolph Hearst, and others that began during World War II and reached their zenith in the McCarthy era of the late 1940s and early 1950s. Most importantly, analyses of those attacks (e.g., Brameld 1944), which ought to be read carefully by curriculum integration advocates today, reveal chilling similarities to the present situation.

Thus the agenda for advocates of curriculum integration involves promoting both an educational approach and the broader social philosophy to which it is related. One aspect of this agenda must be the rescue of the term curriculum integration from its interchangeable use with the multidisciplinary approach. When professional literature and workshop programs use the terms *integration* or *curriculum integration* in reference to multidisciplinary/multisubject arrangements, the deeper meaning of the approach is marginalized and, along with it, the progressive philosophy of democratic general education. By clarifying the differences between these approaches and explaining the integration idea accurately, advocates of curriculum integration have an opportunity to restate and promote the purposes for which the approach was intended.

At the same time, advocates of curriculum integration must speak more visibly about the social principles implied in democratic general education. For example, are there collective purposes for which a democratic society maintains schools that transcend the self-interests or desires of individual parents and which, therefore, suggest that the concept of "citizen" may override that of "consumer" in school decisions? Is it not the case that a central tenet of democracy is collective seeking of common good and purpose by diverse individuals? If that is a central tenet, then shouldn't the school program emphasize a common, general education program? Is collaborative and thoughtful problem solving an aspect of the democratic way of life and, if so, should not much of the school program use that process as a central method?

Lest this analysis be viewed as inappropriately introducing politics into a curriculum conversation, we should remember that all curriculum work is political. Curriculum decision making is an expression of our philosophic beliefs and values, our vision of a good life and a desirable society. This is no more or less true for decisions in favor of progressive, democratic aims of curriculum integration than it is for those in favor of the classical, high-culture interests of a discipline-based separate-subject curriculum. In this sense, then, advocates of curriculum integration must engage with the politics of democracy and education without apology if they expect to create a larger space for their approach. To leave the philosophy behind the approach unstated simply reduces it to a collection of methods that cannot survive the scrutiny of a one-sided ideological attack.

At the same time, more work is needed to advance understanding and practice in regard to the curriculum integration approach itself. Certainly, a growing body of literature by teachers and administrators is available for those who wish to know more about the approach. Yet two areas are in need of substantially more work. The first involves an analysis of existing accounts to more fully understand what kinds of knowledge most frequently surface in curriculum integration, how students organize knowledge within the context of personal issues, how teachers mediate decisions made in collaborative planning with students, and other questions that persist inside the approach in practice. While some important research on such questions has emerged recently (Powell and Skoog 1995; Powell, Skoog, and Troutman 1996; Powell, Skoog, Troutman, and Jones 1996), much more is needed.

The other area that advocates of curriculum integration must address is the feasibility of the approach on a school or district scale. With few exceptions, the work of curriculum integration has been done within isolated classrooms or teams in scattered schools. This leaves open such questions as how a school or district might pursue coordination when a large dose of the curriculum is planned in each classroom, or whether themes can be repeated across school years if they recur in classroom planning. While such questions do have responses (Beane 1997), they are not acknowledged often enough by advocates of curriculum integration and, therefore, can easily paralyze even preliminary discussions about the approach.

Popular opinion often describes the comings and goings of educational ideas in terms of a swinging pendulum. However, as Kliebard (1986) points out, the history of curriculum over the last century is actually a struggle among competing visions, all of which are present at any given moment. Given that, we might safely predict that the future of non-separate-subject approaches will have at least two features. One is that they will never gain complete ascendance in the struggle over curriculum designs. The other is that they will not disappear from the educational scene. Instead, they will continue to be among the various curriculum designs that educators choose to pursue particular goals and promote particular cultural and political philosophies.

In the very near future, moreover, it is unlikely that non-separate-subject approaches will continue to experience the kind of rapid growth they did in the late 1980s and early 1990s. As the standards movement implies, this is a conservative era in which nostalgic yearnings for social, cultural, and economic security are awash across social institutions, including the school. Thus, while non-separate-subject approaches will persist, their advocates will face serious opposition from those whose nostalgia includes the classical separate-subject curriculum and all of its institutional trappings. Moreover, until the dust settles from the first wave of standards-setting activity, it cannot be known what and how much effort will be required to reconstruct the content and skills involved in the context of non-separate-subject formats.

In the longer term, I believe that multidisciplinary arrangements will be used with increasing frequency in schools and are even likely to become commonplace. Again, as emphasis on specialization and fragmentation decreases in influential business and higher education settings, the related trend toward generalization cannot help but enter into the school curriculum. In addition, the possibility that this approach can provide more efficient ways of accomplishing increased skill expectations will also support its expanded use.

The future of curriculum integration is far more complicated. Certainly it will continue to have advocates, but in order for the approach to have a secure place for some portion of the school program, rather than to exist as a network of localized progressive moments, the public and the profession will have to have a change of heart about the purposes of the curriculum. Perhaps the day will come when the desire for the democratic way of life, and a school curriculum to go along with it, will become so widespread that general education will be defined not as a collection of separate subjects but as a program in which diverse young people come together for a common experience focused on personal and social integration. Only in such a scenario can curriculum integration, as I have defined it, once again be considered as an appropriate design for general education and subsequently gain a wider place in the schools. It is hard to imagine such a time, especially immersed in the present one.

Meanwhile, advocates for all kinds of alternative approaches must continue to expand and clarify the meaning of their work and its potential for enriching the lives and learning of young people. And they must continue to protect the reputation of such approaches from unwarranted attacks by those who for one reason or another simply do not see this potential. No matter the future, though, those advocates may rest assured that theirs is a significant story in the history of curriculum, both past and present.

Recommended Readings

- Brodhagen, Barbara L. 1995. "The Situation Made Us Special." In *Democratic Schools*, edited by Michael W. Apple and James A. Beane, 83–100. Alexandria, Va.: Association for Supervision and Curriculum Development. This essay is the best contemporary example of teacher writing about curriculum integration as it might look in the classroom.
- Faunce, Roland C., and Bossing, Nelson L. 1951. *Developing the Core Curriculum*. New York: Prentice-Hall. The classic work from the great midcentury "Core Curriculum" movement, this volume lays out theoretical and practical ideas and issues in creating a problem-centered curriculum for general education in a democracy.
- Hopkins, L. Thomas, and others. 1937. *Integration: Its Meaning and Application*. New York: D. Appleton-Century; and Hopkins, L. Thomas. 1941. *Interaction: The Democratic Process*. New York: D. C. Heath. These two volumes should be read as a pair since they bring together perspectives on integration from a number of fields with a view of how the concept relates to curriculum theory and democratic education.
- Noar, Gertrude. 1948. *Freedom to Live and Learn*. Philadelphia: Franklin Publishing and Supply Co. In this volume, one of the leading early advocates and practitioners of curriculum integration explains both theoretical and practical issues regarding curriculum integration, including the teacher's role, teacher-student planning, and the use of the disciplines of knowledge.
- Smith, Meredith. 1927. *Education and the Integration of Behavior*. Contributions to Education 261. New York: Teachers College Press, Columbia University. Probably the first professional education book to use the term "integration" in the title, this volume suggests how the project method, organismic psychology, and other forces converged to promote the concept of integration in education.

4

Introduction to *Interdisciplinary High School Learning in an Information Age*

High school has traditionally been more resistant to interdisciplinary approaches than the rest of K–12. In 1997, Allyn and Bacon published a new book that documents why interdisciplinarity is becoming more familiar in the final years of secondary education. Written by John Clarke and Russell Agne, *Interdisciplinary High School Teaching: Strategies for Integrated Learning* defines the shift from a subject-based to a process-based curriculum. They grouped ten innovation strategies into three major themes: making connections, focusing on processes, and solving problems. Rich in contributions from a network of New England educators, the book is a hands-on resource complete with curriculum models, teacher checklists, exercises, and graphic tools for professional development and classroom use. Like Rebecca Burns, Clarke and Agne ground the conceptual case for integrated teaching and learning in a constructivist view of how we assemble knowledge of ourselves and the world. Like Burns and Heidi Jacobs, they also believe that interdisciplinarity and constructivism can work in concert with the standards movement.

Since they wrote *Interdisciplinary High School Teaching*, Clarke and Agne have found three streams of influence to be converging—the constructivist approach, the information revolution, and the standards movement. In Chapter 4, they situate this convergence in terms of a topic of wide concern, assessment, and a relatively neglected topic in discussions of interdisciplinarity, the use of technologies in the classroom. Their discussion of assessment is informed by the Vermont *Framework of Standards and Learning Opportunities* for K–12 curriculum. The Vermont *Framework* defines both "Vital Results" in all content areas—intellectual skills that include communication, reasoning and problem solving, personal development, and social responsibility—and "Essential Learnings," which meet specific content requirements. In an interdisciplinary design, content remains "essential" to making meaning and solving problems, but the process of managing information also becomes "vital" to education. The Web project in Vermont provides a striking model of how technology and assessment can be merged. Student performances can be collected on a Web page or a CD-ROM, generating public dialogue on the quality of content acquisition and intellectual process.

To guide educators in working with technologies, Agne and Clarke provide a graphic model of software programs arranged to answer questions of purpose, process, fact, and interpretation. Their explanations and illustrations are arranged around four quadrants of technology: for data analysis, for theory development, for creative expression, and for supporting communication and problem solving. At present, few secondary school Web courses have a strong interdisciplinary character. Yet, as high school libraries continue to be transformed into media centers, this tendency will change. And as the Web becomes more and more central to the classroom, Agne and Clarke predict, integrative management of knowledge and information will become increasingly central factors in curriculum design.

Interdisciplinary High School Learning in an Information Age

Russell M. Agne and John H. Clarke

Since we wrote the introduction to *Interdisciplinary High School Teaching* in 1996, three streams of influence we mentioned separately at the time have continued flowing together. First, constructivist views of learning have become widespread among high school teachers, leading them to explore methods of instruction and assessment that accommodate the wide range of individual differences visible in their classrooms. Second, the standards movement has produced a set of purposes for high school learning that is not constrained by conventional disciplinary boundaries. Third, the information revolution has allowed individual students and teachers to gather information from a wide array of sources and represent what they have learned in a wide array of media. The largely unforeseen confluence of these trends has allowed both teachers and students to envision and pursue a most improbable goal: individualized learning plans for all high school students—based on individual goals, organized to demonstrate success against common standards, and presented on student Web pages accessible to parents, students, and teachers. The confluence of these three streams of influence adds more force to the movement toward reforming high school learning than any one source alone (Clarke et al. 1998).

New Trends in Integrative Learning

The challenge of interdisciplinary high school teaching is to prepare all students to gather and assess information from a wide variety of sources, fitting a strategy they have designed to a clear purpose they have set for themselves. While a complete prototype of high school teaching following individual student goals, meeting common standards, and mediating by computer technologies may not yet exist, evidence of the convergence is more accessible now than it was just three years ago:

- University Heights High School in the Bronx has developed a flexible process of individual learning that allows different students to meet the same common standards in their own way, explaining and defending their achievement in a series of public "Roundtables" (Clarke and Agne 1997).
- The Metropolitan Regional Career and Technical Center (Met) in Providence, Rhode Island, allows students to design their own learning plans, supported by small advisory groups and linked to community-based learning in business and public service.
- University City High School in Philadelphia is becoming "virtual," using Web-linked computers to develop and represent student learning in the school and community (http://www.u-city.com/ucity1.html).
- Web66, a project of the University of Minnesota, maintains a Web site to link students and teachers to the World Wide Web servers in K–12 schools (http://Web66.umn.edu/). Also, during the 2000–2001 school year the Massachusetts-based Concord Consortium's Virtual High School identified 150 schools and 300 students taking net-based courses (http://vhs.concord.org/). What experimental schools have shown to be feasible, others are adapting to change the face of subject-based curricula in conventional high schools.

The commonalities among these three high schools reveal a similar inspiration of their origins. All are urban schools serving students who differ so widely in background that attempts to group them in useful "tracks" prove futile. All respond to the needs of students who have become disaffected by schooling that emphasizes memorization and recitation. All the programs also include a large component of experience in the surrounding community, either well-developed school-to-work internships or community-service programs, to motivate students toward achievement of the standards. Each school emerged from a partnership between the local business community or a K–16 collaboration with a higher education institution, reducing the insularity of the high school experience. Each, moreover, has been able to demonstrate success for students who do not "fit" into a conventional curriculum organized around "seat-time" in a sequence of subject-area courses. In Vermont and elsewhere, conventional high schools are now adapting constructivist teaching strategies, standards-oriented curriculum, and information technology from urban experimental schools—aiming to create independent learning opportunities for all their students.

In May of 1998, we went to Providence to participate in the year-end roundtable presentations by which Met Center students demonstrate their achievement of the school's standards. For nearly two hours, we watched a bright but angry young sophomore explain what she had learned while serving as a Spanish-language interpreter for patients in a city hospital. Daily, she had traveled room to room helping patients with no English explain to doctors and nurses how they felt about their pain and their treatment. During the year, this sophomore, who had not been recognized previously for academic drive, discovered that she wanted to become an advocate for Hispanic people in her community. What would she need? Written fluency in English and Spanish? Biology? Basic statistics? Computer applications? Her advisor, community mentor, English teacher, and science teacher took careful note of her assertions and our comments, setting up the elements of a plan for her next year. As they adapt their teaching to her purposes, they are moving toward an integrated curriculum.

From a curriculum built to reflect the structure of what is known—and therefore, what exists for young people to memorize—we are turning to a curriculum based on the processes of managing information, featuring strategies that individual students can use to make sense of information and put it to work in ways that are consistent with their own purposes. Will we recklessly abandon the substance of the subject areas for the empty allure of process—again? No. Interdisciplinary teaching at the high school level simply bows to necessity—allowing the process of inquiry to subordinate the wild profusion of information that now strains both the boundaries of the subject areas and our own ability to understand complexity. Subject-area courses may still exist, but increasingly they serve interdisciplinary motives: analyzing real issues in the students' experience with adult roles, and using information to solve problems. The confluence of constructivist thinking, standards-based curriculum, and interactive technology is pushing high school teaching toward an interdisciplinary design. To understand this confluence, first we need to know more about constructivist thinking.

A Constructivist Perspective on Formal Learning

For a curriculum to work, it must be comprehensible to students. Few adolescent learners can connect the array of subjects they face in the high school curriculum to the lives they have begun to imagine for themselves after high school. A glance at a typical sophomore schedule can reveal how disjointed the curriculum might appear to a student. A typical eight-period day might begin with a class in physical education, followed by a discussion of *Huckleberry Finn*. Then Algebra 2, then Chorus, then Federalism in Early America, divided in half by a split-period lunch. Afternoon might begin with a study hall, move to an examination of sexuality and relationships, and end with a review of irregular verbs in French 2. For a typical sophomore, the only real effort at coherence occurs in the three-minute breaks between classes, when persistent social problems can be quickly raised and resolved. Is Tim going with Alice or Felicia? The answer and its follow-up questions can be established before afternoon buses roll. Against any single measure—SAT scores, tests of basic competency or math skills for the workplace—high school students appear less prepared than they should because their years in school aim to prepare them for no organizing purpose, not even for success on norm-referenced tests. Because knowledge is created by the knower, schools must shift focus to the question of how each of us develops discrete perceptions into a coherent, reliable worldview (Brooks and Brooks 1993).

Constructivist theories of learning emphasize the unique nature of individual learning, which computers accommodate more easily than most teachers. A constructivist approach to teaching emphasizes that learners need to be actively involved, to reflect on their learning, and to experience cognitive conflict as they struggle to reconcile alternative perspectives (Fosnot 1989). As a learning theory now emerging to guide teaching, constructivism focuses teaching on the processes students can use to develop and manage a working model of the world in which they live. Developing complex "models" of how the world works requires students to sift through increasingly complex information and solve increasingly complex problems (Cognition and Technology Group of Vanderbilt University 1990).

In constructivist learning theory the idea of basic knowledge is still prominent. "All new learning depends on prior learning," David Ausubel (1968) observed near the dawn of constructivist thinking. What we already know determines what we learn and how we learn it. We learn not so much by filling gaps in an idealized curriculum, but by testing and extending what we already know. In constructivist theory, therefore, "basic knowledge" shapes all new learning—and remains thoroughly idiosyncratic to the individual learner. Inferences that individuals draw from facts create personal meaning, not the facts themselves. By creating the governing structures that form the basis of meaningful learning, early childhood experience—hardly uniform in a multicultural society—begins to govern the processes of formal school learning. High school students cannot all learn the same content in the same way because their prior knowledge restricts what is possible for them to know. They have to continue constructing knowledge from the structures they have already built, whatever they might be.

Constructivism is a theory of learning devised largely from cognitive psychology, research in brain physiology, and complex systems dynamics (Caine and Caine 1991). Unlike developmental psychology, which stresses common trends in the process of growth from infancy to adulthood, constructivism asks us to look first at individual variations, aiming to comprehend the baffling array of differences that characterize individual students in any classroom. As every high school teacher knows, students may be perfectly happy not struggling to reconcile new information with their existing knowledge. Teachers must act skillfully in order to engage the learning process among a class of individuals who learn, think, and understand quite independently.

Neural physiology explains the paradox by which one standardized physical system—a modularized brain—creates such a wild variety of different minds (Pinker 1996). The human nervous system is nicely wired to allow individually adaptive constructions of experience and meaning. Neurons reach to the borders of the human frame via all five senses, searching the world for evidence of threat, sustenance, or delight. Mental functions related to sight use up to about 70 percent of our mental effort. Hearing provides us with a second way to see—scanning the environment equally well day or night (Sylwester 1995). We can often smell a threat long before we see or hear it. Our sense of smell is hard-wired to long-term memory, bypassing short-term memory to speed our reaction time. Taste is confined to four basic qualities, those that help us make fine distinctions between pleasure and poison. The world rubbing on our skin brings excitement or pain. To touch is to take the measure of trust. All the senses reach into the same environment, but they bring back different kinds of information that the brain then weaves into a simulacrum—a mental model of how things work and what they mean.

Our brains are built to fold together a multilayered model of the world outside. (The cerebral cortex alone uses six layers of interconnected nerves to help us understand and make decisions). The modeled world we construct in our minds seems real. We often act as if our circling on a boundless stage—woven into schemata that connect ideas and images, concepts, and modeled impressions—is equivalent to physical experience, but the elements of the schemata are composed only of energy passing across synapses in multilayered networks of neurons, firing away in patterns that create the impression we live twice—first in experience and thereafter in an endless symbolic drama of construction and reconstruction (Jensen 1998).

In the life of the mind, recollected images, sounds, smells, and sensations become actors, memories. If new impressions resemble older memories, we assimilate them, strengthening the ideas we use to organize mental clutter. If new impressions conflict with prior knowledge, we experience disequilibrium. We are forced to question. Questions force us to reconcile new information with prior knowledge. The answers we develop to resolve conflicts change the entire structure of what we know.

If the workings of our environment prove radically inconsistent with our mental models, we may suffer and die. Our chances of survival are heightened by the fact that the physical world and the internal dramatization interact constantly; they are mutually self-regulating. If some part of the world threatens our safety, we adjust the world. If we are surprised when some expectation fails to materialize, we may simply change our minds. Working in behalf of our individual survival, expectation and actuality are mutually self-correcting in the process we call learning.

Knowledge construction, then, results from a complex interaction between prior knowledge and the flow of new information through the senses. Neither prior knowledge nor the flow of information can be regulated from the outside, by a teacher or a curriculum. From a constructivist perspective the products of student learning will always be unique to the individual. Requiring a uniform response from a group of 25 students, therefore, is probably as ill advised as it is impossible. Yet this is the mistake carried forward by discipline-based teaching that insists each subject area consists of a codified body of knowledge that can be transmitted intact to any group of students (Hirsch 1987).

Interdisciplinary teaching provides the best context so far for moving from what students know to what they don't yet understand. In interdisciplinary teaching, we can help students focus their questioning. We can arrange a vast array of material for them to look at and test. We can ask them to express what they see in forms that communicate effectively. Still, we cannot forget that the most important determinant of new learning remains fixed in the mental structure of the learners; the objects they choose to "see" depend as much on their initial understanding and curiosity as on our curricular blueprints. At the end, each student will leave high school with a wholly unique conception of the purpose, structure, and content of the learning he or she explored. If all learning is idiosyncratic, how then are teachers supposed to guide learning among diverse students and assess learning equitably? The answer may lie in performance standards for learning.

Performance Standards for Knowledge Construction

The standards movement, now active in most states, is a response to the need for a simplifying purpose for high school learning. A standard is an expression of what all students should be able to do with what they know as a result of their education. At first glance, the idea of "common standards" seems to wrestle uneasily with a constructivist view of individual learning. In actual use, however, common standards allow high school teachers to assess a wide array of student productions or exhibitions, using criteria for each standard that are stated clearly and uniformly to students and parents alike. If student productions are collected on a Web page or CD-ROM, the assessment of student learning can occur in a public dialogue. For example,

> The WEB Project, based in Montpelier, Vermont, is a U.S. Department of Education Technology Innovation Challenge Grant geared toward creating multimedia forms of evidence of student performance. This means using technology to show what students can do through digitizing images, sound, and motion. The WEB Project also hosts this World Wide Web site where teachers, students, and community members can discuss work together.   (http://www.webproject.org/)

Dialogues in the WEB Project increase the clarity of the standards and criteria the participants use to judge student work, while also challenging our conventional sense of what reliability and validity may mean in student assessment. Performance standards for the knowledge construction process give us a way to ensure quality without imposing uniformity on the constructions different students create to organize their learning. In standards-based classrooms, teachers set challenging tasks for students to complete, arrange resources for them to use in completing the task, then measure their progress against a list of criteria that represent the performance standards. Student learning in such a classroom can range widely across the subject areas and result in products that reflect the unique perspectives of individual students—except that each product is measured against the same criteria for the same standard (Stiggins 1998).

Performance standards describe what students "should know and be able to do" as a result of learning. That is, they include measures for both content acquisition and the intellectual processes of applying knowledge. Vermont's *Framework of Standards and Learning Opportunities* was designed around this duality of motive (Vermont Department of Education 1995). The half of the Vermont *Framework of Standards* called "Vital Results" defines the intellectual skills that apply to all the content areas: communication, reasoning and problem solving, personal development, and social responsibility. They are described as flexible strategies for analyzing information so it becomes useful in solving novel problems (Resnick 1989). The other half, called "Essential Learnings," includes a list of content requirements deemed by Vermont educators to be necessary to progress in school. The Vermont *Framework* includes specific content for each of only three "fields of knowledge": Arts, Language, and Literature; History and Social Sciences; and Science, Mathematics, and Technology. Both the "vital results" and the "fields of knowledge" are described as "performance expectations" that help teachers measure what students can do with what they learn, not as facts and ideas to be memorized. The "Learning Opportunities" referred to in the title suggest ways in which students, rather than teachers, can become the focus of classroom work with criteria that favor individualized learning and technological media.

We think there may be more magic in the term "performance standards" than one would first expect. In a politically divided educational context, the term nods happily toward both progressive and conservative educators. It grants to discipline-based educators, who often aim for increased rigor, the promise of a curriculum that will produce measurable results in knowledge acquisition. At the same time, it grants to interdisciplinary teachers, who use questions, projects, and problems to organize learning, a chance to show how individual student work should take center-stage in the classroom. "Standards" leans to the right, while "performance" leans to the left. The "Vital Results" appeal more to interdisciplinary teachers. The "Essential Learnings" appeal more to content-area specialists. When all standards are used collectively to assess student exhibitions, performances, or portfolios, distinctions blur and we achieve a remarkable level of unanimity in public dialogue about the quality of student performance. Welded together, the term "performance standards" ensures that all of us, as one profession, will be able to talk about the same questions at least some of the time. Although it is intimidating at first glance, the term "performance standards" may have the power to bridge disciplinary and interdisciplinary teaching.

The argument that all teaching and learning should aim to meet high standards is both simple and powerful. We can help all students learn at a high level of challenge if we give them challenging tasks to complete, with standards-based criteria that help them see where they are going and recognize success when they get there. Teachers can arrange tasks at increasing levels of complexity for different students, but can meanwhile hold the standards steady, adapting them only as we come to understand them better, reflected in specific instances of student performance. Once embarked on the path toward high standards, the technical adjustments needed in structure, curriculum, and instructional method will become as obvious as they are difficult to complete. We may even arrive at a time when the idea of K–16 performance standards appears feasible. Guinette County (Atlanta) Georgia, has designed a set of performance standards to assess student progress K–12. Each standard devolves from the same question: "What does it take to become a competent adult?" (Clarke and Agne 1997).

The Core Curriculum has had the same general purpose throughout its long and erratic history. Linking K–12 standards to college standards, however, will require more than a technical fix. It will require an expansion of the research and development activity that began, perhaps, with the Eight-Year Study, so teachers gradually develop confidence that they can help students achieve performance standards without sacrificing academic achievement, even as measured by conventional means, such as SATs, GREs, and MCATs. More important, it will require an energetic conversation among teachers K–16 in which we all rediscover our shared purpose—and slowly delineate a structure for our shared profession.

The Information Revolution

Information technologies easily carry out intellectual tasks that would quickly overwhelm a high school student: computers serve as repositories for vast amounts of information that remain stable until adjusted intentionally; they carry out some processes of analysis with almost absolute reliability; they communicate information to others verbatim, without editorial license. The human mind, in contrast, performs at least two tasks well that computers cannot manage at all: we make meaning from information and use it to solve complex problems. Stated somewhat differently, humans develop complex strategies to serve purposes we devise for ourselves. Making meaning and solving problems lie at the heart of human capability; they should hold a similar place in the high school curriculum, supported by technologies that simplify both critical analysis and creative planning. Interdisciplinary high school teaching does not threaten to replace the content areas with processing skills; it switches the order of their subordination, supported by emerging technologies that enhance our ability to ask questions and derive answers in the endless cycle of intellectual revision called learning.

Information remains essential both to making meaning and to solving problems, but the process of managing information using both simple and complex strategies is becoming "basic" to all learning. The simple process of asking questions and deriving answers is basic to all intellectual endeavors, from literary analysis to chemical engineering. By asking more complex questions about earlier answers, each of us constructs a version of "truth" for ourself that explains an expanding range of content and experience. To become a general skill, asking questions and making answers must be learned and relearned in multiple contexts over a long period of time, using the language structure of each subject area and information management strategies that are distinctive to each discipline but adaptable to different situations.

Computers allow students to ask their own questions and construct their own answers, in a wide variety of media. The software and communication hardware being used most in schools today is built to help manage problems in life, not to answer textbook questions. As electronic flashcards built 20 years ago to support subject-area memorization disappear, they are replaced by information management software built to support adults in the workplace. Word processors, spreadsheets, statistical packages, e-mail, and Internet access—designed to help people manage and communicate information—all represent general processing capabilities rather than a specific subject. Software helping students manage rather than memorize information is now much more common in high school courses than earlier drill and practice programs. (High school courses on computer programming have also become a rare specialty.) In high school classrooms, computers and technology are better able to handle individual inquiry than most teachers are. Some social critics such as Theodore Roszak (1997) dispute this contention. While a computer-based curriculum may open locked doors, he fears that unless used in exactly the right spirit it can produce the sort of stultifying result that teaching machines of the past and many forms of computerized instruction currently produce. The new software programs, however, are much more challenging and open-ended than earlier versions. Software programs designed to solve adult problems have no respect for disciplinary boundaries; they gather information wherever they are asked to look. Empowered by far-reaching software capabilities, what high school student would stop at a content border?

As the information age matures and constructivist thinking continues to exert influence on educational practice, the knowledge that anyone calls "basic" becomes harder to describe even in a very long list of specific items. Instead, basic knowledge in an information age consists of knowing how to manage all kinds of information with a clear purpose in view. Managing large, unruly quantities of information is what computers do best. In addition, computer software and communications hardware now mimic many of the mind's intellectual capabilities, creating a medium in which each of us can construct our own meaning, using information from a wide range of media. Having stretched the subjects beyond their holding capacity, we may be saved from incoherence by a constructivist perspective, common standards for learning, and the emergence of processing technologies built to bring order to information chaos.

In *Interdisciplinary High School Teaching,* we proposed a cycle of four connecting questions that high school students can use to organize information from any source:

WHY?: Questions of Purpose

> Why are we doing this? Why do things happen? Why do some live while others die?

HOW?: Questions of Process
> How can I do this? How can I find out? How do things happen? How can we make a difference in the way things occur?

WHERE? WHEN? WHAT? HOW MUCH?: Questions of Fact
> What evidence exists that relates to my questions? What result do I get? How many times has this happened?

SO WHAT?: Questions of Interpretation
> What does the evidence mean? How do the facts connect? How many different interpretations work for these facts?

In addition to connecting inquiry among the disciplines, these four questions in sequence constitute a general strategy for managing information in any subject area (Clarke 1990; Clarke and Biddle 1993). They also represent the kind of intellectual skills that computer software is designed to support. To explain how available software mimics some narrow aspect of human intelligence, we developed the illustration in Figure 1.

Figure1: Cycle of Software

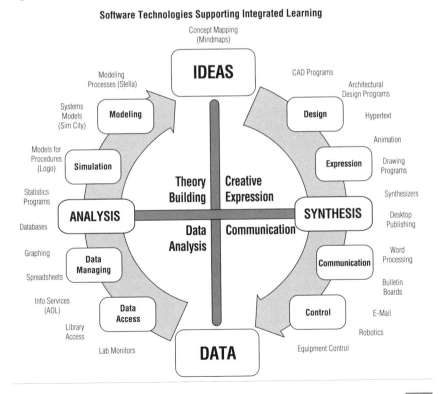

The Cycle of Software in Figure 1 represents a sample of software programs, arranged to answer different kinds of questions. Some software packages, illustrated in the lower left quadrant, help students gather information and organize it for analysis. Other software packages, described in the upper left quadrant, help students generate plausible hypotheses and "models" of how things work. A third group, in the upper right quadrant, help students create a unique expression of what they have learned or understood. The fourth group, in the lower right quadrant, help students solve problems or generate new data. Together, the four quadrants constitute a catalogue of intellectual processes that computers are built to manage. Humans are left to organize these tactical supports into strategies that they can use to serve their own purposes.

Each software package replicates a thin slice of intellectual ability, allowing students to analyze or synthesize information using a narrowly prescribed routine. Computers can handle easily intellectual tasks that would take humans hours or days to perform: gathering data from the U. S. census; calculating means, modes, and standard deviations; or constructing a model that explains the data. If computer and communication technologies had no utility in the workplace or in college, it is less than likely that information technologies would be providing the final push from a content-based to a process-based curriculum. As it is, computers and information exchange have become essential to success in both adult work and secondary learning, making it necessary for students and adults alike to devise valid and reliable strategies for using information. What the computer is unable to do is sequence software routines into a strategy that serves a human purpose.

Interdisciplinary high school teaching relies increasingly on these technologies. High school students in science classes are designing surveys and experiments, producing data they analyze for presentation to their peers. Students in social studies classes are using simulations of city politics and economics to design virtual cities that may actually work. Students are designing advertising campaigns for English classes and travel brochures for geography classes. They are using graphic calculators to predict the future from past events. From an adult or student perspective, the tasks that computers support are both challenging and innately interesting, leading some commentators to label them "authentic" and creating an interdisciplinary movement toward "authentic learning" (Wiggins 1989). In the following section we will describe some of the projects high school teachers have devised to help their students use computers to complete authentic tasks, driving high school teaching further in an interdisciplinary direction.

Using Technology to Support Interdisciplinary Learning

Secondary school teachers throughout the United States have developed many exciting strategies to engage students in interdisciplinary study. Much of this effort has resulted from individual teacher initiatives in schools where computer-based resources have been incorporated into units of study or used to organize entire courses. While one can become very enthusiastic about efforts to wire schools for technology, it is certainly true that access to computer resources is uneven, with many schools falling in the "have not" category. The uneven distribution of computer resources in public schools threatens one of the central purposes of public education, to prepare all students to manage their own lives and participate in a democratic society. Billions of dollars have been spent on the promise of reinventing education. In 1995, for example, the nation's schools spent $3.2 billion on computer hardware, networks, teacher training, and infrastructure (Buckeley 1997). Unfortunately, schools in the inner cities frequently are shortchanged by hand-me-down equipment, limited teacher preparation, and little ongoing technical support. However, little by little, high school teachers are learning to make substantial use of information technologies, a process that must be generalized to all students in all schools. We will describe exemplars of such teaching using all four quadrants of Figure 1 as organizers: Data Analysis, Theory Building, Creative Expression, and Supporting Communication and Problem Solving.

1. Technology for Data Analysis

Students and teachers today have wide access to information, thanks to multimedia such as video tapes/disks and CD-ROMs. While these media will continue to make a wide range of information available to students, many teachers have discovered that fount of virtually limitless information access represented by the Internet or World Wide Web (WWW). With support from government, private foundations, and the telecommunications industry, increasing numbers of schools are being brought online. While the traditional library with print books and copies of real periodicals may continue to exist in public schools, electronic media are being used for information retrieval at an explosive rate. The high school library has been transformed into the "media center." With unlimited amounts of raw information accessible through the Web, students and teachers are shifting their emphasis to the question of making meaning from vast quantities of data of very mixed quality.

Software helping students analyze information is also entering high school teaching from business, industry, and government. Teachers in many traditional subjects are finding ways to use databases such as the government census, voting records, crop data, and information on weather and violent storm events, disease, history, and economic forecasts. Not all sources are quantitative; not all appear in written language either. Other Internet sources feature satellite-gathered pictures, archival collections from art museums and arboretums, music excerpts, interviews with famous people, and newspaper articles, critical reviews, and commentary. For a high school student, access to information shifts our educational priorities toward the intellectual skills of asking clear questions, assembling reliable information from several media, and organizing it into structures in which meaning can be perceived and communicated.

The World Wide Web is an information transfer medium, completely unrestricted by disciplinary boundaries. Once access has been gained by one or more computer stations in a high school, difficult issues of usage must be confronted. Best instructional practice is demonstrated when teachers go beyond content or subject knowledge to prepare lessons based on contemporary views of pedagogy (e.g., using a process approach to teach writing; taking an inquiry approach to science learning; employing manipulatives and graphing calculators such as the TI–81 to teach mathematics).

The existence of massive amounts of information forces the high school curriculum to focus on analytic skill, judgment, and reasoning. Just because some technical material pops up on the screen doesn't make it authentic or reliable information. Indeed, the overwhelming urge some people have to publish on the Web leads to the posting of information with little or no quality control. How do we then determine if it is accurate? Another instructional issue is that surfing or browsing the Web can be an enormous waste of time, resulting in uncertain outcomes and little intellectual accomplishment. These limitations of the "Web" are highlighted by the following example from Roszak:

> I talked with a librarian recently who was approached by a student who had to do a paper on sharks. She found him a couple of excellent books and articles. He insisted on using the Web; his teacher had insisted that he use the Web! After a long search, he came up with scores of hits for teams named "Sharks," software firms called "Sharknet" and such, products called "Shark-," ads for hunting and fishing equipment, some scattered private sites that kept track of shark attacks, beach front spas and hotels featuring shark on the menu, bookstores and video stores selling books and feature films about sharks . . . but no basic, reliable information about sharks—except for the article in the *Encyclopedia Britannica*."
>
> (Roszak 1997, R32, R35)

Facing excess and superfluity, how tempting it is for students to land on the *Britannica* article and press the print button!

Finally, and this is our most serious concern, simply gathering information by any means, in this case via the Internet, is fundamentally a low-level intellectual activity. The derivation of meaning from diverse sources is a higher-level challenge. As Peter Deming has observed, "The Internet is basically an information transfer medium. Knowledge is much more than information, it is the capacity for effective action. People do not consider that you know something unless you demonstrate it by doing it. You need more than the facts; you need the capability to act. As long as the Internet is seen as an information transfer medium, it will be incapable of helping to confer knowledge" (interview in *Educom Review* 1997, 24).

To showcase the *significant* use of databases, we must identify examples where teachers have gone beyond information access and downloading. A higher-order instructional goal is to learn the research skill of *manipulating* data to answer important student-identified questions. Students develop questions about the real world that are important to them and then ferret out information to form a basis for their answer. This process represents constructivist pedagogy in action. In our judgment the more impressive data-centered curriculum efforts have come from teacher-developed materials rather than from off-the-shelf commercial products. Often, large organizations involving researchers in a particular field work collaboratively with teachers to develop such curriculum options. Active school partnerships now include the National Geographic Society, the Colonial Williamsburg Foundation, the New England Aquarium, the Smithsonian Institution, and the London Zoo. Given sometimes difficult access to the Internet when it is needed, many teachers wisely use CD-ROM disks containing archival information (Clarke and Agne 1997, 178).

A rich example of what we believe to be appropriate use of Internet information is the work of Tom Vaughn, a high school teacher in Billerica, Massachusetts. His students used the Internet site maintained by the United States Geological Survey to get access to both historical and "real time" data on earthquake epicenters. Gerald Larson, one of Vaughn's associates at a high school in Wisconsin, developed a "Where Was That Earthquake?" activity with a guide sheet that provided structure preferred by many teachers (Clarke and Agne 1997, 176). Christine Massey and Tracy Rushmer, colleagues at the University of Vermont, have employed the same data sources in teaching an introductory college geology course. Today, the Technical Education Resource Center (TERC) in Cambridge, Massachusetts, is developing instructional options using earth science space data such as the Mars lander and state-of-the-art geographic visualization tools (Barstow 1997).

2. Technology for Theory Development

Modeling: In addition to storing vast quantities of information the computer can represent ideas and the connections between ideas and events so as to "model" some aspect of reality. How can all this information be related, especially when it often includes competing ideas and inconsistent facts? Computer technology has provided tools that help us to develop abstract models that mimic complex systems—for example, food chains, economic systems, or the earth's atmosphere—letting us create simple systems that become increasingly complex as new factors are added. The STELLA II dynamic modeling program has been used by high school teachers for this activity, although its sophisticated power is more routinely used at the college level. STELLA involves students in plotting complex networks of cause and effect, supporting systems thinking and analysis. Because it cuts across all disciplines, it can be used as an integrating tool or vehicle for synthesizing models of natural or human behavior (Stella II 1995)

Simulations: Simulation software lets students envision themselves in situations where they must test and retest their assumptions about some aspect of the human condition. Computer simulations are prebuilt to reflect abstract forces, trends, and general laws at work: in salt marsh ecology, Wall Street crashes, social behavior in an ant colony, or fish-harvesting policy in the Grand Banks. Typically the computer and sophisticated graphics make the models appear real: the air war over the Pacific in 1943, the Battle of Gettysburg, or population ecology in a small pond. The better examples are fun to use, much in the video game tradition, yet their carefully planned structure allows changing conditions with each reenactment to lead to different outcomes.

There are so many such programs on the market today that educational computing journals must provide a steady stream of reviews to assess their quality and potential usefulness. *Classroom Connect* is one such K–12 educators' practical guide to using the Internet in the classroom (http://www.classroom.net). Simulations in use today tend to be based on complex interactions among many interdependent forces. In Vermont, social studies teachers are experimenting with Sim City in their global studies courses.

How does a city "work"? In Sim City, students become the mayor of an urban environment with fluid boundaries. They have to plan out the industrial sections that will support the city, the residential sections that will house the citizens, and the latticework of services that will maintain health and order. If they raise taxes too high, the citizens may cause mayhem in the streets. If traffic gets tied up in the residential sections, their "approval rating" may go down and they may lose the next election. Both building and destroying what has been built entail "costs" to their city. Sim City includes a number of unpredictable disasters—volcanic eruptions or tidal waves, for example—that surprise the most farsighted mayor and cause sudden social or economic collapse. Students may create their own city from scratch or work from an established structure based upon Tokyo or New York. To help students make connections between the simulation and their own world, teachers often develop a set of reflective journal guides that focus on the major issues of urbanization (Clarke and Agne 1997, 179).

What forces direct the future of our cities? Are they manageable? What forces direct the growth of civilization? Are they manageable? Simulation software puts students in situations where they can recognize the importance of information in decision making. Neither the information nor the decisions fall neatly within disciplinary boundaries. No matter what the simulation models, in constructivist fashion students must generate their own questions and their own answers.

3. Technology for Creative Expression

The third quadrant in Figure 1 identifies interdisciplinary technologies that help students express their knowledge in a wide variety of media. CAD (computer-assisted-design) programs have entered high school teaching from industry. Drawing and painting programs have entered education from advertising. "Linking" software allows students to string together words, images, and sounds into an infinite variety of expressive forms. Even a modest investment in these technologies lets students create cartoons, slide shows, movies, and interactive displays. With linking software and video capability, English courses that once emphasized writing now integrate movement, color, and sound as elements of communication.

Tim Comolli's development of an Imaging Lab at South Burlington High School in Vermont represents a highly sophisticated curriculum for creative expression. Comolli, a veteran English teacher with an affection for teaching Shakespeare and a background in media and advertising, now teaches his classes in a computer animation and video production facility producing work of commercial quality. Starting with no material resources, but with the backing of many benefactors, he established a nationally recognized creative expression facility, providing a technological base that now supports a variety of interdisciplinary efforts. Few high schools may be able to emulate such a computer-intensive operation—it has been supported entirely through gifts, grants, and the sale of student work. This operation represents a talented teacher's vision for making schooling fit the challenges of life in this culture. Once an English teacher, what shall we call Tim Comolli now?

The Imaging Lab began in 1992 with a parent-donated Amiga computer capable of representing two-dimensional animations. A FASTRACK motion capture system was donated by the Polhemus Corporation and increased the

Lab's capability for high-end graphics. Today it has state-of-the-art equipment and multiple software tools that engage students in three-dimensional and virtual reality production. The history of the Imaging Lab is illustrative of a frequent developmental pattern for interdisciplinary curriculum with a technological base; i.e., energetic individuals or teams of teachers—fueled by student excitement—accomplish challenging goals without administrative mandate and without much support from the school budget.

Tim Comolli's educational goals have little to do with either technology or English. Instead, they reflect the general intellectual goals or standards—the "Vital Results"—represented by Vermont's *Framework of Standards and Learning Opportunities* (Vermont Department of Education 1995). As we discussed earlier, the Vermont standards emphasize problem solving, communication, social responsibility, and personal responsibility, as well as subject-related goals. In the real-life setting of the Imaging Lab, students produce media projects for their peers and the wider community. In doing so, they must practice and progress simultaneously toward all four "Vital Results," while also focusing on subject-related information. Technology allows the integration of higher-level educational goals as neatly as it allows integration of content knowledge.

Comolli stresses the problem-solving character of learning in creative expression. Media work in the lab builds upon mathematics, moving quickly to involve programming skills in three-dimensional space. Comolli, who is not an expert on most of the recent equipment, is not troubled by his students' mastery of sophisticated equipment and software. Instead, he has become comfortable playing the role of *guide on the side*, learning as his students develop their skills. Not only are more experienced students used to teach beginners in high school courses, they also teach applications of presentation software to teachers, administrators, student teachers, school board members, and peers in after-school and evening programs. His students are often paid to teach courses to local college students and adult education students. Students and the Lab sell advertising videos they have produced to local television outlets. Comolli's students have been invited to participate at national meetings in Seattle, New Orleans, Minneapolis, Tampa, and Boston. And, a video tour of the work of the Imaging Lab is used in efforts to garner additional financial support for the school program. There is concern at the school over the quality and standards of student products. Critics, for example, have said that the students are just making cartoons. Comolli acknowledges that sometimes what students create is "fluff" and is less an intellectual accomplishment than a paint-by-numbers effort. Still, sometimes an outsider does not appreciate the fact that his students are using the same computer code that let NASA's lander "Sojourner" gather and return physical data from Mars.

The Imaging Lab is a powerful example of the integrating power of contemporary computer technology. Problems are posed and solved without conscious attention to whether they are from the domains of art, music, mathematics, English, science, or psychology. This program has been largely the result of one individual's willingness to invest substantial professional and personal energy in making it work. It cannot yet be characterized as institutionalized! Yet the lab accomplishes many of Vermont's educational goals more efficiently than the work of separate teachers working in isolated classrooms. In the hands of students and a creative teacher, technology is pushing the teaching profession beyond the narrow roles that have confined us all since schools became public institutions.

Janet Bossange has captured the transformative power of the Imaging Lab in a high school setting:

> Technology is a teaching tool and also an art form. As a teaching tool, computers allow students to think in layers and deal with many variables related to a complex issue, forcing them to manage multifaceted relationships. Technology involves using communication skills effectively to carry on a cycle of dialogue, guiding a process of literacy that allows students to meet new criteria for knowledge and skill proficiency.
>
> (Clarke et al. 1998, 107–8)

4. Technology Supporting Problem Solving

The fourth quadrant in Figure 1 identifies communication and problem solving as the final arena for using computer technologies in the learning process. Component strategies in communication and problem solving include word processing, electronic bulletin boards, e-mail, robotics, and equipment control. International correspondence involving language and cross-cultural topics has been conducted in many high schools. In schools, the commonplace instrument known as e-mail becomes a powerful conversation that may reach around the globe. Knowledge that really matters is not confined to one geographic region any more than it can be confined to conventional classrooms. If desertification is a concern in Africa, why not make contact with African students about the issue? AIDS is an international problem. Ann Sorrell and her interdisciplinary team of French, social studies, and English teachers at Tim Comolli's high school in Vermont have students conduct public interest surveys on AIDS in cooperation with their peers in Paris. Large and important questions push learners beyond classroom walls in the same way that they force learning to cross disciplinary boundaries (Clarke and Agne 1997, 185). Lists of people seeking educational connections are generally available on the Internet; ePALS Classroom

Exchange is notable in that regard, with 8,000 schools in 80 countries (http://www.epals.com/).

Communication software is leading inexorably toward a "virtual classroom." The opening up of the Internet to formal courses for students has mushroomed recently with "Distance Learning" or "Distributed Learning," in which students are physically removed from the locus of course material, studying material on their own time—termed asynchronous learning. High school and college students take courses through telecommunications channels that would not be available to them in their own schools.

Some students choose to learn with a Web- or satellite-TV-based course even when traditional options are available. The proliferation of Web-based courses has been phenomenal. It is a rare college or university campus today that has not investigated such learning technologies. Unfortunately, our examination of secondary school Web courses found few that are of a notable interdisciplinary character. Many, if not most, are of the advanced placement variety, replicating classroom-bound courses without the desks. We suspect that individual teachers and groups of teachers will eventually choose to develop their own interdisciplinary courses, accommodating their personal strengths and insights about the students with whom they work on a daily basis. Instructional design has the potential not only to use technology but to provide intellectually rigorous methods students can use to construct practical models of their situations and their world.

Concluding Thoughts

High aims cannot be fully served by simple mechanics. The purpose of all education is to allow individuals to manage the work of their own minds, so as to further control their own lives—and positively influence the lives of others. Our interactions with each other, shaped by emerging technologies, are the medium in which we must learn together and solve our shared problems. Technology will push learning beyond classroom walls. It will further erode our dependence on subject areas and academic disciplines as vehicles for knowing. In the meantime, using information to solve problems will remain a human task in a world where human problems grow increasingly complex.

Recommended Readings

- Brooks, David W. 1997. *Web-Teaching: A Guide to Designing Interactive Teaching for the World Wide Web*. New York: Plenum Press. While this resource may be too technical for general readers it is a useful primer for teachers at all levels who are thinking about setting up a Web site for instructional use. Jargon, common in this field, is replaced with ordinary language. Research on teaching and learning is also discussed and reference links are provided.

- *Educom Review*, a bimonthly periodical. Turnkey Publishing, Inc., P.O. Box 2000509, Austin, TX 78720. Of the numerous journals available to K–16 educators on the inroads being made by technology into teaching, this periodical by the Interuniversity Communications Council, doing business as Educom, consistently offers informative and analytical articles about developments in the field. It would be a best journal read for administrators and others who want to "know the technology territory."

- Fosnot, Catherine T. 1989. *Enquiring Teachers, Enquiring Learners: A Constructivist Approach for Teaching*, New York: Teachers College Press. In this volume, Catherine Fosnot uses 20 years of research and theory to develop a comprehensive presentation of constructivist teaching. Though her view is based largely on cognitive psychology, her presentation is tempered by experience in classroom teaching and familiarity with instructional techniques that respond to individual differences among learners.

- Perkins, David. 1992. *Smart Schools: From Training Memories to Educating Minds*. New York: The Free Press. Perkins and his colleagues at Harvard's Project Zero have long advocated teaching strategies that respond to what we know about how individuals construct knowledge from experience, within and outside of school. This short book explains how learning theory challenges the established structure of formal learning—teaching, content structures, curriculum plans, classroom patterns, and assumptions about student motivation. Unlike most books on reform, Perkins focuses on the needs of the learner, rather than the needs of the reformers.

- Pinker, Steven. 1996. *How the Mind Works*. New York: Norton and Co. Steven Pinker writes about the science of the mind in terms that educators and lay people can recognize as human. Pinker's understanding of cognitive process and language development is both broad and deep, but he also understands that most readers need a synthesis of technical research and theory, presented with humor and a deep respect for the gaps that exist in what we know about what it means to be human.

Part II

Current Issues in College

5

Introduction to *Integrating the College Curriculum*

State-of-the-art handbooks are crucial guides in any field. In 1994, the Jossey-Bass series on New Directions in Teaching and Learning (NDTL) published *Interdisciplinary Studies Today*. This NDTL sourcebook was an outgrowth of the first national task force on interdisciplinary studies, affiliated with the Association of American Colleges' (now the Association of American Colleges and Universities) three-year study of undergraduate majors. It is a collection of authoritative essays on interdisciplinary knowledge, course design, program administration, learning assessment, and networking. William Newell, who wrote the chapter on "Designing Interdisciplinary Courses," had previously been reluctant to write a "how-to" guide. By the 1990s, however, interdisciplinarity was becoming more common, especially in general education.

Newell's chapter was a step-by-step guide to designing courses. *Step 1, Assembling an Interdisciplinary Team*, requires building a collaborative relationship and agreeing on a number of essential issues. In *Steps 2* and *3, Selecting a Topic* and *Identifying Pertinent Disciplines*, a balance must be created between disciplinary perspectives and student interests. In *Step 4, Developing the Subtext*, Newell distinguished the substantive topic of a course from its subtext. The substantive topic provides a context for abstract issues. It is the synthesizing glue that holds a course together and motivates students. The conceptual glue is refined in *Step 5, Structuring the Course*. Separate topics and texts must be linked in a coherent relationship that balances breadth and depth. *Step 6, Selecting Readings*, focuses on engaging student interest and balancing separate disciplinary inputs around a core topic. In *Steps 7* and *8, Designing Assignments* and *Preparing the Syllabus*, desired outcomes and skills are orchestrated in a manner that is clear to students. If a course is to be truly integrative, its interdisciplinary objectives also need to be spelled out explicitly and discussed on an ongoing basis.

Like Heidi Jacobs, Newell finds conditions to be changing as he visits campuses across the country. The contexts of practice are becoming more plural, and there is emergent agreement on definition. Proliferation of the literature and new scholarship also make it possible to think with greater clarity and sophistication today. In Chapter 5, he reassesses his earlier guide in light of new scholarship and previously unpublished data from the Institute in Integrative Studies. More than 150 participants from almost 40 colleges and universities have gained hands-on experience designing and critiquing courses at this professional-development program Newell founded. The general lessons of his earlier guide still stand. However, analysis of preliminary and revised drafts of syllabi developed by Institute participants, coupled with the critique of postmodernism and new research in cognitive and developmental psychology, foster a more complex understanding of the dynamics of course development. In presenting his findings, Newell addresses new issues in sequencing and coverage and their theoretical implications. Like his K–12 counterparts who conceive of integration in terms of a continuum, Newell depicts a spectrum ranging from partial to full interdisciplinarity. He views interdisciplinarity as a counterbalance and complement to disciplinarity. He also calls for more research on connections between interdisciplinarity and three other developments: complexity, other innovative pedagogies that foster integration, and the philosophical tradition of American Pragmatism.

Integrating the College Curriculum

William H. Newell

"Designing Interdisciplinary Courses" was written in response to repeated demands from beginning interdisciplinarians for a nuts-and-bolts, how-to-do-it guide. I resisted such demands in the 1980s when interdisciplinary studies was still moving from the "radical fringe" into the "liberal mainstream" of higher education (Newell 1988), since the very conception of interdisciplinarity was still in flux. An interdisciplinary guide would have promoted premature closure on conceptual issues that still deserved exploration.

By 1994, however, interdisciplinary liberal education was widely embraced by bellwether organizations such as the American Association for Higher Education and the Association of American Colleges and Universities as well as state councils of higher education (Miller and McCartan 1990). It was also widely implemented by curriculum committees of small colleges and large universities, public and private, sectarian and nonaffiliated institutions alike throughout the United States (Edwards 1996). Moreover, with acceptance came agreement on some of the basic elements of interdisciplinarity. By the mid-1990s I found clearer understanding of interdisciplinarity when arriving on a campus for a consultancy than I had found when leaving at the end of a consultancy in the 1980s. It was now safe to write a guide.

In the half decade since then, the context and understanding of interdisciplinarity have continued to evolve. Over half of all colleges and universities now have an interdisciplinary component to their liberal education requirement. Several key books and articles have also been written recently that make it possible to think with more sophistication as well as more clarity about interdisciplinarity. While the advice in my earlier guide still stands, this chapter reassesses interdisciplinary practice in light of more nuanced thinking about interdisciplinarity. It offers a coherent perspective on interdisciplinarity, from which it derives practical lessons for the care and feeding of interdisciplinary curricula.

While a majority of interdisciplinarians would accept the perspective presented here, at least in broad outline, disputes among theorists over the role of disciplines and the nature of interdisciplinary integration have been muted in the interests of clarity and consistency. Those disagreements have been examined in detail in an anthology of readings on interdisciplinary education, *Interdisciplinarity: Essays from the Literature* (Newell 1998), especially its concluding chapter on "Professionalizing Interdisciplinarity: Literature Review and Research Agenda," which sifts through the essays to evaluate the current status of interdisciplinary studies.

The strategy here is to address the actual problems that teachers encounter as they develop their first interdisciplinary courses. Key insights from the earlier guide are merged with new lessons from the literature and the Institute in Integrative Studies. More than 150 faculty from close to 40 colleges and universities in Canada, Hungary, and Nepal as well as the United States have developed syllabi through the Institute since its formation in 1992. Those syllabi constitute a unique data source that has not previously been tapped. After developing an extended metaphor for interdisciplinarity and placing it in conceptual and historical contexts, the chapter turns to course development, since interdisciplinary courses are the building blocks of interdisciplinary curricula. Theoretical issues drawn from the anthology are applied to the eight steps identified in the earlier guide. Discussions of sequencing and coverage shift the focus from courses to curricula. Finally, the chapter closes with recommendations for the future.

Introduction

First, a metaphor for interdisciplinarity. Picture a dense fog perpetually swirling around a huge jumble of objects, bizarre-looking objects with strange shapes and varying degrees of translucence. Standing all around the objects are scholars/teachers, all in their established location and with a knot of students behind them, shining flashlights into the fog. The flashlights vary as much as the objects they illuminate. They all have similar wattage, but some emit a thin penetrating beam while others diffuse light over a wider area. (It is no coincidence that the flashlights are different: over the years, they have been adapted to the objects they are used to study. Where the fog is particularly dense or the objects less translucent, flashlights must supply a more concentrated beam.) Each scholar has come to know a particular part of the jumble quite well, developing increasingly elaborate theories to account for all the features visible or inferred from that location. The teachers have also become quite proficient at using their flashlights to point out distinctive features of the landscape to students, who strain to see them through the fog. The students' eyes are not yet fully adapted, and they have not yet learned to visualize the objects as a whole from the facets visible to them.

When scholars/teachers from different vantage points come together to discuss the jumble, they find themselves disagreeing about its nature. But this is no dispute among blind men over an elephant, as in the proverbial tale popular among interdisciplinarians. No one has seen the jumble unobscured by fog; there is no sighted person to identify the elephant. There may not even be an elephant; the jumble may not have overall coherence. Moreover, scholars/teachers may even focus on the same part and still see something quite different because they look from different vantage points; this elephant is not symmetrical, so blind men on opposite sides may find that the trunk feels quite different. Still, for blind men or scholars/teachers examining elephant or jumble, what they find and what vision they construct from it is shaped by where they stand, what they choose to focus on, and how they choose to study it.

Individually, the scholars/teachers represent different disciplinary approaches (each with its own methodological flashlight). Collectively, observed from outside the disciplines, they represent a multidisciplinary approach. Different disciplinary perspectives are brought to bear, but there is no systematic attempt to integrate them. Thus a coal-fired electric power plant may be variously seen as a real-world Carnot engine, a point source of acid rain and greenhouse gases, a component of economic infrastructure, and an alternative to dependence on oil imported from the politically volatile Middle East. If the conflicting disciplinary images are to be reconciled and combined into an integrated vision—if the clashing tones of the multidisciplinary orchestra are to be supplanted by integrative harmony—then another approach is needed.

What scholars and teachers alike require is a process for drawing together insights generated from their different disciplinary perspectives into a more comprehensive understanding. Human behavior follows different principles than the behavior of the natural world; and the search for underlying principles is not even an effective method for appreciating the creative products of the human mind. Moreover, some principles vary with scale and location as well as over time. Thus the jumble is neither consistent nor coherent, so integration must be designed to answer a specific question or solve a particular problem using what disciplinary insights are currently available. In the power plant example, interdisciplinary integration of insights from the various disciplinary perspectives might focus on selecting among alternative sources of electric power for a particular region.

The foregoing metaphor of interdisciplinarity starts from the insight that interdisciplinarity is necessitated by complexity. If the world around us were not complex, there would be no need for interdisciplinary studies. Then again, there would be no need for more than one discipline either. If all phenomena studied by disciplines followed the same underlying principles, operating according to the same rules and thus yielding their secrets in response to the same methodologies, there might be many specialties but only a single discipline. If relationships among those phenomena were additive, so that the whole were equal to the sum of its parts, then those specialties could successfully follow the divide-and-conquer strategy implicit in reductionist scholarship. The disciplines cannot collectively see the jumble as a whole, however, because its parts interact multiplicatively as well as additively: the interdisciplinary whole is greater than the sum of its disciplinary parts. For example, the income, status, power, country of origin, and education of public housing residents are all interrelated. The jumble requires interdisciplinary study to be better understood as a whole: the various aspects not only look different from each vantage point, they follow different principles as well. Each discipline reconstructs its distinctive set of principles; interdisciplinary study uses them to develop an answer to a particular question, an answer that provides a glimmer of new insight into the whole—a more comprehensive understanding.

Interdisciplinarity is the counterbalance to disciplinarity. Disciplinary analysis requires interdisciplinary synthesis as its complement (Newell 1983). Disciplinary fragmentation of understanding necessitates interdisciplinary integration. The disciplinary power generated by narrowing of perspective and restriction of assumptions can be fully harnessed only through the interdisciplinary development of a more comprehensive understanding, one that embraces and reconciles the full range of disciplinary assumptions. Ideally, disciplinarity and interdisciplinarity should become symbiotic: focused disciplinary scholarship should be guided and corrected by interdisciplinary perspective, which in turn becomes sharpened and more comprehensive as it draws on new disciplinary scholarship.

As academic disciplines differentiated and institutionalized themselves in the late nineteenth and early twentieth centuries, they developed distinctive worldviews or perspectives. Scholars trained in disciplinary graduate programs, teaching in disciplinary departments, and publishing in disciplinary journals have produced and passed on to subsequent generations expanding collections of powerful but limited insights. They are powerful because of the greater focus, resolution, and penetration made possible by disciplinary lenses, but limited because the price of that power is narrowed range of vision and restrictive assumptions. The power of economics to evaluate alternative sources of electrical power is grounded in a rational self-interest model of the individual and an impersonal market-based model of society, which blind the discipline to other sources of human motivation (such as concern for future generations, desire for political power, religious intolerance, and xenophobia) and societal organization (such as wealthy corporations controlling political regulators or nongovernmental organizations promoting sustainable growth). Where a discipline stands (the assumptions it makes), the lens through which it looks (its perspective), what it chooses to look at (its characteristic subject matter), and why it chooses to look there (its values) all limit as well as define that discipline.

The distinctive worldviews of disciplines have become blurred in the last quarter century but have not disappeared. First, from inside the discipline differences between competing schools of thought loom large and the notion of an overall disciplinary worldview seems atavistic . . . until one tries interdisciplinary team teaching. Then the shared implicit assumptions of the discipline become apparent by their clash with the conflicting assumptions of others on the team. They also become evident when one violates them in a manuscript submitted for publication to a disciplinary journal. Like a set of overlapping Venn diagrams, a discipline has extensive areas of nonoverlap that obscure important commonalties.

Second, disciplines are borrowing at an accelerating rate from one another, and more and more scholarship can be described as "boundary work" (Klein 1996). While the clear-cut dichotomy between disciplinarity and interdisciplinarity is being eroded, an important distinction remains: researchers in each discipline are borrowing concepts, theories, and methods from other disciplines while still holding on to its characteristic world view. Furthermore, in contrast to cutting-edge research, most disciplinary education (especially in the natural sciences, but also in many social sciences and even in parts of the humanities) still presents the disciplines much as they have traditionally been presented. Instead of a monolithic conception of interdisciplinarity, it is becoming useful to think in terms of a spectrum between disciplinarity and full interdisciplinarity, with varying stages of partial interdisciplinarity in between (Newell 1998). Full interdisciplinarity involves looking at an issue through different disciplinary lenses, comparing their insights for commonalties and conflicts, using each lens to expose and critique the other's assumptions, forging new commonalties that bridge the conflict, and integrating them into a new, more comprehensive understanding of the issue. Partial interdisciplinarity utilizes some but not all of the steps in this process.

Individually, then, disciplines have produced depth of insight. Collectively, they have produced a piecemeal understanding of the world. The implicit assumption underlying the divide-and-conquer strategy of the disciplines—that the parts exposed by separate disciplines will naturally or automatically come together to produce a whole—has proven inaccurate. Since the disciplines have controlled education as well as scholarship, most members of the next generation have specialized in one discipline. Consequently, few have been prepared for the task of pulling together disciplinary insights into a more comprehensive perspective. Integration, it turns out, is neither automatic nor easy. It happens only when teachers and scholars make it possible. They must value synthesis in a world that focuses on analysis, creating space for it in educational institutions and assisting their students in developing the requisite skills.

Interdisciplinary Course Development

The earlier recommendations in "Designing Interdisciplinary Courses" can now be reassessed in light of practical lessons from syllabi designed through the Institute as well as theoretical insights from the anthology. First, interdisciplinarity should be understood as a multidimensional concept. One dimension is breadth, epitomized in the distinction between broad and narrow interdisciplinarity (reflecting the epistemological distance between disciplines from which insights are drawn). Thus, a broadly interdisciplinary course draws on disciplines with highly divergent epistemologies, perhaps from the humanities, social sciences, and natural sciences, while a narrowly interdisciplinary course might draw only from the physical sciences. Another dimension is completeness, captured in the distinction between partial and full interdisciplinarity. A multidisciplinary course is an example of partial interdisciplinarity, since it draws on more than one discipline but makes no attempt to integrate their insights. Second, interdisciplinary study draws its insights not only from disciplines, but from various kinds of interdisciplines and antidisciplines as well. Third, discussions of interdisciplinarity need to incorporate the results of recent research in cognitive and developmental psychology. Fourth, thinking about interdisciplinarity needs to take into account the critiques of postmodernists (e.g., that the context provided by interdisciplinary studies is itself a text and thus problematic) and left-wing theorists (e.g., that issues of power pervade interdisciplinary studies as they do the rest of the educational enterprise).

Each step of the foundational guide may now be re-evaluated.

Outcomes: It seems likely that the same educational outcomes of interdisciplinary courses will be enhanced by broader interdisciplinarity (a difference in degree) while additional outcomes will be produced by shifting from partial to full interdisciplinarity (a difference in type). After all, different cognitive functions are involved in seeing through a disciplinary lens, in shifting from one discipline's lens to another's, in using one discipline's lens to critique the lens of another discipline, and in synthesizing the insights from the various disciplinary lenses. Greater epistemological distance (i.e., more divergent assumptions, criteria for evidence, methodologies), on the other hand, makes each of those cognitive functions more challenging to carry out. Students' eyes adjust more slowly when there are bigger differences in the prescriptions to which the disciplinary lenses are ground. In practical terms, then, it is preferable to introduce students to interdisciplinary thinking by starting them on a course that is narrowly but fully interdisciplinary, rather than on one that is broad but partially interdisciplinary. John Ritter and Marilyn Svigney start out their environmental studies students at Oregon Institute of Technology (Klamath Falls) with a course on Acid Rain that draws exclusively on the natural sciences to trace fossil fuels from cradle to grave before exposing them to more broadly interdisciplinary courses that integrate insights from the social as well as natural sciences.

Teams: Differences in power among individual members on an interdisciplinary team can be cross-cutting (gender and race) or hierarchical (tenure and rank) or reflect their disciplines (which vary in status), or departments and divisions (which differ in access to outside funding), or even personal characteristics (e.g., who talks loudest). Power differentials can bias every decision from selection of topic and choice of disciplines to the integrated understanding students take away from the course. Thus a topic might reflect too much of the disciplinary perspective of tenured male faculty members. Similar problems confront student teams engaged in an interdisciplinary group project.

The centrality of democracy to the educational vision of philosophical Pragmatists such as John Dewey holds for interdisciplinary studies as well. Every member (and discipline) on the team needs full participation and equal voice for a course to fulfill its interdisciplinary potential. In practical terms, faculty members need to embrace democratic principles as a precondition for serving on an interdisciplinary team. Team process needs to be monitored by its members and attention called to nondemocratic behavior. Decisions of the team should be reviewed when they reflect disproportionately the positions of its privileged members.

While equality is essential to the process of developing interdisciplinary courses, equity is more appropriate in their implementation. In team-taught interdisciplinary core courses of the doctoral program in public administration at the University of LaVerne in California, Jack Meek takes professional aspirations, personal traits, and family crises as well as expertise into account in allocating team responsibilities. Instead of trying to fit all faculty members into the same mold by treating them as interchangeable parts, he focuses on who is best in front of a large lecture, or leading small discussion groups at a field site, or schmoozing with community leaders to set up new programs. Student teams face similar problems and the successful ones often come up with comparable solutions—students who cannot seem to research their section of a group paper may carry their weight by typing it up.

Topic: Narrow topics should not be confused with narrow interdisciplinarity (Newell 1994, 38). Breadth of topic refers to the range of substantive material (i.e., the number of sub-issues, the quantity of facts) under examination, while breadth of interdisciplinarity refers to the range of disciplinary perspectives brought to bear on that substantive material. A narrowly interdisciplinary course might examine a broad topic (e.g., global warming studied from the perspectives of the physical sciences). Conversely, a broadly interdisciplinary course can fruitfully focus in on a narrow topic (e.g., a particular power plant studied from ethical, historical, economic, and social as well as physical science perspectives). The broader the interdisciplinarity, of course, the greater the "creative tension" that emerges by contrasting disciplinary perspectives, but also the greater the challenge in integrating their insights.

With sufficient interdisciplinary experience, however, one can design a general education course that is both broadly interdisciplinary and focused on a broad topic. In his honors course at Southwest Texas State University (San Marcos) on Religion, Science, and the Quest for Meaning, Chris Frost narrows the focus to how we can avoid choosing between "naive acceptance of religious tradition" and "total rejection of any system of meaning that extends beyond confirmation of sensory experience." The course is broadly interdisciplinary because it draws on the widely divergent epistemologies of science and religion, yet focused because the scientific perspective is drawn only from the discipline of psychology. The course is fully interdisciplinary in that it presents students with a "dialogical model" they can use to develop their personal strategy for bridging the intellectual gap between science and religion.

Disciplines: Interdisciplinary study may function differently when it draws from different kinds of disciplinary perspectives. It can make a difference, to borrow the categories of Jill Vickers (1997), whether perspectives are drawn from disciplines with compatible or incompatible epistemologies (e.g., history and literature versus economics and sociology) or from interdisciplinary fields (e.g., culture studies), congealed interdisciplinary fields (e.g., biochemistry), antidisciplines (e.g., Native American studies), or nondisciplinary sources such as cultures, communities, and political ideologies. It is tempting to argue that, like roses, a perspective is a perspective is a perspective; that it makes no difference how you came by it, because all that counts is that your perspective affects what you see and the value you place on it. But perspectives differ in their inclusiveness, their moral and affective content, their attitude toward other perspectives, and thus the tenacity with which they are held.

The conflict in perspectives (and the challenge in integrating their insights) will be greater between a discipline and an antidiscipline than between two disciplines, so the course that includes both is more broadly interdisciplinary. When the conflict between disciplines and antidisciplines is embodied in faculty or student participants in the course, however, the dynamics of the interdisciplinary process itself change. Here again, the Pragmatic commitment to democracy in education becomes essential to interdisciplinarity, not only in adjudicating difference but in establishing sufficient trust in the process to allow it to proceed. Similarly, nondisciplinary sources of perspective may be more resistant to integration than disciplinary perspectives, since their assumptions tend to be more deeply embedded and fully integrated into a world-taken-for-granted: challenges to their assumptions are more threatening and thus resisted. On the other hand, congealed disciplines seem no different from other disciplines in their participation in interdisciplinary study. The fact that biochemistry emerged out of an interdisciplinary process seems to have little effect on its openness to perspectives of other disciplines.

In her Gender and Epistemology course at Wooster College in Ohio, Nancy Grace models for students how to draw on disciplinary, antidisciplinary, and nondisciplinary perspectives to work toward an integrated perspective. She shows that the perspective of a woman such as herself reflects the discipline in which she was trained, the feminist critique of disciplines (including her own), and her personal experiences as a woman. By being self-conscious, deliberate, and informed about each of these perspectives and the process of interdisciplinary integration, a student can draw on the disciplinary perspectives of philosophy and science featured in the course, the perspectives of disciplinary feminists in each field, and personal experiences to work toward a new epistemology.

Subtext: A postmodern sensibility is at once a delight and an irritation because of its tendency to make problematic what might otherwise remain unexamined. In interdisciplinary course development, the two-edged postmodern sword slices open subtext and context alike, revealing hidden assumptions while complicating the process. The subtext of a course (Newell 1994, 42) is what the faculty decide the course is really about. When seen through postmodern eyes, however, the subtext may turn out to be more than a device for fulfilling institutionally-mandated general education goals. It may also reflect, for example, an attempt by faculty to bootleg their research interests into the course, interests that serve them more than the students. Watchdogs are essential. On the other hand, the deconstruction of premises must be balanced against the need to get on with developing the course. Of more fundamental challenge to interdisciplinary study is the postmodern insight that context, like any text, is itself socially constructed and thus problematic, since interdisciplinary integration can be thought of as a process of contextualization. Thus, interdisciplinary study is recognized as a human process responsive not only to the insights of disciplines and the reality to which they respond, but to the biases of the interdisciplinarian—personal, gendered, class, cultural, and so on. Out of that recognition comes the demand for procedures that minimize the impact of such bias—peer review, replication of experiments, free exchange of information—but also humility, since no procedures can completely eliminate biases when they are widely shared. Such procedures can be institutionalized in general studies councils and curriculum committees (like Miami University's Liberal Education Council) that have come to see themselves as nurturing as well as enforcing interdisciplinarity.

Readings: Criteria for choosing readings include how clearly they explain and utilize relevant concepts or theories from the discipline, how well they embody that discipline's perspective, how sophisticated they get while still being accessible to a lay audience, and how sharply they contrast with other readings, as well as their distinctive contribution to the topic. Not every reading can or should meet all these criteria: courses may start off with a "hook" (Newell 1994, 46), and some readings can focus narrowly on a specific disciplinary theory or set of concepts. Nonetheless, most readings should contribute on more than one level, so that students can develop proficiency at reading texts from more than one perspective. For examples, see the set of syllabi developed through the Institute in Integrative Studies by faculty at Georgia College and State University (Milledgeville) displayed at <http://www.gcsu.edu/acad_affairs/coll_artsci/int/>.

Since the articles and chapters chosen as reading assignments for an interdisciplinary course have seldom if ever been written for that purpose, students have to learn to read and study differently. Instead of focusing merely on mastery of subject matter and letting the author dictate the direction of their thought, students in interdisciplinary courses need to assert some control over the text, reading it for their purposes as well as for the author's. This resistance to the author includes deciding what aspects of the reading are relevant to the course, asking why as well as what the author is saying (thus exposing assumptions and reconstructing worldviews), and contrasting all of these to earlier readings from different disciplines. It is no wonder that educational researchers consistently find that interdisciplinary courses promote critical thinking skills. (For a large-scale quantitative study, see Astin 1993. For a survey of previous studies, see Pascarella and Terenzini 1991, 619.)

Structure: In disciplinary courses not already structured around a textbook, the logic of the course structure is often dictated by the subject matter: chronology, information, or theories that must be mastered before other information or theories can be understood. The structure of even the most rudimentary interdisciplinary course is complex: it must present the insights of more than one discipline into the subject matter (i.e., relevant facts, concepts, and theories), give students a feel for the disciplinary perspectives out of which these insights emerge; probe the assumptions underlying them (often by contrasting one discipline with another); and help students integrate all the foregoing into an answer to the question or solution to the problem posed by the course, one that reflects a more comprehensive understanding of the subject. Thus, the structure of an interdisciplinary course moves back and forth between the dimensions of subject matter and disciplines, and between discussions and metadiscussions; it also builds dynamically to a crescendo or epiphany at the end. Teaching an interdisciplinary course is more like writing and putting on a play than setting up exhibits or conducting a museum tour.

The intellectual movement within an interdisciplinary course can be facilitated by shifting students back and forth between lectures or seminars and a range of other activities. In Georgia College and State University's The Gothic Imagination, Greg Pepetone, Bob Viau, and Tina Yarborough structure the course around such themes as the cult of madness, the gothic hero, death and dying, and the grotesque and fantastique. Within individual units, students are introduced to architecture, film, literature, music, painting, and theater as they embody a particular gothic theme. Interspersed throughout the course are listening labs, viewing labs, a joint public lecture from three disciplinary perspectives, a piano recital, a film festival, an organ recital, a student contest, a poetry reading, a one-man show, and a production of Byron's *Manfred*—all connected through integrative journals, reaction papers, and e-mail discussions as well as seminars.

Assignments: Evaluative assignments play a special role in interdisciplinary courses. Since interdisciplinary study is fundamentally a multistep process, paper or essay exam topics can be designed sequentially to lead students through those steps. In his bioethics course at Southern Illinois University Edwardsville, Doug Eder takes students through five stages of writing assignments:

1. *description/narration* of an ethical problem personally encountered;
2. an *analysis* of Isaac Asimov's *The Relativity of Wrong* (to take apart and differentiate the components of disciplinary style and content, communicating an appreciation of the scientific perspective);
3. *comparison/contrast* of two essays on the bioethics of reproductive technology (to analyze viewpoints grounded in different disciplinary perspectives, separating their standards);
4. *application/case study* choosing between competing sites for a nuclear- and toxic-waste-disposal facility (to draw on insights from biology, economics, political science, sociology, and ethics, showing how separate disciplinary standards can contribute to a better interdisciplinary interpretation);

5. *application transfer* to an issue not discussed in the course (to write a take-home final exam on teaching evolution vs. creationism in schools or choosing whether to have an abortion). For the complete syllabus, see <www.siue.edu/~deder/index.html>. For a detailed discussion of sequenced writing assignments in interdisciplinary courses, see Haynes (1996).

The sequencing of assignments is all the more important because the steps of the interdisciplinary process lead students through more advanced stages of cognitive development. On scales of intellectual and moral development, students are led from concrete or absolute thinking through dualism and relativism to relativism with commitment. (For the classic discussion of these stages, see Perry 1970. Similar movement is evident in stages that take into account differences between males and females; see Baxter Magolda 1992.) Because interdisciplinary courses ask students to develop new cognitive strategies as well as to learn new subject matter, they need more assistance from sequenced evaluative assignments than in most disciplinary courses.

Pedagogy: By focusing on the development of interdisciplinary courses, "Designing Interdisciplinary Courses" overlooked their implementation. Interdisciplinary study is reinforced by a number of innovative pedagogies such as collaborative learning, experiential learning, learning communities, living-learning, multicultural learning, service-learning, and study abroad. They are all integrative studies in the sense that they draw on diverse perspectives for insights that they integrate into a more comprehensive understanding. Interdisciplinary study draws its insights from the perspectives of disciplines, while the various pedagogies draw theirs as well from perspectives based on experiences of the self and others. Because they share a common method, if not a common epistemology, with interdisciplinary study, they reinforce the interdisciplinary way of thinking with a multiplicative effect on educational outcomes. When students encounter integrative thinking only in one or two interdisciplinary courses, its effects may be limited. However, when integrative thinking is demanded as well in their group project outside of class, in the residence hall, in group experiences off campus, and in the community, there is a synergistic effect on learning that can be quite powerful. In practical terms, that means interdisciplinary faculty should utilize several of these pedagogies at the same time and learn to structure them so their integrative effect is enhanced.

Interdisciplinary Curriculum Development

Sequencing Interdisciplinary Courses: There are no hard-and-fast rules about the appropriate number of interdisciplinary courses in each kind of curriculum, or about their ideal location within the curriculum. Most of the literature on interdisciplinary education talks about individual courses, not curricula. An exception is Armstrong (1980), who describes four strategies for interdisciplinary majors: disciplinary courses drawn from different departments, an adisciplinary capstone, interdisciplinary courses serially taught by disciplinary faculty, and a sequence of fully interdisciplinary courses. Newell (1990) goes further, identifying factors promoting interdisciplinary curricula and discussing sequencing of interdisciplinary courses, resource requirements, and creation of academic community. The foregoing discussion suggests several additional considerations in designing interdisciplinary curricula.

Regarding the number of interdisciplinary courses in the curriculum, it should be evident that an intellectual process which asks students to move up several levels of cognitive development requires more than one experience with the process. The required number of interdisciplinary experiences obviously depends on where the students start out: a program that draws students who are predominantly concrete thinkers will require more interdisciplinary courses to move them up to relativism-with-commitment than a program that attracts predominantly relativistic thinkers.

By the time they are in an interdisciplinary doctoral program, students operate at a high enough cognitive level that a course can move beyond a topic and take the interdisciplinary method itself as its subject. In her Introduction to Interdisciplinary Research at the University of Missouri-Kansas City, Pat Hovis introduces students in the interdisciplinary doctoral program to the professional literature on interdisciplinary study, then breaks them into teams to analyze pertinent research questions from multiple worldviews reflecting their different disciplines, synthesize the disciplinary perspectives into an integrated response to the question, and engage in intellectual dialogue to resolve conflicting positions. They also address issues of ethics and professional responsibility related to their research question. Group presentations are critiqued in light of issues raised about the professional literature.

In addition, curriculum planners must consider the appropriate extent of interplay between disciplinarity and interdisciplinarity. A general education curriculum may be most effective if it alternates disciplinary and interdisciplinary courses. A disciplinary major may require only a couple of interdisciplinary courses to contextualize the discipline. An interdisciplinary major in environmental studies, on the other hand, might intersperse a few disciplinary courses among its predominant interdisciplinary courses, or require a disciplinary minor in addition to the major comprised exclusively of interdisciplinary courses.

The key locations for interdisciplinary courses in a mixed curriculum are at the beginning and at the end. An introductory interdisciplinary course is important, especially in the first semester of college, because it can respond affirmatively to the preconception of many students that college is a place where they can address big issues. It also signals to students new to college that the multiple perspectives and integrative thinking of interdisciplinary studies are a legitimate part of the college experience, before the barrage of disciplinary courses convinces them otherwise. Finally, an initial interdisciplinary experience can provide a context for subsequent disciplinary courses.

Interdisciplinary courses at the beginning of the curriculum are also an effective means of integrating instruction in basic skills into the rest of the curriculum. Faculty teaching basic reading and writing skills at the University of the Virgin Islands work closely with faculty developing interdisciplinary first-year core courses in the natural and social sciences, organizing their basic skills courses to prepare students to complete individual assignments in the topical core courses. They meet weekly with core faculty to see where students are experiencing difficulty in applying skills, then adjust their instruction accordingly. Instead of feeling like second-class citizens, students taking basic skills courses feel advantaged because the payoff is so immediate. Introduction to Intercultural Communications, the next-level skills course, asks "Can Knowledge of Cultural Difference Reduce Cultural Conflict in the Virgin Islands?" Valerie Combie introduces students to a wide range of humanities, fine arts, and performing arts while training them in speaking, listening, reading, and writing. Students develop an appreciation for the practical implications and aesthetics of cultural expression as they learn communication skills.

At the end of the curriculum, interdisciplinary capstones play the key role of recontextualizing the disciplinary expertise students have so assiduously developed in their majors. This curricular contribution is enhanced by capstone courses that deliberately bring together majors from different disciplines to work in teams on an interdisciplinary project. Majors from biology, engineering, philosophy, and history might evaluate a new biotechnology. Here students come to appreciate both the power and the limitations of their new-found expertise, as other members of their team react to their contributions. Before we send disciplinary majors out into the world to apply what they have learned in college, it is important for them to develop some humility at the same time that they feel empowered, by realizing the relative strengths and weaknesses of their discipline.

In an interdisciplinary major, students may also be well served by individual interdisciplinary capstone projects in which they draw upon both disciplinary and interdisciplinary skills to address an interdisciplinary topic different from any they have studied before. Given sufficient time and structure, nonhonors students can complete every phase in the interdisciplinary research process and produce a written project commensurate with disciplinary honors theses. The School of Interdisciplinary Studies at Miami University (Ohio) devotes five credits a semester for two semesters to senior projects, which are a graduation requirement for all its majors. A senior workshop leads the students through the steps of project proposal, annotated bibliography, literature review, project outline, thesis-and-argument presentations, and separate due dates for each chapter, culminating in public oral presentations. Those presentations take place in a professional conference format, complete with discussants drawn from disciplinary departments across the university. Throughout the year, seniors meet individually each week with their project advisors and twice a week in senior workshop. At each step in the process, they receive written feedback from peers as well as from individual faculty advisors and the workshop director. Worcester Polytechnic Institute in Massachusetts and the Interdisciplinary Studies Program at Wayne State University in Detroit, Michigan, offer equally elaborate senior projects. While most institutions invest fewer faculty resources in that part of the curriculum, the potential for impressive capstone projects is present in all fully interdisciplinary programs because they stretch students so far cognitively.

"Coverage" in Interdisciplinary Curricula: A disciplinary curriculum "covers" the characteristic subject matter of the discipline, using its concepts, theories, and methods developed for that purpose. In the process, students become initiated into the discipline's way of thinking—imbued with its values, predisposed to its assumptions, and accustomed to its perspective. Since many interdisciplinary curricula are likewise focused on subject matter such as a geographical area (e.g., American studies), a group (e.g., women's studies), a time period (e.g., eighteenth century studies), or a problem (e.g., environmental studies), there are important parallels between coverage in disciplinary and coverage in interdisciplinary curricula. Since interdisciplinary study works through multiple disciplines using both its own special set of skills and those of the disciplines, there are important differences as well.

The boundaries and content of a discipline's subject matter are defined by convention: physics is what is studied by physicists. In contrast, the boundaries and content of the subject matter of interdisciplinary studies are defined by contention. The same subject matter might be seen by an economist as unemployment, by a sociologist as low socioeconomic status, and by a political scientist as powerlessness. The interdisciplinary common ground might be poverty for the economist and sociologist, and it might shift to inequality when political science is included. Thus the very subject matter of interdisciplinary studies is determined through multiple disciplinary perspectives integrated by the creation of common ground.

Interdisciplinary boundaries as well as content shift with each disciplinary perspective. Inequality, to continue the example, can be more narrowly studied by economists, political scientists, and sociologists, or it can be placed in cultural context by including anthropology, or in the context of time and space by including history and geography as well. Moreover, in each case, that additional context can be relatively narrow or broad. The inequality within and among various Western nations can be examined for recent decades, or the contrast can be expanded to include Eastern nations or more isolated traditional societies, and its historical context can be expanded to the entire modern era or even to the broad sweep of Western civilization. Where is interdisciplinary study to stop? What determines its boundaries? Does it even have boundaries?

Obviously, interdisciplinary study is bounded by pragmatic considerations of time and money. A semester or quarter has only so many weeks, and only so many faculty can be assigned to teach in a single course. If those were the only bounds, however, every interdisciplinary course would be fundamentally inadequate because it would necessarily be incomplete. But since interdisciplinary courses attempt to integrate the insights of disciplines into a specific problem to answer a specific question, they are bounded as well by the question they ask, by the problem they choose to confront.

The skills required to answer interdisciplinary questions and solve interdisciplinary problems are, in part, the skills of the disciplines on which an interdisciplinary course is based. The nature of the interdisciplinary process, however, requires some distinctive skills as well. Klein identifies a number of the basic cognitive tasks—differentiating, comparing, contrasting, relating, clarifying, reconciling, and synthesizing—involved in the multiple step interdisciplinary process of

1a. *defining* the problem [question, topic, issue];
b. *determining* all the knowledge needs, including appropriate disciplinary representatives and consultants, as well as relevant models, traditions, and literatures;
c. *developing* an integrative framework and appropriate questions to be investigated;
2a. *specifying* particular studies to be undertaken;
b. *engaging* in "role negotiation" (in teamwork);
c. *gathering* all current knowledge and searching for new information;
d. *resolving* disciplinary conflicts by working towards a common vocabulary (and focusing on reciprocal learning in teamwork);
e. *building* and *maintaining* communication through integrative techniques;
3a. *collating* all contributions and *evaluating* their adequacy, relevance, and adaptability;

b. *integrating* the individual pieces to determine a pattern of mutual related-
    ness and relevancy;
c. *confirming* or *disconfirming* the proposed solution [answer]; and
d. *deciding* about future management or disposition of a task/project/patient/
    curriculum.   (1990, 183,188–89).

For other models of the interdisciplinary process, see Hursh, Haas, and Moore
(1983) and DeWachter (1982). All of these models feature numerous feedback
loops, which bring out the iterative nature of the process. To return to the opening example, an interdisciplinary examination of a coal-fired electric power plant
may conclude that it was posing the question too narrowly: instead of asking
about alternative means of generating electrical power for the region, it might
have asked about alternative sources of energy in general.

Newell (1998) identifies a broad range of cognitive and affective characteristics developed in carrying out these steps. The cognitive skills include:

> critical thinking, problem-solving, synthesis or integration,
> contextual understanding, coping with complexity, making
> connections, reflexive thinking, unconventional or original
> or creative thinking, facility with analogy and metaphor, sen-
> sitivity to bias and ethical issues, awareness of embedded val-
> ues, receptivity to new ideas, broadened horizons, tolerance
> of ambiguity (embracing irony or tolerating paradox), recog-
> nizing commonalties and differences, ability to identify and
> willingness to challenge assumptions, ability to see all sides of
> an issue, ability to shift perspective, evaluation of expert tes-
> timony, openness of mind, and a wide range of traditional
> academic skills.   (Newell 1998, 538)

Requisite affective traits include self-confidence and empowerment, empathy
and compassion, respect for difference, ability to work on a team, and investment
in a political and ethical agenda.

Where Do We Go from Here?
The Future of Interdisciplinary Studies

The discussion in this chapter suggests some roles that interdisciplinary study
needs to play in the decades ahead if higher education is to live up to its potential.
Interdisciplinarity must be integrated into disciplinary and general education
curricula alike. Tacking on an interdisciplinary course or two to a fundamentally
discipline-based curriculum will not suffice for a liberal education, nor will it

produce satisfactory professional education. If disciplinarity and interdisciplinarity are to feed off one another, so that interdisciplinarity can play its roles as corrective and contextualizer (and thus guide) for the disciplines—as sense-maker of a complex reality and as our best hope for solving complex problems—then we need to develop curricula in which there is an ongoing, systemic interplay between disciplinary and interdisciplinary education. More advanced interdisciplinary courses should be able to presume greater disciplinary knowledge, and more advanced disciplinary courses should be able to build on awareness of their assumptions and worldviews developed through interdisciplinary courses. That means creating a more equal balance of disciplinary and interdisciplinary education. More importantly, it means we must develop pervasive linkages between disciplinary and interdisciplinary courses. In short, we must think in terms of the curriculum as well as individual courses if we are to take full advantage of interdisciplinary education.

To achieve that potential, we also need to improve interdisciplinary education. In part, this is a matter of being more conscious of the nature of interdisciplinarity when we design and sequence interdisciplinary courses. It is not enough to create interdisciplinary courses that merely explore interesting topics. We need to be clear about the skills and sensibilities interdisciplinarity requires, then develop systematic strategies for inculcating them. Students should be familiar with some basic concepts, theories, and methods of several different disciplines. They should have some awareness of the fundamental assumptions (implicit as well as explicit) of those disciplines, and some feel for their perspective or worldview. They need to be skilled at using one discipline to critique the insights of another discipline. And they need to develop some proficiency in reconciling conflicting insights and integrating them into an answer to the question or solution to the problem. The focus of interdisciplinary educators must expand from exploring interdisciplinary topics to include the training of students in interdisciplinary study.

Improving interdisciplinarity also requires understanding more clearly and fully how it relates to other intellectual developments. One is its connection to complex systems theory. Interdisciplinarity is seen increasingly as a response to complexity, but the implications of complex systems theory for interdisciplinary activity remain largely unexplored. A second development connects interdisciplinarity to a variety of pedagogical innovations. Interdisciplinarity shares a common integrative impulse with learning communities, collaborative learning, living-learning, service-learning, study abroad, and multicultural learning. Again, however, the implications for practicing interdisciplinarity and for employing those pedagogies most effectively are unexplored. A third places interdisciplinarity within the philosophical tradition of American Pragmatism.

In a review of the College Board book *Education and Democracy: Re-imagining Liberal Education in America*, I suggested that interdisciplinarity fulfills the educational vision of philosophical Pragmatism. Explicit linkages between progressive thinking and interdisciplinary theory could enhance teaching K–16.

Students should graduate from college trained in both a specialty, quite possibly a discipline, and in interdisciplinary studies. They should be able to go back and forth with ease between analysis and synthesis, focused inquiry and contextualization, using each to inform the other. They should also be proficient at viewing the world through more than one disciplinary lens. Their eyes should adjust rapidly as they take off one lens and don another. Then, when they become employed in business or government or even education, and they confront complex problems, they should be able to draw competently on a range of experts or constituents or disciplines to construct a better solution (Hershberg 1988). We need to design curricula with those skills and that goal in mind.

College graduates should also be prepared to work on an interdisciplinary team, even if they play the role of disciplinary expert. More and more projects in the corporate sector are carried out through what are called "cross-functional teams." Task forces are increasingly common in law enforcement and government. The team approach is becoming popular in the practice of medicine as well as in medical research. And research teams have long been common in the natural sciences. In short, the more any field confronts complex problems, the more likely it becomes that it will organize itself into interdisciplinary teams. Beyond disciplinary competence, successful participation on an interdisciplinary team requires characteristics such as breadth of perspective, flexibility, and respect for the capability of others, as well as willingness to expose ignorance and learn from others (Armstrong 1980, 56). Experience in interdisciplinary courses that provide self-conscious reflection on the interdisciplinary process would obviously help as well.

Recommended Readings

- Since many key articles and chapters are already compiled in my 1998 anthology, my top selection is William Newell. *Interdisciplinarity: Essays from the Literature*. New York: The College Board. Twenty-nine authors contributed essays on the philosophy, administration, and disciplinary contexts of interdisciplinary studies in humanities, social sciences, and natural sciences, plus lessons from specific fields such as environmental studies, women's studies, peace studies, German studies, critical theory, and multicultural studies. The "Guide to Syllabus Preparation" developed through the Institute in Integrative Studies is included as well.

- The most comprehensive single book remains Julie Klein. 1990. *Interdisciplinarity: History, Theory, and Practice*. Detroit, Mich.: Wayne State University Press. Its 100-page bibliography alone makes it a standard reference work, though it is unique in its eclecticism, giving voice to a variety of conceptions of interdisciplinarity.

- The most stimulating collection of articles is *The Journal of General Education*. 45:2 (1996), contributed by alumni of the Institute in Integrative Studies—Tom Paxson, Jim Kelly, Don Richards, David Sill—as well as Julie Klein and me. Key issues emerging from the literature are highlighted and explored, such as the role of disciplines, the goal of integration, the role of creativity, types of interdisciplinarity, and its future in the academy.

- My favorite articles from *Issues in Integrative Studies* that have not already been anthologized are Guy Beckwith, "The Generalist and the Disciplines: The Case of Lewis Mumford," and Carolyn Haynes, "Interdisciplinary Writing and the Undergraduate Experience: A Four-Year Writing Plan Proposal," both from volume 14 (1996), and Tom Murray, "Confessions of an Unconscious Interdisciplinarian," from volume 4 (1986). Beckwith probes the intellectual strategies of Mumford for lessons about integration. Haynes develops a sequenced approach to introducing students to the steps of the interdisciplinary process, one that is grounded in developmental psychology and educational theory as well as in the professional literature on interdisciplinarity. Murray draws on his own experience to make the case for learning about interdisciplinarity through studying its practitioners. See www.muohio.edu/ais/ for a complete listing of articles published in *Issues in Integrative Studies* and for ordering information.

6

Introduction to *The Joys and Pitfalls of Team Teaching*

Like William Newell, James Davis presents new reflections on the raw data of teaching and curriculum design across the country. Davis is the author of *Interdisciplinary Courses and Team Teaching: New Arrangements for Learning.* Published in 1995 by Oryx Press and the American Council on Education, this book was the first comprehensive study of the topic in college. Davis explained the rationale and nature of interdisciplinary courses, applied insights from the wider literature on groups and teams, and described the dynamics of teamwork. He also illustrated the variety of arrangements, ranging from a single course to a clustered sequence of courses that together constitute a learning community. In addition, he presented criteria for judging degree of collaboration in four major areas: planning, content integration, teaching, and evaluation. The greatest degree of integration, he found, occurs when collaboration is high across all four areas. Typically, though, degrees of collaboration vary. Planning is the area of greatest cooperation. Collaboration varies in teaching, and the most neglected area is evaluation of student work.

Davis illustrated the criteria with five examples from the University of Denver. As their titles suggest, the courses span a range of contexts. Making of the Modern Mind and Multiple Voices of America are available to first-year and sophomore students fulfilling a 12-hour humanities requirement. The Origin and Evolution of Life is offered to undergraduate nonscience majors as an option for meeting a 12-hour core requirement in science. The Quality Panorama is offered to graduate students in business, and The Lawyering Process is required of all first-year law students. In addition to presenting an in-depth study of these five courses, Davis annotated 50 examples from responses to a survey of geographically disbursed postsecondary institutions in the United States, along with citations in Canada and Mexico. In the book, he described the nature and intended audience of each course, the disciplines represented, personnel, course topics, and distinctive features. In Chapter 6, he reflects for the first time on the fuller implications of the survey data.

Faculty engage in team teaching for varied reasons—a commitment to collaborative pedagogy, personal philosophies of education, and their own intellectual curiosity. Because many are used to working alone in classrooms, becoming a member of a team often feels like a "bootcamp in collaboration." The ideal team-taught course has a galvanizing idea at the center that becomes the focal point for collaboration on all aspects, from planning and developing the central organizing concept to making decisions about scope and sequencing, defining learning outcomes, and creating appropriate assessments. Davis illustrates principles of good practice in a remarkable range of contexts—general education, professional and technical programs, integrative studies programs, women's and gender studies, multicultural and ethnic studies, international studies, capstone and integrative courses, and electives. Even with the clear picture of teaming that emerges, there is still an unresolved philosophical debate on the relationship of existing disciplines and the new subjects that are "invented" in interdisciplinary courses. To help frame discussion of these differences, Davis concludes by defining core philosophical issues surrounding the theory of team teaching and offers recommendations for practice.

The Joys and Pitfalls of Team Teaching

James R. Davis

Recalling the writing of *Interdisciplinary Courses and Team Teaching* provoked unexpected nostalgia for a time in my career when I was involved with a team of enthusiastic colleagues and teaching assistants in planning and delivering a course called Social Science as a Craft. The course paralleled two other examples I discussed in the book, Making of the Modern Mind and Multiple Voices of America. It was an option that undergraduates could use for meeting general education requirements in the University of Denver core curriculum. My memory is of seemingly endless discussions about what should be included in the course or omitted, conscientiously attended planning sessions that somehow always left important details uncovered, and heated disagreements about student issues—such as, Can they be trusted?—which revealed our fundamental differences in educational philosophy. There were also magical moments in the classroom, notably the day we forgot to invite the guest lecturer and improvised a spontaneous dialogue that drew raves of "best class so far" from students. Most memorable was the sustained interest we all developed in the process of teaching and learning, signified by the daily recap question: Well, how do you think it went?

Social Science as a Craft was the result of efforts by three teachers—one each in education, sociology, and speech communication—to introduce students to common methods of research and topics of interest typically pursued by social scientists. The course followed a time-tested model for elementary school social studies known as the expanding social horizons curriculum. The order of topics moved from the individual to family units, small groups, organizations, and eventually society and culture. The contributions and perspectives of various social science disciplines were identified and sometimes contrasted—this is how the psychologist sees it, but this is how a sociologist would look at it. In general, though, the emphasis was on the commonalty of the tools, concepts, and approaches that social scientists bring to study of social phenomena. As the topic shifted, for example, from groups to organizations, the sociologist on the team would remind students that they were riding in an imaginary helicopter that enabled them to rise to a slightly higher vantage point each time a course transition was made, changing the unit of analysis and requiring new methods, perspectives, and concepts. Should the instructors have been delighted that students were finally catching the hallmark skepticism of the social scientist when they informally renamed the course Social Science as Crap? Perhaps this new name helped at least one team member, slightly bewildered by the whole experience, to deepen his resolve to leave the course to write a book on interdisciplinary team teaching.

In this chapter, the discussion of team teaching moves beyond illustrations from the University of Denver to reflect comparatively on some of the 50 examples collected in Part II of the book.

Motivations for Team Teaching: Why Educators Get Involved

Why do colleagues go to all this trouble to generate interdisciplinary courses? It is a daunting question because interdisciplinary courses are indeed "trouble," but there are also fleeting joys and deep satisfactions. The main answer to the question is that some teachers, at least those who get involved, find traditional teaching to be so very inadequate in so many ways. What is traditional teaching?

For years, the typical college classroom has involved one teacher alone teaching his or her disciplinary specialty, usually through lecture or discussion. The established paradigm for traditional teaching and learning at the postsecondary level is characterized by high levels of autonomy for individuals. Teachers determine what specialties they are competent and willing to teach. They select the subject and organize it as they see fit. They usually develop their own syllabus, their own reading list, and their own means of evaluation. They usually lecture, relying heavily on the spoken word, although sometimes saving time at the end for questions or "discussion." Any feedback they get from students usually comes at the end of the course through an evaluation form. They almost never get feedback from colleagues because no one has the time or inclination to visit another teacher's classes. Integrating what is learned in one course with what is learned in another is essentially "the student's problem." If this description seems harsh and to border on caricature, one need only ask: Have you seen such teaching—and how frequently—in your own institution?

How widespread is "traditional teaching"? In *College: The Undergraduate Experience in America*, a comprehensive report written on behalf of the Carnegie Foundation for the Advancement of Teaching, the late Ernest Boyer notes with a tone of discouragement that traditional teaching was encountered frequently and almost exclusively during site visits to the 29 colleges and universities in the study:

> Today the lecture method is preferred by most instructors. With few exceptions, when we visited classes, the teacher stood in front of rows of chairs and talked most of the forty-five or fifty minutes. Information was presented that often students passively received. There was little opportunity for positions to be clarified or ideas challenged. When discussion did occur in classes we visited, a handful of students, usually men, dominated the exchange.   (Boyer 1987, 149–50)

Boyer opens chapter 9 of the book, entitled "Creativity in the Classroom," with this description:

> At a freshman psychology lecture we attended, 300 students were still finding seats when the professor started talking. "Today," he said into the microphone, "we still continue our discussion of learning." He might as well have been addressing a crowd in a Greyhound bus terminal.   (Boyer 1987, 140)

The lecture method is still widely used, but today teams of faculty are exploring a subject from many viewpoints and collaborating in the use of different teaching strategies. Why is that? Why are teachers seeking alternatives to traditional teaching in interdisciplinary team-taught courses?

Much of the rationale draws on arguments for interdisciplinarity, discussed in depth in other chapters of this book and in other books. Those arguments are well crafted and often run deep. Sometimes they become quite philosophical, taking those who become engaged in them—academics love this discussion—into profound explorations of epistemology, cultural criticism, and even . . . ontology. At a rather different level, however, some faculty prefer to work as part of a team, as opposed to working alone, for rather mundane reasons. From formal interviews with faculty as well as comments gathered informally, a list of rather simple personal reasons emerges. Faculty like to explore new interests. They find stimulation in branching out into fields that go beyond their graduate school specializations. Some comment favorably on being able to read books they might not otherwise have time or inclination to explore. Some are actively seeking new ways of teaching. They want to watch others teach and enter into a dialogue about their own teaching. They become impassioned about a subject that goes beyond their own solitary expertise, and they get excited about creating large, complicated courses that have high potential for significant impact on students. Many admit that they simply crave the intellectual and social stimulation that comes from team teaching.

Team teaching is a lot of trouble, but for these reasons, as well as deeper intellectual reasons, faculty become drawn to it. When that happens, it helps to enter the process with some awareness of what to expect. For those who wish to get involved, there is something to be said for careful and systematic preparation—learning what questions to address, what issues to raise, and what steps to take. Above all, it is useful to anticipate what team membership is likely to entail.

The Ideal Team-Taught Course: Covering All the Bases

If one were to embark on planning and carrying out the "ideal" team-taught interdisciplinary course, what factors must be addressed? Most such courses begin with a great idea. Someone, not necessarily even a team member, must have or find a great idea, a central organizing concept around which the course can be planned. A course at the University of Michigan (Ann Arbor) called Words and Music brings together graduate students in music and poetry to study songwriting—a rather simple and natural arrangement, but also a brilliant idea. One or two people get a great idea for a course and then find the team members who can make it happen; and it usually works this way, rather than assembling a team that is expected to think of a great course.

When an appropriate team is assembled they take the general idea for the course and elaborate it in detail. This is where the real collaboration begins, and there is often much give and take needed to hammer out the course. In some cases, as in a course entitled What is Life? Biological and Philosophical Perspectives at the University of St. Thomas (Houston, Texas), two faculty bring together the views of their respective disciplines. In many instances, however, the team is "inventing a new subject" and the crucial task of content integration begins here. Contrast the course at St. Thomas with a course from the University of Maryland at College Park called Elements of Nutrition, where the disciplines represented are chemistry, biochemistry, psychology, social sciences, epidemiology, as well as molecular, cellular, and integrated physiology. What faculty often bring to the course is their own disciplinary perspective and a certain anxiety about "coverage"; what they must learn to do is see how their own expertise can be drawn on in creating a new subject or a new approach to an old subject, in this case "nutrition." In the ideal interdisciplinary course, the subject grows out of the idea; it is invented and elaborated by the faculty who participate in the course; it is more than the sum of the interdisciplinary parts; and it is presented to the students, as nearly as possible, as an integrated whole.

Like any course, the ideal team-taught course will have well-established and clearly stated learning outcomes. These are not so easy to define, because university faculty are more accustomed to thinking about content than outcomes, and if a truly interdisciplinary course is intended, special and unique outcomes should be anticipated. In a course at the University of South Dakota (Vermillion) called Rural Real Estate Appraisal, presumably students will actually be able to do appraisals for their final projects. In establishing learning outcomes, faculty can be more articulate about the special features of the course as an interdisciplinary course.

Likewise, decisions need to be made about scope, depth and breadth, and sequencing of topics. These are challenges in designing any course, but now, because the faculty are inventing a new subject, the old rules don't always apply. Consider Making of the Modern Mind at the University of Denver as an example: Just where does "modern" begin, and how much of the "mind" is considered? Which topics are most important among all that could be selected from art, literature, philosophy, and religion, and in what order should they be presented? It takes time and good listening skills to debate and resolve such issues.

Eventually the course, like any course, will need some organizational structure, but team-taught courses, especially those involving many participants, can get rather complicated. Consider The Lawyering Process, with eight simulated law firms, regular lectures, firm meetings, and 57 faculty, staff, and student assistants. Decisions must be made about structure, and logistics must be worked out.

Ultimately, decisions also must be made about methods of instruction. Ideally, shouldn't a "team-taught" course involve at least some team teaching? Surprisingly, some so-called team-taught courses don't involve much collaboration in instruction. When students see only serial teaching, they tend not to see it as a team-taught course, no matter how much collaboration has taken place behind the scenes in planning. Furthermore, many opportunities for enriching the classroom experience are missed when faculty fail to collaborate in instruction. Although there are often obstacles to overcome, such as lack of time and know-how, the benefits of team teaching can be enormous when special efforts to collaborate are made. Collaboration does not necessarily mean agreement.

A course called simply Introduction to Humanities at Cuyahoga Community College (Cleveland, Ohio) features two teachers from opposite ends of the political and intellectual spectrum. As one teacher presents the topic, the other serves as commentator and devil's advocate. A true team learns to differentiate faculty roles—some faculty are better at preparing materials, some are stars at lecturing, while others excel at leading inquiry or facilitating groups. Some teams divide up the subtasks of instruction. Effective teams also learn to do things together—to carry on debates, dialogues, and panels (instead of lectures), to conduct role plays and simulations, to work simultaneously in facilitating breakout groups or supervising the work of students in leaderless groups. All of this takes imagination and a collaborative attitude that gets beyond the usual question, What do I do when it is not my turn to lecture?

Finally, the ideal team collaborates on assessing student learning, not only in designing, administering, and evaluating student work for grades, but in assessing the more comprehensive outcomes of the course for students. Again, this is a necessary task in any course, but in an interdisciplinary course there ought to be some special outcomes to identify and measure. The ideal course will include assessment activities that stress integration and synthesis, such as logs and diaries, case studies, critiques (using multiple viewpoints), proposals, team projects, panel discussions, and creative works. If the goal of interdisciplinary learning is integration, then students should be given assignments that give them the opportunity to make connections, to "put Humpty Dumpty back together again." That is what interdisciplinary learning is all about: connections, patterns, broader perspectives, and integration.

Effective assessment focuses on these outcomes. In addition, because interdisciplinary courses are often innovative and complexly structured, it is important to develop and use ongoing assessment techniques for the course itself. This includes not only the typical end-of-course evaluation form—which usually needs significant modification to be relevant to a team-taught course—but also a wide range of classroom assessment techniques to find out how students are responding to the course while it is in progress. In this regard, many of the Classroom Assessment Techniques (CATs) found in the book of that title by Thomas Angelo and K. Patricia Cross (1993) can be adapted for use with interdisciplinary courses, keeping in mind that what instructors want to find out especially is how students perceive the interdisciplinary connections.

For example, when assessing prior disciplinary knowledge is important, a Background Knowledge Probe or Misconceptions/Preconceptions check can be used. For quick assessments of synthesis of interdisciplinary material, Concept Maps or Invented Dialogue can be used. Assessment should focus both on student learning and (because the arrangements may be unfamiliar and complex) on student satisfactions. Likewise, when several faculty are involved, assessment should provide opportunities for students to comment on the effectiveness of each of the players. Although one might believe that interdisciplinary courses provide a higher quality of education, they are, in fact, only an opportunity for higher quality. The opportunity becomes a reality only when appropriate assessment measures are used to document quality and stimulate continuous improvement.

The Ideal Team: Bootcamp in Collaboration

Team teaching involves collaboration, and a team of teachers shares many of the characteristics of groups and teams found in other walks of life. What social scientists know generally about group behavior and teamwork applies quite aptly to team teaching. All teams are groups, but not all groups are teams. A team is a group with a mission. People who gather on Friday nights for square dancing are a group. They have no particular mission. Teachers who draw together to offer a course collaboratively have a mission: to offer the course as effectively, creatively, and efficiently as possible. The ideal team has a clear goal and a strong commitment to it.

One thing we know about groups is that they generate more ideas than individuals thinking things through on their own. No one says the ideas generated by groups will necessarily be better, only that there will be more of them. This is at once a blessing and a curse for team teaching. Having a plethora of rich ideas increases the possibility of an attractive and valuable course, but it also leaves the team with a problem: How will certain ideas be retained and others rejected? More important, how will these decisions be made? How much time will be allotted for the generation and discussion of all these ideas? How and when should closure be reached? Sometimes these issues are resolved naturally, but at other times there is struggle and tension. The ideal team sets norms about its own behavior. It usually needs one person to play the role of facilitator and to help the team make and abide by norms for making decisions.

All groups engage in communication. Some of that communication is about the task, in this case the real work of planning and delivering the course. Other communication is about process, the informal chitchat and social interaction that takes place in any group. Process communication is extremely important in groups because it helps individuals feel comfortable in the group and builds group cohesion. Groups need to build a certain level of cohesion in order to be able to work on the task. As one might guess, the higher the level of cohesion, the better the task outcomes—but only to a point. When process behavior begins to dominate, task behavior diminishes. As group members begin to enjoy the process too much, they neglect the task. The ideal team recognizes the need to use time wisely and stay on task.

Groups and teams vary in size. Some arrangements for team teaching involve only three or four faculty, but other teams have many members and complex arrangements. The ideal team is large enough to draw in the needed expertise to accomplish course goals, but small enough for all members to participate in a significant way. Courses with large teams need a strong facilitator who oversees communication.

Participants in groups tend to find their niche and take on roles. This gives the group structure. After working together for a while, team members know what they can expect of each other and how the team works best together. On the ideal team, participants differentiate their roles clearly, capitalizing on individual strengths while dividing up tasks in a way that maximizes overall effectiveness.

Most groups and teams face problems. Typical disturbances are conflict, apathy, social loafing, and "groupthink." Problems develop when two or more members are in conflict with each other, the group, or the leader on a continuing basis. Apathy occurs when members of a team lose interest in and enthusiasm for a course. Social loafing occurs when one or more members fail to carry out responsibilities in a timely way and rely unfairly on other members to do the work. Groupthink occurs when a team reaches consensus too rapidly without giving consideration to alternatives. The ideal team recognizes all of these dangers, faces problems and resolves them directly when they arise, and designates a leader who helps the team recognize and resolve its problems.

Teamwork is learned. It doesn't always come naturally, and it usually needs to be cultivated consciously over a period of time. Some faculty who have always worked alone may need a "bootcamp in collaboration" in order to become effective team members. In general, however, most faculty work in a culture that values democratic resolution of issues through rational discussion, so most teams work fairly well. By learning more about teams, facing problems honestly, and taking swift and appropriate action, most of the pitfalls can be avoided.

Mainstreaming Team Teaching: All Corners of the Curriculum

One important development in team teaching is that it is now making its way into all corners of the curriculum (Davis 1995). Consider the following examples. The most conspicuous place for team teaching is in the general education programs that have a "core curriculum." Briar Cliff College (Sioux City, Iowa) offers The Human Person, a provocative shared experience for first-year students exploring the human species. Teachers from theology, biology, mathematics, chemistry, English, sociology, and other fields plan and carry out this course.

Eight teachers at Syracuse University (Syracuse, New York), mostly from the social sciences, collaborate to offer a core course entitled Critical Choices for America. Three teachers at Oklahoma State University (Stillwater) work as a team to offer nonscience honors students a course in Scientific Inquiry.

Sometimes team-taught courses are offered as introductory studies for majors. At the University of British Columbia (Vancouver, Canada), students planning to major in one of the sciences begin their studies with Science One, a course that integrates the equivalent of first-year biology, chemistry, mathematics, and physics in an interdisciplinary format. And of course some majors are interdisciplinary majors, such as the Interdisciplinary Program in Information Sciences at the University of Wisconsin at Green Bay and the Basic Humanities Degree Program at Marshall University (Huntington, West Virginia).

Team-taught courses are frequently found in professional schools or career-oriented undergraduate majors as well. Carnegie Mellon University (Pittsburgh, Pennsylvania) draws on teachers from design, marketing, and engineering for a course entitled Design, Marketing, and Manufacture of New Products. At the University of Alberta (Edmonton, Alberta, Canada) teachers from a wide variety of health-related disciplines offer a course on Team Building and Ethics, enabling students to learn team-centered and patient-focused health care delivery. The Northwestern School of Law at Lewis and Clark College (Portland, Oregon), draws on the skills of two law professors, a practicing attorney, and a psychiatrist to explore legal issues growing out of medical and mental health situations in a course called Law and Psychiatry. Students in journalism and graphic design at the University of Hawaii-Manoa (Honolulu) learn about Editing and Design in Publications and work together in teams to produce actual publications incorporating text, headlines, photos, and artwork. At South Dakota State University (Brookings) five teachers from wildlife and fisheries sciences, range sciences, park management, environmental management, and plant science collaborate to help students work on team projects in a course entitled Integrated Natural Resource Management. At Harvard University (Cambridge, Massachusetts) students learn about Inclusionary Education and At Risk Children: Mapping a Process of Change from teachers in education, law, government, and medicine, and through carefully selected practicum placements.

Team-taught interdisciplinary courses are also common in gender studies and women's studies programs. At the University of Hartford (Hartford, Connecticut) teachers from a variety of disciplines work in teams to help students, both male and female, trace gender socialization from childhood through adolescence and adulthood. Williams College (Williamstown, Massachusetts) offers an introductory issues-oriented course in women's studies entitled Introduction to Feminist Thought. Two teachers at the University of Southern

California (Los Angeles), one in law and one in sociology, offer a course for graduate students across many disciplines entitled Feminist Theory. Interdisciplinary teams are often used to present multicultural or international topics. A course at the University of Arizona (Tucson) on American Indian Studies draws on the disciplinary expertise of teachers from history, political science, law, anthropology, and literature to explore personal, social, cultural, political, economic, philosophical, and religious issues relating to the Native American experience. At Ithaca College (Ithaca, New York) an interdisciplinary team from history, art history, literature, anthropology, philosophy, religion, and economics offers Introduction to Japanese Culture.

Some colleges use interdisciplinary activities as "capstone" courses for seniors to help integrate the college experience. Sarah Lawrence (Bronxville, New York) offers a series of Senior Seminars on selected interdisciplinary topics. One example, The Modern City—Technology, Democracy, and Political Economy, explores the workings of megacities, such as Tokyo-Osaka, New York, Shanghai, Djakarta, Los Angeles, and Mexico City.

Although most interdisciplinary courses have their "home" in some corner of the curriculum, a few are not "required" as part of any program and draw their enrollments simply because they are interesting. At Hobart and William Smith Colleges (Geneva, New York) an art history and a geology teacher team up for a fascinating course about how the geological formations of the region produced the building materials for a rich cobblestone architecture. This attractive course is simply entitled Pieces of Landscape: Upstate Cobblestones. At Oberlin College (Oberlin, Ohio), students are attracted to a course called The Meaning of Life because it is developmentally appropriate and offers them an opportunity to explore a sublime question seldom raised in the disciplines.

This brief review illustrates clearly the variety of team-taught courses offered in colleges and universities today, and is a tribute to the imagination and creativity of teachers who have discovered the benefits of collaboration.

Issues and Recommendations

Although most interdisciplinary team-taught courses have a clear niche within the curriculum—general education, the major professional programs, multicultural, international, or women's studies—their academic home in the institution is often unclear. The organizational structure for the discipline is the department. What is the organizational structure for the team-taught course? A course such as Models of the Mind: Anthropology, Psychoanalysis, and Psychiatry at Vanderbilt University (Nashville, Tennessee) not only cuts across departments and divisions but colleges as well. Everyone knows that General Psychology belongs to the Psychology Department, but where is the home for a course that spans the colleges? Whose course is it?—the dean's? the provost's? Who approves it, who staffs it, who pays for it, and under what conditions? If a college or university generates a significant number of team-taught courses, establishing a workable home for them becomes an important matter. Departments, with their tendency to dominate organizational matters, may not provide a friendly home for interdisciplinary work. In fact, departments are often hostile to interdisciplinary efforts, both philosophically and organizationally, and may prevent the "release" of faculty from departmental responsibilities to engage in interdisciplinary collaboration.

Recommendation 1: Those who are in leadership positions in administration, and who also believe that interdisciplinary arrangements are important, should make special efforts to facilitate cross-departmental collaboration. This is an issue that deserves further study, inventiveness, and sharing of successful arrangements among institutions.

Closely related to the issue of organizational structure is the matter of faculty assignment (load) and financial arrangements. To put the matter bluntly, if six teachers work together to teach one course, do they all get credit for one course in their teaching load, or do they get credit only for a fraction of a course? For teachers to earn full credit, it is often necessary for the course to have a large enrollment; for example, a course with a team of four may need to have a course enrollment of 100 to support a teaching load equivalent to 25. A student-to-teacher ratio of 25 to 1 is used in this manner for interdisciplinary courses at the Evergreen State College (Olympia, Washington). The College of Business at the University of Denver uses a point system to award credit for participation on teams. At some institutions, and for some courses, this may work; but other teachers argue that team teaching is so much more work than ordinary teaching, that "equivalence" arrangements are unfair. Some institutions apparently find it easy to work out these arrangements because they value team teaching, while others, with bureaucratic rules about "full-time equivalents," seem to get hung up endlessly on this issue.

Recommendation 2: Institutions should develop flexible, fair, and equitable arrangements for assigning teachers to team-taught courses. This issue also requires further research and sharing of solutions among institutions in appropriate forums.

An urgent matter for faculty committed to team teaching is the development of more collaboration within the classroom. Faculty appear to collaborate most in planning, but when it comes to teamwork in the classroom—to actual team teaching—they often don't know what to do or how to feel comfortable doing it.

Recommendation 3: Faculty should balance the time spent collaborating in planning with more time devoted to collaboration in teaching, so that students can experience models of interdisciplinary integration. Workshops and conferences that focus on creative classroom collaboration would be valuable in stimulating more creativity in this area and would provide a forum for activities that work.

Like many new arrangements in education, team-teaching is something that inspires belief among those who participate in and experience it, but it is time to get beyond the gut-level feeling that it is a "good thing." If it is a good thing, what is good about it and how might that be documented? Some courses provide unusually inviting opportunities for assessment of outcomes. For example, a course at Universidad de Las Americas in Mexico provides an interdisciplinary approach to Child Evaluation. It raises several questions. Do students who have taken this interdisciplinary course approach the testing and diagnosis of children in a more integrated and holistic way? Exactly what are the special outcomes of team teaching, and how can these be more fully elaborated and carefully described? In other words, how can the quality—the excellence we expect from team teaching—be documented?

Recommendation 4: Faculty involved in team teaching should spend much more time developing classroom assessment techniques and student assignments that measure the unique outcomes of interdisciplinary study. This is a fertile area for quantitative and qualitative research studies designed to describe the unique outcomes of interdisciplinary learning. Those who are "unconvinced" about team teaching will be more impressed by documentary evidence than by undifferentiated enthusiasm. Furthermore, it is crucial to describe what is taking place when team teaching is well done. Team teaching needs more assessment.

Unresolved Debates

To what extent is interdisciplinary teaching about making connections between existing disciplines and to what extent is it about inventing new subjects? The example mentioned earlier, Science One, is an integrated core course for science majors at the University of British Columbia that stresses connections among biology, chemistry, physics, and mathematics. This academically rigorous 21-credit course covers the equivalent of first-year studies in the participating disciplines but does so in a way that demonstrates connections among the sciences and commonalties of method. By contrast, a course offered at Carnegie Mellon University entitled Design, Marketing, and Manufacture of New Products, though it draws on faculty from design, marketing, and engineering, does not have those disciplinary perspectives as its main focus. Rather, it draws on those disciplines to create a new subject. Both faculty and students are drawn from the represented disciplines and are mixed together in groups composed of two students from each discipline. Although the disciplinary perspectives are valuable and are drawn on, the focus is on how to use those perspectives in an integrative manner to create new products. Hence, a new subject has been invented in this course.

On the one hand, some faculty insist that before students can engage in interdisciplinary studies, they need to have strong foundations in the disciplines involved. Thus, to engage in the study of literature in an interdisciplinary context, one must first understand literature, then history, then art, in order to bring the three areas together in a productive way. There is some merit to the argument and examples of this kind of interdisciplinary teaching and learning are widely available. Others say it is possible and desirable to use disciplines only as resources or perspectives for studying a new subject. The subject—quality improvement, the Native American experience, cobblestone architecture—is what is important. It is not only possible to study new subjects without previous background in a discipline, these faculty argue, it may also be necessary to leave disciplinary moorings to invent new subjects. This is one of the more compelling philosophical issues to arise from interdisciplinary studies. Where one stands on this issue reveals the strength of one's attachment to disciplines as primary means of organizing knowledge for instruction. Are interdisciplinary studies primarily about coordinating the knowledge we gain through the disciplines, or are they about creating new ways of knowing?

Is team teaching primarily an effort to bring together disciplinary specialists to present their methodologies for viewing that subject, or is the goal of team teaching to create new methods for examining and teaching about a subject, new or old? In a course entitled Law and Economics at the University of Alberta in Canada, public policy created through legislation is examined for economic implications. Economics is used to study the economic implications of law, and one has the impression of a stimulating but traditionally taught course where one discipline examines another. By contrast, a course entitled The Lively Arts, offered by the University of Massachusetts at Amherst, finds new ways to prepare students for a lifetime spent understanding and enjoying concerts and exhibits. Although students are exposed to the vocabulary, stylistic issues, and historical contexts of various art forms, the course has a distinctly multicultural and international flavor. By drawing on regular programming of a Fine Arts Center representing African American, Asian American, Latino, and South Asian cultures, the course creates a broader world view of art and music. Students attend concerts and exhibits and are expected to write about them. One has the sense that the teachers have tackled an old problem—cultivating appreciation for the arts—but are addressing it in a new way by exposing students systematically to new art forms and types of experiences they otherwise wouldn't have. The course is not only interdisciplinary but also innovative.

These two courses, each remarkable in its own way, also raise the issue of pedagogy. Is the pedagogy of team teaching simply a serial presentation of disciplinary pedagogies, or is the goal to create not only a new subject but also new ways of teaching that subject? This is another interesting philosophical issue, and the way people respond to it reveals how much emphasis they wish to place on classroom collaboration. Some would argue that two lectures on a subject, side by side, perhaps involving also some dialogue from two disciplinary perspectives, is the goal of team teaching. Others would say more emphasis needs to be placed on synthesis, new insights, fresh perspectives, and unique ways of teaching and learning. Clearly, the type of collaboration and pedagogical outcomes of teamwork are likely to be very different for teachers with such different philosophical views.

Where is interdisciplinary study taking us and what is its place in the larger enterprise of education? One way to explore this question is to examine the extent of interdisciplinary team teaching within a particular institution. In some cases one finds only a few courses, maybe some electives or an occasional course in an area such as women's studies. In other cases one finds a major portion of the curriculum—for example, the entire general education program at the University of Denver—delivered this way. Colorado College (Colorado Springs) offers a host of interdisciplinary majors and minors. Seniors at Sarah Lawrence College take a series of interdisciplinary capstone courses to round out their education. Wayne State University provides undergraduate and graduate degrees in an Interdisciplinary Studies Program for adult learners. Miami University (Oxford, Ohio) has a separate college for interdisciplinary studies. These institutional differences, between minimal and extensive offerings, reflect a larger debate about the importance and direction of interdisciplinary studies.

Some see interdisciplinary work, and team teaching in particular, as an interesting minor phenomenon, a way of accomplishing certain tasks and achieving certain connections that might not otherwise be achieved. For them, it is a useful, albeit somewhat distracting, effort for those who want to get involved, but it will never upset the basic disciplinary paradigm as a way of organizing knowledge. Others argue that although interdisciplinary studies may have begun in an unthreatening way, the movement has gone much further, with intriguing methods of studying old subjects and inventing new ones that may indeed shake, if not shatter, the disciplinary structure. There are new subjects now that students and teachers want to study, and need to study, that won't be easily "shoe-horned" into old structures. The knowledge explosion of the information age will not be easily contained within disciplinary structures. Besides, they would argue, the disciplines themselves are already in trouble for other reasons.

Having been attacked by feminists for gender bias, and by cultural studies critics for work that has proven to be highly conditioned by time, culture, political outlook, and power, the disciplines are also scrambling to reestablish their credibility in a context where "relational knowing" and "the social construction of reality" are more important than "ultimate truth." The once clear boundaries between the disciplines, both with regard to method and domain, have already been blurred, and the paradigm shift of the late nineteenth century that created the disciplines is now being recapitulated in a new paradigm shift toward other ways, perhaps multiple ways, of organizing knowledge for research and instruction. Some would say it is too early to know where all of this will lead because we are too much in the middle of it. Although we may not know the exact form of the outcome, it is reasonable to conclude that interdisciplinary team teaching, along with technology, may be one of the important driving forces in the reengineering of traditional teaching in the next century.

Team-Taught Courses Revisited: The Constancy of Change

Some team-taught courses live and die, never to be reborn. Alas, Social Science as a Craft at the University of Denver disappeared eventually and nothing similar has replaced it. Other team-taught courses live on, seemingly forever. Western Humanities at Reed College (Portland, Oregon) has been in continuous operation for nearly 50 years. Even if team-taught courses endure, though, they usually change, playing out some internal necessity for re-creation. The team-taught courses at the University of Denver discussed above, and the major examples in my book on the subject, are all still in existence.

The faculty who taught Making of the Modern Mind took a collective "sabbatical" from the course and did not offer it one year. They came back refreshed and designed an alternative version of the academic-year course (still available) which is offered in spring quarter on campus and summer quarter in London. Multiple Voices of America now has an important service-learning component that provides students with opportunities for cross-cultural experiences to accompany their cross-cultural study of American history. The Origin and Evolution of Life no longer draws on teachers outside the Department of Biology and only one of the creators of the course continues to teach in it.

The Quality Panorama continues as a core course in the MBA program, and instructors have made significant advances in their use of technology. Students enroll online, PowerPoint presentations are used in class, the textbook has an accompanying computer disk, and students work through an elaborate case on CD-ROM. A second CD-ROM lets them discover how the case actually turned out. Students are also introduced to standard software packages for examining quality operations. After several changes in personnel, The Lawyering Process is still searching for a way to make the large lecture sections better, although the simulated law firms remain intact. The lesson in all of this, it would seem, is that team-taught courses seldom stand still. Faculty come and go, new purposes are identified, assessment provides feedback on needed changes, and bright new ideas occur. Nothing is as constant as change whenever human beings are working in teams. Teams are inherently dynamic.

Team teaching is still teaching, and the guidelines for the general improvement of teaching still apply. When teachers work in teams they often experience valuable social pressure from students and colleagues to become more sophisticated about the process of teaching and learning. This is perhaps the greatest benefit of all that derives from team teaching: the enriching dialogue about learning that inevitably takes place.

Recommended Readings

My recommendations for further reading are mostly from outside what might be called the "mainstream literature" on interdisciplinary studies.

- To understand interdisciplinary studies it helps to know something about the academic disciplines, how and when they came into existence, and why they became so well established. This fascinating story appears in Burton Clark. 1987. *The Academic Life: Small Worlds, Different Worlds.* Princeton, N.J.: The Carnegie Foundation for the Advancement of Teaching.

- For more background on undergraduate education in general, including an interesting chapter on the transition to college, see Ernest Boyer. 1987. *College: The Undergraduate Experience in America.* New York: Harper & Row and The Carnegie Foundation for the Advancement of Teaching.

- Two books on teamwork are especially valuable for learning more about the dynamics of collaboration. For a fascinating study of high-performance teams, see Carl Larson and Frank LaFasto. 1989. *Teamwork: What Must Go Right/What Can Go Wrong.* Newbury Park, Calif.: Sage. Or consult the now-classic study of teams in the business world, Jon Katenbach and Douglas Smith. 1994. *The Wisdom of Teams.* New York: Harper Business, 1994.

- Two books on classroom teaching techniques offer useful strategies. Discussion of assessment methods is valuable in Thomas Angelo and K. Patricia Cross. 1993. *Classroom Assessment Techniques: A Handbook for College Teachers.* San Francisco: Jossey-Bass. For help on linking teaching strategies to well-established theories of learning, see my earlier work: James Davis. 1993. *Better Teaching, More Learning.* Phoenix, Ariz.: The American Council on Education and The Oryx Press.

7

Introduction to *Developing and Administering Interdisciplinary Programs*

Like William Newell and James Davis, Beth Casey reassesses the lessons of an earlier guide in the context of new practices. In the 1994 Jossey-Bass sourcebook *Interdisciplinary Studies Today,* Casey wrote the chapter on administration and governance of programs. She established principles for effective administration in four areas: interdisciplinary studies programs, general education, interdisciplinary schools, and interdisciplinary colleges. The principles were accompanied by practical suggestions about faculty concerns, budgetary supports, and administrative leadership. Casey urged administrators in all four areas to examine their institutional and college mission statements while asking two questions. How well do those missions serve current knowledge needs? And how well do they serve civic and social ends of academic study?

In Chapter 7, Casey reflects on recent developments. The trends she noted earlier continue. Moreover, the principles of oversight, structural flexibility, organizational culture, program protection, and administrative leadership remain integral to long-term stability. Today, though, Casey places greater emphasis on the role of new scholarship and on two needs that are catalyzing structural reform for interdisciplinary learning. The first is the need to accommodate and support boundary crossing related to the urgent problems and challenges of our time. The second is the need to restructure and revalorize undergraduate liberal education through learning communities capable of realizing a democratic civil society. Meeting these needs will require nothing less than a new social contract.

Even in a time of downsizing and retrenchment, Casey reports, interdisciplinary programs have increased in number and variety. Many are still isolated and dependent on external funding. Yet the trend toward greater fusion in academic programs has resulted in more support structures that resolve older problems of staffing and budget. Both new and established programs are enacting new meanings, collaborative work modes, and administrative supports. In general education, in particular, the learning community movement continues to provide fresh impetus to interdisciplinarity. Some educators, in fact, regard this development as nothing less than a paradigm shift. Interdisciplinarity has also been a major variable in comprehensive reforms of undergraduate curriculum. And nontraditional student populations are being served, including working adult students in formats that allow for self-designed concentrations, independent studies, and internships, along with traditional seminars and workshops.

Administrative structure is still inherently conservative. Today, however, it is being pressured by the need to accommodate disciplinary boundary crossing on an unprecedented scale, to provide intellectual community, and to acknowledge the varied learning styles of today's students. The developments Casey describes are complementary modes capable of transforming the current "multiversity" into a genuine "transversity."

Developing and Administering Interdisciplinary Programs

Beth A. Casey

In 1994, when I contributed the chapter on administration to *Interdisciplinary Studies Today*, I defined the growing significance of interdisciplinary studies in terms of increased enrollments in programs and national calls for integrative curricula. In 2002, however, it would be more accurate to report that interdisciplinary study has entered the mainstream of higher education as the full and necessary complement of disciplinary study, generating courses, majors, and degree programs, and catalyzing connections across departments and colleges. Crossing boundaries is, as Julie Klein (1996) states, "a defining characteristic of our age." Boundary crossing, however, is still a formidable task because it implies reorganization of the institutional structures that support production of knowledge and innovations in the practices involved in its dissemination.

With supportive structural change, interdisciplinary study can reinforce the vision of a college or university as a collaborative learning community enhancing communication, cooperation, and interaction among departments, schools, centers, and programs, as well as faculty, students, and the public world. Complementary rather than competitive modes of relationship can thus be fostered, collegiality enhanced, and intellectual community embraced both within and without the academy. Such coherence can result in greater economy as well—repairing the expensive fragmentation created by specialization and disciplinary implosion, which I discussed in 1994. It could even result in transforming the present multiversity into what has been termed a "transversity." Such an institution would seek to overcome the barriers that impede connections across disciplines and emphasize linkages to K–12, community colleges, industry, state governments and agencies, and society in general (Scott and Aubrey 1993). In so doing a new social contract can be forged, creating a different understanding of a people's relationship to its institutions of learning from kindergarten through college.

Administrative structure in higher education, however, is inherently conservative. Necessity is the primary if not the sole agent of transformation, though we are certainly not without precedent for functional innovation. Structural change for interdisciplinary learning today is being catalyzed by two related needs. The first is the need to accommodate and support the practice of disciplinary boundary crossing, which increases in direct relation to our attempts to resolve the most pressing problems and challenges of our time: climatic change, environmental and energy problems, technology assessment, the integration of minority populations on a local and global level, the effort to stabilize a global economy, or the challenges of the information revolution. The second is the need to restructure and revalorize the liberal education of undergraduates by creating more effective learning communities directed toward a democratic civil society. It is this civil society I had in mind when I called in my earlier chapter for mission statements directed toward purposeful—that is, civic or social—ends.

In response to these forces for structural change—particularly the latter one—Stanley N. Katz, former president of the American Council of Learned Societies, called recently for a new investigation of whether the present organization of intellectual life in universities is the best for cultivation of responsible citizens. In doing so, he called for a closer relationship between secondary and tertiary educational institutions and for "the provision of greater continuity in the schooling of college-bound students," perhaps by seeking to reconceptualize the last two years of high school and the first two years of undergraduate education as a single unit. The unprecedented rate of change today's college graduates will face indicates clearly that education must be sufficiently liberal and unspecialized to create broadly knowledgeable citizens capable of critical thought. Katz called for the inclusion of multicultural perspectives, a broader range of pedagogical techniques, a reexamination of the departmental structure as an artifact of a period of distinct disciplines, and a broadening of the curriculum by consolidating faculty from different departments along thematic lines. Increasingly we organize research around the subjects we study—in the manner of urban studies or women's studies—rather than around a particular set of investigative techniques. Instead of organizing general education around introductions to disciplines such as sociology, psychology, or biology, why not organize it around a theme such as "models of human behaviors"? "We have to find ways," Katz urges, "to make the organization of the university look more like our own minds" (1996, 85).

Calls for structural change supporting interdisciplinarity increased toward the end of the decade and often occur in a new context—one that emerged in the late 1980s, gathered new significance in the late 1990s, and will surely continue for the foreseeable future. Some administrators and faculty view this new context as a radical paradigm shift, a move from viewing an institution of higher learning as an instruction provider to viewing it as a learning producer. We might avoid, if we wish, the puzzle of paradigms and simply refer to this as the Learning Community Movement. Whether we choose a radical or a more conservative view, the new context can be defined, as Barr and Tagg have done, as a development that allows administrators and faculty to think about creating learning environments rather than simply offering courses; to view knowledge as constructed and created rather than "delivered"; and to define learning as the result of interactive frameworks in collaborative, cross-disciplinary environments, not as courses and programs in independent disciplines or departments (1995, 16–17). The learning community movement is more about integration than about interdisciplinarity, but it is helping to bring about structural change supportive of the latter.

Early in 1990, Faith Gabelnick, Jean MacGregor, Roberta S. Matthews, and Barbara Leigh Smith issued a germinal book entitled: *Learning Communities: Creating Connections Among Students, Faculty, and Disciplines.* They defined the communities as purposefully restructuring the curriculum to link together courses or coursework so that students find greater coherence in what they are learning and experience increased intellectual interaction with faculty and fellow students. Very modestly, they noted that learning communities can address the structural features of the modern university that undermine effective teaching and learning through collaborative learning, team teaching, and interdisciplinary themes (5). In my 1994 chapter on administration and governance, I noted the importance of developing learning communities for both students and faculty when building general education programs. Today, this movement is further enhancing the development of interdisciplinary programs, schools, and colleges as well as general education where a variety of models and connective strategies are emerging. The movement itself fosters an overarching principle of cooperation, enhanced collegiality, and intellectual community, while creating a new reciprocity between academic and student life and between the university and the community, often through experiential and service learning. As it reconnects students and faculty, this in turn increases retention in colleges and universities and has a positive impact on budgets—another motivation to create change.

With these shifts in mind, let us revisit the major areas of interdisciplinary programs, general education, and interdisciplinary schools and colleges to see what new developments are occurring.

Interdisciplinary Programs

Interdisciplinary programs have continued to increase in number, even during a time of downsizing and retrenchment, especially in general education, the humanities, women's and gender studies, and American studies (Edwards 1996). A new role has been found for ethnic studies—including African American, Latin American, and Asian studies—and for such programs as urban, environmental, or international studies in the extensive support they provide general education programs. Scholarship and teaching in both interdisciplinary and general education programs are enhanced by curricular fusion in these areas, although the isolation of programs within universities and colleges does not often lend itself to such cooperation. Successful efforts, however, are indeed made, often receiving external funding. These fusion efforts have begun to influence the development of supportive structures to resolve the staffing and budgetary problems of many interdisciplinary programs.

In 1995, for example, the Ford Foundation funded a project known as the Women's Studies, Area, and International Studies Curriculum Integration Project (WSAIS), which encouraged curricular transformation through integration. By integrating the experiences, knowledge, and research of and about women from Africa, Asia, Latin America and the Caribbean, and Central and Eastern Europe, Ford sought to enhance the capacities of U.S. women's studies scholars to include comparative international perspectives in their research, to develop the abilities of area studies faculties to incorporate issues of gender in their research, and to mainstream comparative gender research in both undergraduate women's studies and general education courses through interdisciplinary faculty and curriculum development activities. New course syllabi and new scholarship resulted, and some mainstreaming of international and gender research occurred in general education curricula in the 12 universities and colleges funded, including Arizona, the University of California at Berkeley, the University of Maryland at College Park, the University of Michigan, the University of Minnesota, Princeton University, Rutgers University, Spelman College, and the University of Wisconsin–Madison.

Many new administrative structures have been developed recently to permit interdisciplinary programs to enhance and enrich one another in the manner suggested by the Ford grant. Let us examine three of these structures that address the program isolation and budgetary shortfalls I discussed in 1994.

- First, at Appalachian State University in Boone, North Carolina, a Department of Interdisciplinary Studies was formed to offer 14 concentrations in the most common interdisciplinary areas, including women's studies, Asian studies, and environmental studies as well as Appalachian studies and Individually Designed Studies. Four of the concentrations offer a minor. The department includes nine full-time faculty, about 86 majors, and five core courses. Faculty receive tenure within the IDS department, thereby solving the staffing problems of many interdisciplinary programs, and the Watauga College program, which is overseen by the department chair and by the program director, has the authority to create courses without going through the full institutional review process.

  The core courses are required of majors in all concentrations and range broadly, utilizing the talents of all interdisciplinary program faculty. Courses such as Science and Culture, Interdisciplinary Thinkers and Thinking, or Interdisciplinary Approaches/ Contemporary Issues are offered. Majors must also complete 24 credit hours in one of the interdisciplinary program concentrations and undertake a separate minor. Still more interesting is the fact that the same faculty and numerous part-time faculty offer an alternative, two-year, residential interdisciplinary general education program to 200 students in a cluster college format called Watauga College. First-year students enroll in 10 course hours per semester. These classes are all subsumed under two course numbers, one in the fall and one in the spring. The fall consists of Watauga Chautauqua, which is integrated with various campus cultural activities; American Stories: Narratives of Family; Tools of Human Understanding; and one interdisciplinary area studies course. The spring semester consists of a second Watauga Chautauqua: Civilizations East and West, and another interdisciplinary area studies course. Sophomores choose from a variety of interdisciplinary courses and enroll in a service-oriented Chautauqua. The area studies include women's studies, gender studies, environmental studies, and the like. The courses get their unusual name from nineteenth-century traveling lecture circuit tours called "Chautauquas."

- Seeking to enhance collaboration and strengthen interdisciplinary programs, Virginia Polytechnic Institute and State University (Blacksburg) created the Center for Interdisciplinary Studies. The center is a tenuring unit with approximately 46 full-time faculty and a smaller number of on-loan faculty participating part-time. It offers courses to more than 600 majors in two B.A. degree programs in Interdisciplinary Studies and International Studies. Eight previously independent centers and programs in the College of Arts and Sciences were brought together to create the center. Such programs as Latin American studies or Russian studies provide degree options for the majors, while others, including black studies, religious studies, and American studies, offer concentrations and minors. The majors provide a continuous student body for the center, while participating on-loan faculty may refresh themselves by teaching interdisciplinary courses. Each program maintains its own identity and offers its own core courses and electives, making the center director a Director of Directors. All new faculty hired by the center are formally connected to at least two programs to increase collaboration and cooperation. Naturally, some struggle for program identity ensues, but program collaboration reduces this.

- Finally, Colgate University's Division of University Studies (Hamilton, New York) illustrates how a unit in a small private liberal arts college can be formed to strengthen disparate interdisciplinary programs, including African and Latin American studies, Asian studies, peace studies, women's studies, Jewish studies, Native American studies, and environmental studies. In addition, the faculty offer a four-course interdisciplinary Liberal Arts Core General Education Program focused on questions of identity, culture, and knowledge, in which students select two courses on Continuity and Change in the Western World, one course in the Cultures of Africa, Asia and the Americas and one topics course from a series on Scientific Perspectives on the World. Numerous upper-level general education courses are also available, as well as courses related to the study areas. Students may pursue distinction in the Core Curriculum by completing advanced work, including an integrative examination of topics relevant to the contemporary world.

All three of these structures make it possible to tenure faculty in interdisciplinary programs without some of the intense follow-up dual appointments require—though these appointments are still possible—and they have simultaneously supported cooperation and rich curricular fusion among programs. Faculty external to the units may be located there for a semester or a few years or more to teach in one or more of the programs. The directors can work to encourage program collaboration and foster program consistency for students. Too often students enrolled in such programs as American studies or environmental studies cannot obtain courses necessary for completing their majors because the units are dependent on departmental course schedules. Deans wishing to protect interdisciplinary programs can make it clear that evidence of serving interdisciplinary programs is essential for requesting faculty replacement, though some kinds of faculty absence are beyond the reach of the most supportive of deans.

Cooperative units not only enhance and enrich faculty scholarship and teaching but provide more consistency for students as well. Such units, with the power to offer tenure-track lines, are much more likely to achieve budgetary parity with departments. They can hold seminars at the boundaries and interfaces of disciplines, foster new programs, and assure faculty development for interdisciplinary pedagogies and team teaching. The center or division directorship might even be a revolving office, thus assisting in maintaining a more flexible and less hierarchical structure.

In short, interdisciplinary faculty and program directors greatly increase their chance of achieving budgetary parity and equitable treatment by joining forces in a comprehensive unit. Faculty in interdisciplinary programs are still too often isolated, unrewarded, and unsupported. These conditions can be mitigated through more cooperative structures. If such interdisciplinary administrative units cannot be created, then at the very least a council of interdisciplinary programs headed by a coordinator—a recommendation in my 1994 set of principles—should be initiated.

Interdisciplinary General Education

The learning community movement has given fresh impetus to the development of interdisciplinary general education programs, encouraging a rich variety of new structures and connective strategies, bringing about a cultural transformation in our ability to view a university or college as a collaborative unit, and enhancing our ability to provide programs with explanatory power for students. Many communities link general education courses with courses in writing or speaking and courses in the major, often along thematic lines, and strive to integrate clustered courses to create cognitive coherence. Students may share the same residence hall and be actively involved in course-connected programs or projects at these sites and many engage in service learning in the community. In addition, some colleges are experimenting with course clustering in particular interdisciplinary majors, forging links with general education. Learning communities involving students, faculty, and peer advisors serve to integrate programs at the University of Missouri at Columbia, Texas A & M at Corpus Christi, California State University at Sacramento, Clarion University of Pennsylvania, and the State University of New York at Potsdam—in other words, it is a genuinely national movement. The movement fosters the conditions necessary for interdisciplinary program design, and it flourishes in a wide variety of educational settings and among a wide variety of students.

In 1994, as universities and colleges began to move in more integrative directions, AAC&U summarized the key characteristics of the best general education programs in *Strong Foundations: Twelve Principles for Effective General Education Programs* (Gaff Project on Strong Foundations). The principles actively support new strategies for connecting courses, faculty, and students and, if applied, can foster interdisciplinary work. The first six imperatives emphasize programs and answer the question, "What is the point of General Education?" Programs that provide a compelling vision of general education embody a well-defined institutional mission, strive for educational coherence, teach social responsibility, attend carefully to student experience, strive to be value-based, and design for continuous evolution. The next six principles emphasize community. Strong programs require and foster academic community, assure strong faculty and administrative leadership, cultivate substantial and enduring support from multiple constituencies, engage in dialogue across academic specialties, involve student cocurricular experiences, and monitor and assess progress toward an evolving vision.

Let us look now at the administration and design or redesign of three programs where interdisciplinarity flourishes: a new residential learning community at Bowling Green State University (Bowling Green, Ohio); a set of revisions to extend the success of an interdisciplinary required course sequence at Skidmore College (Saratoga Springs, New York); and a comprehensive program redesign for interdisciplinarity at Portland State University (Portland, Oregon). All three make manifest the AAC&U principles and demonstrate the influence of the learning community movement.

- In the fall of 1997 Bowling Green State University opened the Chapman Residential Learning Community with the goal of addressing the need, as Director Tom Klein put it, "for a seamless learning community fostering the education of the 'whole person.'" An interdisciplinary five-credit course addressing Voyages of the Imagination, a linked writing course, and shared common experiences with music, art, literature, debates, and theater structured the fall semester. Students were introduced to the languages of the arts, their communicative possibilities, and their interdisciplinary connections. Interdisciplinary courses addressing rationality, critical thinking, and the examination of social controversies—Voyages in Science and Asking the Right Questions—along with continued work in writing and other curricular options fulfilled the spring semester. All classes met university general education requirements, and students were able to begin professional programs and majors in additional courses outside of Chapman.

The administration funded redesign of the residence hall for the learning community and constructed faculty offices and new spaces where students and faculty could gather for films, debates, performances, and other activities linked to the curriculum. Students who select the Chapman experience are charged a nominal fee in addition to regular university charges to defray the cost of the construction. Additional financial support is gained through the high retention rate of students returning for the sophomore year—7 percent higher than the usual rate—the pattern in most residential communities where faculty and students are in close connection with one another. Ten instructors from different disciplines joined the staff at Chapman, including tenured faculty, graduate students, instructors, and adjunct faculty.

In its second year, Chapman added interdisciplinary general education courses for returning sophomores who would continue to live in the community and mentor first-year students. All students also participate in service-learning experiences as part of developing the program's commitment to future citizens. Discussions have also been initiated concerning the possibility of a new four-year Baccalaureate for Professional and Liberal Studies as an option for those who wish to continue in the program for an undergraduate degree. Clearly, administrators seeking to begin such an interdisciplinary first-year general education community could either stop at the end of that year, continue to the sophomore year, or offer the option of a full four-year degree. Costs are nominal and one does not need a full panoply of new tenure-track lines.

- Skidmore College has for years required all first year students to take the interdisciplinary Liberal Studies I: The Human Experience, plus three additional interdisciplinary courses over four years. Liberal Studies I was intended to involve the entire college community and serve as a "signature" course for the institution, making manifest what was best about Skidmore. The program's mission was described by Skidmore President David Porter as capturing the spirit of intellectual adventurousness and risk-taking, the habit of open-ended questioning, and interdisciplinarity. Eventually, however, the faculty came to realize that four courses were more than they could comfortably staff and still meet other responsibilities. The requirement was cut back to two courses: Liberal Studies I and one additional integrative course from a creative series of offerings, many of which were team-taught. The option of an interdisciplinary capstone experience was also added.

Often, when interdisciplinary general education programs are formed, the comprehensive design is too ambitious to continue to deliver. Initial enthusiasm needed to drive the program wanes. Some streamlining has to occur. Faculty in this case, with the help of consultants, have undertaken a plan still in progress to administer the program with increasing college involvement and enhanced creativity. Most of the new efforts involve administrative enhancement and program redesign to protect an interdisciplinary experience that faculty and administrators realize is central to Skidmore College.

The key course, Liberal Studies I, was refocused and revitalized by assuring that its curriculum was situated squarely within the institutional mission of Skidmore. Faculty investigated ways to include more of their colleagues in collegewide discussions of course redesign to assure participation and incorporate suggestions for change from as diverse a group as possible. A long-term assessment plan will be created, and new supports for faculty development, emphasizing pedagogical strategies for the delivery of the interdisciplinary program, will be put in place. Residential experience had always been connected to Liberal Studies I, but fresh efforts will be made to have student projects presented in residence halls with the assistance of the dean of the freshman year experience, who is eager to be of assistance to the program. Residential programs for Liberal Studies I will be expanded, including film series and other artistic presentations. A new Teaching Museum and Art Gallery that opened on campus in 2000 encourages integrative exhibitions from different departments for use in the classroom, thereby helping more faculty participate in the curriculum. The central administration agreed to establish guidelines for departmental contributions to program staffing.

Such administrative maneuvers to guarantee continued success can be adopted by any institution striving to keep interdisciplinary general education programs alive. It is always wise to require occasional comprehensive examination of the curriculum as a whole, including inquiries into the growth of majors and course proliferation. A major initiative to streamline and create program coherence promotes economy and preserves a college's ability to maintain a valuable interdisciplinary general education program of importance to the offices of admissions and development as well as the intellectual vitality of students.

- The interdisciplinary general education program at Portland State University offers an excellent example of a fully developed four-year sequential model. It also demonstrates how a university with declining retention rates and budgetary shortfalls can design an interdisciplinary program to restore fiscal security and initiate a learning program that benefits not only students and faculty but the community as well. An urban university such as Portland often has difficulty establishing a clear identity and a sense of involvement for its many part-time students. It also must deal with large numbers of transfer students and these must be carefully guided into appropriate levels of a complex program. The cohesive three-tiered University Studies curriculum reduced barriers among disciplines, promoted active student learning and teamwork as well as faculty development, and fostered a new sense of purpose and mission for the entire university. Retention rose to 80 percent for first-year students and is expected to continue to grow. Applications have increased by 40 percent.

Portland State's administrators undertook massive measures to encourage this curriculum and followed up thoroughly with appropriate supports. They reduced administrative support staff by 13 percent and middle management by one-third to generate substantial savings of more than $35 million, a move accompanied by increased academic productivity and utilization of small classes. The system of student credit-hour funding is presently being revised so that departments need not fear losing budgetary support by lending faculty to the program. Tenure and promotion guidelines for faculty have been changed to support the new mission, and faculty replacements are being linked for departments to program participation—a necessity for success and survival. A Center for Academic Excellence was also created to support faculty and departmental teamwork in the development of interdisciplinary curricula and pedagogies and to provide portfolio-based program assessment that would create a culture of evidence.

In the first curricular tier, first-year students enroll in one of five year-long thematic interdisciplinary courses covering such topics as Values in Conflict: Knowledge, Power and Politics, in which faculty from five disciplines explore the conflicts that emerge in a society when perspectives collide (Iannozzi 1997). Students remain with the same faculty, classmates, and mentors throughout the year. Courses are five credit hours per term for a total of 15 hours for the sequence. Sophomore Inquiry creates the opportunity to explore topics of interest that are different from yet complementary to the major. Students choose three, one of which will serve as a foundation for a cluster of courses—most often disciplinary—to be pursued in the junior and senior years. Three or four courses are chosen from the upper division clusters and a required Senior Capstone is designed to build cooperative learning communities by taking the student out of the classroom and into the field to apply learning from the major and general education to issues and problems in the community. Interdisciplinary program courses play a large role in the curriculum at Portland, and many students opt for a minor in such areas as Latin American studies on their way through the upper division clusters.

Carol Schneider, in a recent reflection on the difficulties of achieving coherence in liberal education through the major alone, noted that it may well be that general education, rather than departments, should assume responsibility for linking departmental communities in larger, intercommunity dialogues (1996, 256). Interdisciplinary general education can and should provide the curricular architectures nurturing the generative connections of a liberal education. The fact that courses in any general education program—even in a distribution model—are now increasingly interdisciplinary augments this possibility. International and multicultural education, for example, constitutes at least a quarter of most general education programs. The move toward global education has also influenced the humanities, which provide another quarter of most programs, and assisted the rise of cultural studies (Miller 1997), establishing new links with the social sciences. New developments in philosophical, literary, and historical theory have also created metalanguages in the humanities, reinforcing their connective power with other disciplines (Casey 1986). As new integrations create new matrices and establish further opportunities for connections, the curriculum needs imaginative organization.

Interdisciplinary Schools and Colleges

As I noted in 1994, when discussing Miami University's School of Interdisciplinary Studies (Oxford, Ohio) and the Evergreen State College in Olympia, Washington, these complex enterprises must provide strong cohesive curricula and seek constantly to maintain and develop their original goals for collaborative interdisciplinary learning. The overall degree programs must provide breadth, depth, and focus (Zemsky 1989), while providing experiences that bridge theory and practice. Features of these models have been emulated nationwide. The classic shape of the curriculum at Miami can be seen in many new learning communities emerging across the country, including the previous examples of Watauga and Chapman. Evergreen's Coordinated Studies programs focused on such themes as Political Ecology; Space, Time, and Form; Common Problems in the Arts and Science; Freedom, Causality, and Chance; and Environmental Design, then followed up at the advanced level with specialty areas discovered to be essential to students. These practices have also been frequently emulated. Two examples of growing interdisciplinary schools that focus on nontraditional-aged student populations in innovative ways follow.

- The Interdisciplinary Studies Program (ISP) at Wayne State University (Detroit, Michigan) has established a national and an international reputation for excellence in providing a university education accessible to adults with family, work, and other responsibilities. The program focuses on teaching adults how to use disciplinary, professional, and interdisciplinary knowledge to solve problems and explore complex issues. The average age of the approximately 625 undergraduate students is 41. The student population is 50 percent African American, 25 percent white, and 25 percent other or unknown. About 63 percent are female and 37 percent male. A typical ISP undergraduate student is a married African American female between the ages of 31 and 45 who is working on a Bachelor of interdisciplinary studies degree and will very likely seek a graduate degree as well. Employers of ISP students include Ford, General Motors, Michigan Bell, and the city of Detroit. Wayne State's ISP has made diversity a top priority in its push to educate and inform adult students about community issues and our nation's growing minority population.

  The curriculum design for the ISP Bachelor of Interdisciplinary Studies (BIS) and the Bachelor of Technical and Interdisciplinary Studies (BTIS) degrees enables students to focus on themes and issues using interdisciplinary methods. The curriculum of the BIS degree focuses on historical, contemporary, and cross-cultural issues in the humanities, social sciences, and science and technology. The program places special emphasis on critical thought and analysis, writing ability, and research skills. The course of study focuses on humanistic and social consciousness and scientific and technological literacy, while drawing upon the maturity and experience of the adult learner. The BIS-Capstone and BTIS degrees are both designed to help holders of two-year Associate of Applied Science degrees earn a four-year college degree. The Capstone concept, essentially a reverse 2+2 degree, consists of a core of interdisciplinary studies, training in fundamental skills, and opportunities for advanced study in areas of special interest.

  All ISP courses draw upon several disciplines and use a combination of innovative teaching formats: weekly workshops, directed studies, weekend conferences, and distance learning. Most weekly workshops are scheduled in the evenings to provide after-work opportunities to engage closely with professors and exchange ideas with other students. They usually meet one evening a week at the main downtown Detroit campus or extension centers throughout the metropolitan area. A smaller number of morning workshops are held on campus for students who prefer to attend class during the day. Each workshop carries four semester credits. Directed Study options enable students to do reading, research, or other creative work with individual professors on topics of special interest. Weekend conferences are held on the main campus and provide special opportunities to hear presentations from a variety of speakers, including leading authorities on issues of vital interest. Most conferences meet throughout the day on Saturday and Sunday three times each semester. Web-based courses and extensive use of e-mail enable distance learning as well.

An orientation to the program and concepts and methods of interdisciplinary studies is provided for all students, relieving the anxiety returning adults experience. Most significantly for interdisciplinary studies are the reports of graduates of Wayne State's ISP program. They indicate that their education has been extremely valuable to them in their professional capacities and in pursuing graduate studies. They point especially to the ability to solve problems more readily in their areas of interest by applying multiple perspectives to a situation, evaluating the testimony of experts, perceiving the essential boundaries of specialization, and recognizing the complexity of the issues they confront. Above all, graduates report having learned to communicate clearly the results of their deliberations to diverse audiences and having developed a capacity for collaborative learning and teamwork—one of the most valued outcomes of interdisciplinary programs and one in high demand in industry.

- A second innovative interdisciplinary school worthy of study is the Gallatin School of Individualized Study at New York University, which initially emerged from a University Without Walls program, then attained division status when a graduate program was initiated in the mid-1980s. Gallatin attained the status of a school in 1995 and with it the power to grant tenure. Gallatin offers self-designed concentrations of interdisciplinary courses, independent studies, and internships as well as seminars and workshops. A small number of faculty and a larger number of part-time faculty are appointed solely to the school. About 200 faculty advisors from throughout NYU assist with developing student programs.

First-year seminars at Gallatin focus on aspects of the human experience and include "great books" from various periods, cultures, and disciplines. Interdisciplinary seminars are theme-based and often focus on the history of ideas, and numerous arts workshops are taught by urban professionals. Individualized concentrations may also include most NYU courses, as well as internships, independent study, and private lessons. The Senior

Colloquium involves an oral examination by three faculty based on themes or issues and on reading from ancient and Renaissance classics as well as modern works. A symposium in the senior year prepares students for the colloquium. The school has a dean and associate dean with support from administrative staff. Gallatin's organization displays an extraordinary combination of classic and innovative approaches to interdisciplinarity.

When an interdisciplinary school or college becomes established, it often continues to flourish and excel. The Hutchins School of Liberal Studies at Sonoma State University (Rohnert Park, California), Wayne State University's Interdisciplinary Studies Program (Detroit, Michigan), Hampshire College (Amherst, Massachusetts), St. John's College (Annapolis, Maryland), Western Washington's Fairhaven (Bellington), and the Paracollege at St. Olaf's (Northfield, Minnesota) have lengthy and rich histories. Attempts to develop such separate colleges or schools on a campus today will result in strong enrollments, high retention rates, and stimulating development for both faculty and students. We need the results of interdisciplinary study: self-reliant learners competent to address a world characterized by rapid change and transformation, tolerant of ambiguity yet able to conceptualize and resolve new problems, comfortable with diversity, and committed to the public good. Furthermore, students today are increasingly pragmatic and respond well to the underlying praxis of interdisciplinary learning. Our efforts will no doubt redouble to balance disciplinary with interdisciplinary study.

Conclusions

Most important for development of interdisciplinary study, as I noted at the beginning, is the need for a corresponding redevelopment of at least the last two years of high school education, so that university and college interdisciplinary connections and learning communities will be more familiar to incoming students. A secondary school determined to increase learning might restructure time and form simple learning communities among course units. A pre-culture for moving toward interdisciplinary study would doubtless follow. Any of the general education learning communities that link writing and speaking themes with disciplinary course content could be emulated in an elementary or secondary school. However, as Heidi Jacobs cautions in this book, what usually happens is that time is laid out in schedules that predetermine the possibilities of intellectual life in the classroom. We know that other time sequences can be achieved. Why do we seem to lack the will to change on both the secondary and the postsecondary level? I believe Jacobs has answers to that question. The characteristics and needs of learners are not considered prior to design of formats for learning. Rather, disciplinary units in postsecondary, secondary, and elementary schools set the time sequences—not learning outcomes or the needs of students who will become future citizens. The shape of the discipline and faculty customs determine time sequences, and the curriculum mirrors these separations.

We should also consider the fact that today schools and colleges are admitting students whose learning styles are characterized by a preference for concrete experiences, sequentially connected learning, clarity and specificity of direction, a low tolerance for ambiguity, and "a practice to theory route" rather than the reverse, as noted by Charles Schroeder in a seminal article in *Change* in 1993. Relatively nonselective institutions of higher learning now have a solid majority of such students, bringing a dramatic change to the classroom. Schroeder adds that 75 percent of the general population has been estimated to prefer the sensing learning pattern on the Myers-Briggs type Indicator—not the intuitive mode that has been more traditional among both faculty and students in higher education. These students prefer direct, concrete experiences; moderate to high degrees of structure; sequential learning; and a practice-to-theory route (22). Problem-focused interdisciplinary learning, with its frequent links to experiential learning, can be enormously helpful to the majority of today's students in both secondary and higher institutions of learning. Connected sequences of interdisciplinary learning would better address the learning styles of the general population in elementary and secondary schools and the larger percentage of students now attending college.

Finally, one might also ask if recent graduates of colleges of education will have experienced anything in their training that would encourage them to pursue integrative experiences in secondary or elementary curricula. Many states are now asking that students preparing to teach take two 18-hour minors and an assortment of introductory courses rather than majoring in particular traditional disciplines. They may undertake a social studies or language arts or multidisciplinary science major, which could be promising for integrative studies in schools if the programs in colleges were integrated and some interdisciplinary work encouraged. Such integrations could and should be undertaken by arts and sciences faculty working with education faculty to achieve these results. If not, such preparation may instead result in teachers who are uninterested in pursuing integrative study in K–12, and the absence of higher level thinking skills in these new minors and assorted disciplines might well inhibit interdisciplinary studies. Clearly, there is a lot to be done but, as the current record of courses and programs documents, a lot that has been accomplished.

Recommended Readings

The following works will help readers with the design and administration of interdisciplinary programs.

- First, I recommend James R. Davis. 1995. *Interdisciplinary Courses and Team Teaching.* This is a splendidly detailed study examining the structure and delivery of interdisciplinary courses and providing numerous examples of course designs and syllabi. Interdisciplinary instruction means collaboration among departmentally separated faculty, and organizing for such curricular delivery can seem to be a very formidable and unfamiliar task. This text is genuinely enabling for those who wish to make a beginning in this direction.

- Second, I recommend Julie Thompson Klein and William H. Newell. 1997. "Advancing Interdisciplinary Studies." In *Handbook of the Undergraduate Curriculum,* edited by Jerry G. Gaff and James L. Ratcliff. San Francisco: Jossey-Bass. This essay provides a detailed description of the way in which systems in higher education are evolving from simple to complex ones based on networks, webs, and systems of knowledge. This development, in turn, has changed the way many faculty members think of knowledge and the academy while fostering more interdisciplinary research and teaching. Klein and Newell also address the many hybrid communities and interactions that are often not visible today on organizational charts but which support interdisciplinary thinking. And, they provide a detailed overview of interdisciplinary teaching, curriculum design, pedagogy, and assessment.

- Third, for general administrative assistance, see David Seymour. 1988. *Developing Academic Programs.* Washington, D.C.: AAHE-ERIC Higher Education Report. This is an invaluable text for all aspects of administrative development. Designing and administering interdisciplinary programs involves a holistic look at everything from budgetary issues to assessment, and this text is very helpful.

- Fourth, I admire Jerry Gaff. 1994. *Strong Foundations: Twelve Principles for Effective General Education Programs.* Washington, D.C.: Association of American Colleges and Universities. Though not addressed specifically to interdisciplinary program developers, this is a work of great practical assistance. The 12 principles so carefully described are made operative for program designers and work very effectively to assure success.

- Finally, I would suggest a reading of Stanley Katz. 1996. "Restructuring for the Twenty-First Century." In *Rethinking Liberal Education,* edited by Nicholas Farnham and Adam Yarmolinsky. New York: Oxford University Press. This, more than any other reading I can recommend, addresses issues applying to K–16 most effectively and optimistically and does so in an appropriate historical context.

Part III
Toward a K–16 Dialogue

8

Assessing Interdisciplinary Learning K–16

Julie Thompson Klein

Learning assessment is a topic of considerable debate across K–16. When it comes to interdisciplinary education, the debate intensifies. Until recently, there were no clear guidelines for assessing integrative learning. Reports from classrooms are rich in success stories. However, there is not a large body of empirical evidence or longitudinal studies on interdisciplinary assessment. The evidence remains primarily anecdotal and inferential. Even so, a consensus on an appropriate logic of assessment is emerging across K–16. Four commonly asked questions frame the discussion:

> What is the context of interdisciplinary assessment?
> What criteria are being used to assess quality of learning?
> What assessment tools and strategies are being used?
> What should we do about the standards and assessment movement?

The Context of Interdisciplinary Assessment

Assessing interdisciplinary learning is a complex task. To begin with, more than one subject or discipline is involved. Each carries specific and sometimes conflicting assumptions about how to evaluate learning. Quality of integration must also be considered, and innovative pedagogies often require new approaches to evaluating what students have learned. Contexts differ as well. A full-scale model of K–12 curriculum integration has a different dynamic than a high school or college course centered on the themes of the environment or democracy.

Furthermore, educators disagree on the definition of interdisciplinarity and the purpose of integration. Some emphasize fusion of skills and content. Others stress interaction of knowledge and experience, while others highlight particular theories or methods.

Recently, a task force of the Association for Integrative Studies (AIS) conducted a study of interdisciplinary assessment (Field and Stowe 2002). The task force focused primarily on postsecondary education, though it was unique in having a K–12 expert on board. Gordon Vars, former president of the National Middle School Association, brought the longer history of thinking about assessment of integrative learning in K–12 to bear on the project. Over a two-year period, the group consulted with experts and analyzed results of a national survey of AIS members, directors of interdisciplinary programs, and participants in related projects. The results indicate that assessment practices are still in their infancy. In fact, the task force received more pleas for help than established plans.

Members of the task force, and an earlier study group commissioned by AIS, grappled with the gap between traditional thinking about assessment and the complexity of interdisciplinary learning. The cornerstone of traditional thinking about assessment is measurement of progress toward clear and operationally defined learning outcomes. Knowledge of content and concepts is theoretically easy to evaluate if there is wide agreement. Interdisciplinary curricula, however, tend to be unique. No standard model supplies a universal index. Many teachers, in fact, question whether acquisition of knowledge is the primary goal. They regard intellectual maturation and cognitive development as the appropriate conceptual framework for assessment. Furthermore, complex learning outcomes do not match up with standardized tests, and goals are sometimes combined in a way that makes analytic and reductive measures difficult to implement. A narrow scientific, experimental mode of evaluation fails to capture the intellectual multiplicity, discovery-orientation, diffuse skills, and complex goals that are typical of interdisciplinary education, as well as general and liberal education (Farmer and Napieralski 1997, 597–99).

Over 200 studies on effects are listed in a bibliography of the National Association of Core Curriculum and, over a 50-year period, more than 80 normative or comparative studies have appeared in K–12 (see Vars 1996). The Eight-Year Study, sponsored by the Progressive Education Association, produced the earliest evidence that students in problem- or issue-focused curricula have better attitudes toward learning. Launched in 1933, the study involved 30 progressive or experimental high schools. Students in these schools did as well or better in college than graduates of schools with separate-subject curricula. They were also more involved in social and extracurricular activities. Graduates of the six schools that moved most dramatically in the direction of curriculum integration showed the largest advantage (Beane 1997, 28; Ellis and Stuen 1998, 20). Drawing on more recent data, Rebecca Burns earlier presented new evidence from schools using Interdisciplinary Teamed Instruction, including increased scores on standardized tests, and from reports in the literature on team teaching. Fewer studies have been done in college, though William Newell noted Pascarella and Terenzini's discovery that integrating learning around a central theme elicited greater growth in critical thinking. In the first major study to include interdisciplinary variables, Alexander Astin found the interdisciplinary core approach to be linked statistically with favorable effects on general education outcomes.

These studies parallel the claims that teachers have been making. In K–12, they report gains in the following abilities:

- to make comparisons, contrasts, and connections across disciplines;
- to see relations and patterns;
- to synthesize learning into a meaningful whole;
- to engage in higher-level thinking and abstraction;
- to work collaboratively;
- to grapple with complex questions and problems;
- to be creative and exhibit responsibility for their own learning.

K–12 teachers also report greater enthusiasm for and engagement in learning plus fewer disciplinary problems and improved attendance. Teachers themselves benefit too. They speak of professional renewal, a greater sense of enthusiasm and empowerment, increased creativity and collegiality, and more emphasis on learning not just teaching.

College teachers report similar results. When the earlier AIS task force surveyed the claims made in a variety of interdisciplinary courses and programs, they identified the following educational outcomes:

- tolerance of ambiguity or paradox
- sensitivity to ethical dimensions of issues
- the ability to synthesize or integrate and to think contextually
- the capacity to work with multiple and conflicting sources of information and tools
- broadened perspectives or horizons
- greater creativity, original insights, or unconventional thinking
- improved cognitive skills of higher-order critical thinking
- a better balance between subjective and objective thinking
- greater humility
- the ability to demythologize experts
- increased empowerment   (Field, Lee, and Field 1994, 70)

Teachers also report improvements in conventional outcomes such as writing competency, proficiency in oral communications, and computer literacy.

The question of criteria follows directly on the heels of claims. What are benchmarks of quality in integrated teaching and learning?

The Picture in K–12

Few integrative designs are as comprehensive as Susan Kovalik's year-long model of a theme-based curriculum. However, the "3 Cs of Assessment" in her model apply generically:

The 3 Cs of Assessment

Complete: the work called for by an inquiry meets all requirements or specifications of the inquiry, including timeliness;

Correct: the work contains accurate information, the most recent available information, and use of more than one source;

Comprehensive: the work reflects thoroughness of thought and investigation, not a singular response or point of view.   (Kovalik 1994, 115)

The second criterion—correctness—speaks directly to the criticism that interdisciplinary courses are not just shallow but may be inaccurate. The concern is legitimate. In an elementary school unit on whales, knowledge of cetology must be sound. In a K–12 unit on American civilization, facts about historical events must be correct. This criterion extends to college. In a course on globalization, information about world trade must be exact and current. "Requisite" disciplinary knowledge, a term Jill Vickers (1997) used in the context of Canadian studies, must be defined and clarified. Some familiarity with pertinent concepts, methods, and the way a discipline constructs reality are also important. Content alone does not comprise a discipline. The level of sophistication will vary across age levels. Yet, as James Beane noted earlier, even in a multidisciplinary design teachers can reach beyond the surface of disciplines to engage their substantive resources and tap major concepts.

The question of disciplinarity looms large in discussions of interdisciplinary assessment. In identifying intellectual criteria for quality in integrated curricula, David Ackerman (1989) began with the importance of concepts in disciplines and a design model that enhances them. Concepts must not simply relate to a discipline but be integral to it. They must also be more effectively learned in an integrative design than if taught separately. Educators differ on how far beyond disciplines design models should go. Howard Gardner and others who share his concern for disciplinary integrity argue that disciplinary and interdisciplinary perspectives can work in concert. Yet, they maintain that students should devote most of their energy to "mastering" individual disciplines (Boix-Mansilla, Miller, and Gardner 2000).

The question of quality does not rest entirely on the ground of disciplinarity. The remaining two criteria in Ackerman's scheme were learning that transcends concepts to create a metaconceptual bonus and activities that contribute to development of desirable intellectual and personal dispositions. Martin-Kniep, Feige, and Soodak's (1995) criteria for conceptual integrity in teaching themes, which Rebecca Burns applied earlier to sample units, add to the picture. They identified three criteria: significance, relevance, and coherence. Beyond significance of concepts for disciplines, the integration of learning goals, activities, and assessments must be coherent. Cognitive and affective connections also need to be made between course material and students' experiences and backgrounds. A curriculum is relevant when it personalizes content, making the abstract concrete and enlivening the search for meaning and engagement in the learning process. Beyond correctness, Kovalik's other criteria come into play as well. The interdisciplinary task at hand is the ground for determining completeness and comprehensiveness. Thoroughness of thought and investigation, not a single response or point of view, are required for the production to be broad in scope and integrative.

Quality in interdisciplinary study also requires moving beyond a commonsense understanding of a theme or problem. Boix-Mansilla, Miller, and Gardner (2000) illustrate this movement in a unit on Nazi Germany and the Holocaust in an eighth-grade social studies course. Students progress beyond the commonsense reaction of anger to comprehend sociopolitical, cultural, economic, psychological, and biological dimensions of the Nazi totalitarian state. The concept of obedience to authority and the science of eugenics are core topics in their investigation. Interdisciplinary study is also not simply an organizational consideration. It engages questions about both disciplinary and interdisciplinary knowledge, asking what disciplines contribute to understanding important problems, how multiple disciplines compensate for limitations of individual disciplines, and the purpose of interdisciplinary work.

Quality in Integrative Learning

A fuller picture of what kind of learning is valued in interdisciplinary classrooms emerged when two groups of K–12 teachers defined indicators of quality. In the Rutland, Vermont, Northeast Supervisory District 230, teachers gathered for a day of in-service training focused on quality in student work. To support the effort, teachers brought examples of the kind of work they valued. The variety was striking, including films, geographic maps and tabulations, models, books, computer programs, essays, scientific studies, songs, and games. Then, working in cross-grade groups, they generated a definition of quality intended to serve as a goal for the entire school system. The definition that emerged has little to do with test scores measured against a set norm or convention. It has, as Clarke and Agne observed, "the look of life itself—in the workplace, in the home, and in the community." It also has the "look of intelligence." Five categories emerged.

Quality Indicators

- *Uniqueness:* The work is infused with individual spirit.
- *Communication:* The work has an impact on others.
- *Integration/Connectedness:* The work employs multiple sources and multiple media.
- *Challenge:* The work results from invention with some risk.
- *Growth:* The work reflects a process by which the student has changed.

(Clarke and Agne 1997, 109–10)

These indicators were also evident when a teaching team at Soquel High School in California developed criteria of authentic learning. They taught a three-hour interdisciplinary block combining biology, U.S. history, and American literature for 90 tenth-grade students. Their immediate task was to critique favorite assignments, with the aim of developing new and more powerful ones. The new assignments illustrate the dialogue of content and process that occurs in integrative learning. Weeks of brainstorming, arguments, and revisions in assignments resulted in a list of criteria for authentic learning in interdisciplinary contexts:

Criteria of Authentic Learning

1. articulate purpose of activity;
2. analyze and practice what they do know;
3. acknowledge what they do *not* know;
4. formulate questions that lead to further knowledge;
5. synthesize connections between knowledge and life experience now and in the future;
6. evaluate what was learned, how it was learned, and how it could be more effectively learned as a formal part of the assignment.

(Krovetz et al. 1993, 73–76; in ASCD 117–20).

In one of the new assignments that emerged, on immigration and genealogy, students are given protocols for collecting information and conducting an interview. In a year-end final project, they synthesize learning from the disciplines of history, biology, and English around a complex, issue-oriented question. Their answers to the question are presented to the class, the teaching team, and some parents and other educators. At an end-of-year portfolio evening, students present work they feel best demonstrates their reflective thought and personal style. The meaning of appropriate assessment lies in the verbs in the designated criteria— *articulate, analyze and practice, acknowledge, formulate, synthesize,* and *evaluate.* Integrative learning is a dialogue of content and methods that builds connections across disciplines, school knowledge and life experience, prior and current learning, research, and reflection.

Assessment Tools

Heidi Jacobs's earlier array of assessment devices across the K–16 continuum echoes in Nancy Cornell's report on the assessment tools that the Vermont teachers were using. Like Jacobs, Cornell found an immense variety:

- teacher-made quizzes and unit texts, pretests, and textbook tests;
- reading conferences and writing conferences;
- interviews and informal observations;
- science logs and reading journals;
- running records;
- a social studies assessment and a U.S. history assessment;
- general portfolios and the Vermont math and writing portfolios and uniform tests.   (Clarke and Agne 1997, 109–11, 304–7).

Despite suspicions to the contrary, tests are not missing from this picture. In addition to their own tests, teachers use standardized tests and the essay portion of recognized instruments. They also conduct conferences, interviews, and surveys. Comparison of entrance and exit essays and tests affords a view of learning over time. One particular tool—portfolio assessment—has gained wide favor. Coupled with journals and logs, portfolios combine the best features of introspective self-reports and objective data. The lack of fit between state goals and norm-referenced testing has prompted several states to develop portfolio systems based on state outcomes that include performance events. The K–12 New Standards Project (NSP) combined content-specific standards with portfolios that demonstrate work for a particular district school or student, work prescribed in NSP projects and extended learning activities, and student performances cued to a set of matrix-examination tests (Clarke and Agne 1997, 302).

In two states, new assessment plans accounted for both integrated and subject-specific outcomes. The Bloomfield Hills School District in Michigan created specified goals for each level in K–12. "Broad learner outcomes" included both discipline-based concepts/skills and generic, interdisciplinary performances. "Discipline-based learnings" specified fundamental concepts and skills for individual subject areas. In defining discipline-based learnings for elementary, middle school, and high school levels, teachers drew on the Michigan State Board of Education's Model Core Curriculum Outcomes. "Common Learnings" are generic skills, concepts, and attitudes that can be demonstrated in a variety of activities or contexts. The skill of decision making, for example, requires making informed choices in and across multiple content areas, after considering alternatives and related facts and ideas. Common Learnings may be employed in virtually all discipline areas, providing connective threads for integrated study and learning (Pickard, Travis, and Lang 1994 in ERS).

The Vermont Standards that Agne and Clarke described earlier are a more recent example. "Essential Learnings" provided discipline-based educators with measurable results of content acquisition. "Vital Results" defined intellectual skills applicable to all content areas, such as communication, reasoning and problem solving, personal development and social responsibility. In both the Michigan and Vermont examples, the conventional meaning of reliability and validity was balanced with the need for integration. Discipline-based educators gain measurable results in knowledge acquisition, while interdisciplinary educators using themes, problems, questions, or projects gain opportunities to recognize individual work. A wide array of productions and performances can be used, insuring quality without imposing uniformity on the different ways that students construct knowledge.

The Comparative Picture in College

College educators are behind their K–12 counterparts in dealing with interdisciplinary assessment, but there are significant parallels. Most of the discussion in college centers on general education, not particular fields.

General Education

The trend in general education today is toward multiple outcomes. Greater emphasis is being placed on liberal arts and science subject matter, more skills and competencies are being taught, interdisciplinary scholarship on multiculturalism and global perspectives is being incorporated into the curriculum, and the ethical dimensions of subjects are being explored. As general education has extended across all four years, greater attention is also being paid to differing levels of integration. Breadth of knowledge and thematic studies are emphasized at entry level. Higher-level exploration of connections among the major, general education, academic study, and the "real world" occurs in senior capstone seminars (Gaff 1999).

The trend toward multiple outcomes is evident in assessment plans at the University of South Carolina in Columbia and California State Polytechnic University in Pomona. At South Carolina, students are expected to attain standard proficiencies in written and oral communication, numeracy, and computers and technology. The plan also calls for multidisciplinary breadth of knowledge across the physical and/or life sciences, social and behavioral sciences, history and culture, and literary, visual, or performing arts. In addition, students must be able to communicate in another language and, at the capstone level, to address personal and/or professional ethical problems and global issues. Their abilities are benchmarked as Outstanding, Effective, Adequate, or Ineffective (data from AIS national survey).

The Interdisciplinary General Education Program (IGE) at California State Polytechnic University in Pomona generated one of the earliest plans. Targeted educational outcomes include competence in communication skills and critical thinking, along with historical and social consciousness, multicultural understanding, and understanding of aesthetic experiences and values. The program also promotes independent integration of knowledge and experience through active learning. Progress is evaluated over a multiyear program. In the first year, basic understanding of themes and concepts is emphasized; at the sophomore level, the ability to compare, connect, and analyze; and at the culminating point, the ability to formulate original interpretations and carry out sustained, independent inquiry.

The conceptual model of assessment at Pomona, like many other interdisciplinary approaches to general education, is development of a holistically educated person. Consequently, learning process takes center stage. Learning is defined as a cumulative process characterized by stops and starts, not a linear progression. Each outcome is a node that draws together members of different disciplines, facilitating faculty development and providing realistic benchmarks for measuring both faculty and student work. The most crucial indicator of quality has been critical scrutiny of colleagues in workshops, planning sessions, retreats, public presentations, and team teaching. At Pomona, assessment is rooted in the same kind of public conversation that K–12 teachers in Vermont experienced in their district-wide deliberations (*IGE: Program Assessment;* Manley and Ware 1990).

Assessment Methods

Like their K–12 counterparts, college educators use a variety of methods. The latest AIS task force affirms a fundamental premise of what "appropriate" assessment means in interdisciplinary contexts: Multiple and complex outcomes require multiple strategies. Direct methods, which assess whether students have achieved learning outcomes, include exams as well as performances. Indirect methods, which ask learners to reflect on their experience and achievement, include surveys and questionnaires, interviews, telephone surveys, and focus groups. Exams may be multiple-choice, true-false, standardized, or locally developed tests. Many interdisciplinary environments—senior seminars, internships, field placements, simulations, juried presentations, written projects, case studies, oral presentations, and portfolios—are conducive to performance-based assessment. Observational protocols and scoring rubrics may be used, with analytical ratings of activities, holistic appraisal, or both. Portfolios are valued in college for the same reason they are in K–12. A portfolio provides a longitudinal picture of learning, capturing development of knowledge and skills over time. Learning can be evaluated formatively, over the course of the process, and summatively, at the end. Moreover, evidence of unanticipated outcomes may emerge, an effect not captured by most standardized instruments (Field and Stowe 2002).

The IGE at Pomona uses a combination of direct and indirect approaches: portfolios, journals, student self-evaluations, first- and second-year papers, projects and presentations, participant surveys and questionnaires, focus groups, and data from student writing, test scores, longitudinal studies of alumni, and reports by outside evaluators. Oral defenses of senior theses provide further evidence of learning. Two institutions that participated in the AIS national survey also combine methods. The General Education Program at Morehead State University in Morehead, Kentucky, uses course-embedded performances along with standardized testing, pre-/post-skills assessment, and faculty and student surveys. At the Evergreen State College in Olympia, Washington, where the assessment effort began with existing data on cognitive development of first-year students and their self-evaluations, pre- and post-testing using the Measure of Intellectual Development instrument measures progress in cognitive development. Retrospective studies rely on students' narrative self-evaluations.

In addition to portfolios, comparison of essays written at entrance and exit levels provides a longitudinal picture. In the honors program at Bemidji State University (Bemidji, Minnesota), the comparison is coupled with a systematic protocol for portfolio assessment. Comparison provides evidence of improvement in analytic and evaluative thought, written and spoken communication, as well as student satisfaction with the program. At the University of North Carolina at Asheville, comparison of essays written in the first and senior years in general education courses reveals progress toward designated goals. These goals include appreciation of the diverse human heritage and historical development of the modern world, plus competence in oral communication, written communication, critical reading and evaluation, and arriving at "considered options" using evidence from several disciplines. In addition, videotaped classes are reviewed for evidence of student growth. Douglas Eder, director of assessment at Southern Illinois University at Edwardsville, describes the senior assignment as a scholarly process that results in a tangible product. Faculty can also deal with senior projects descriptively, asking not just "how well" but "what is" (Field and Stowe 2002 and AIS survey data).

These examples underscore another parallel with K–12. Tests play a role, including tests that measure generic liberal arts skills. The College Outcomes Measures Project (ACT-COMP) evaluated a wide range of intellectual skills, not specific content. The phasing out of ACT-COMP, though, means other tools are needed. The General Intellectual Skills test measures critical thinking and communication skills, and the Academic Profile measures college-level skills. The latter, though, is discipline-based. In interdisciplinary fields, parts of relevant disciplinary and professional tests may be appropriate, as well as measures of critical thinking and reflective judgment. However, many measures are not standardized or supported by sufficient research on validity and reliability. Even the best test of liberal arts skills, Karl Schilling (2001) cautions, ends up reflecting general intelligence as much as or more than the impact of a specific curriculum. Rebecca Burns called earlier for "direct and palpable evidence of cross-disciplinary connections." James Davis suggested a potential tool. Many examples in Angelo and Cross's book on *Classroom Assessment Techniques* (1993) can be adapted to focus on connections. When assessing prior disciplinary knowledge, the Background Knowledge Probe or exercise on Misconceptions/Preconceptions may be useful, as well as Concept Maps and Invented Dialogue.

In contrast to general education, little has been written about assessment in specific interdisciplinary fields. There are, though, important parallels.

Interdisciplinary Fields

Despite the relative lack of work on assessment in interdisciplinary fields, the topic has been addressed at length in women's studies. *Students at the Center* (Musil 1992) contains results of a national study, complete with sample instruments and design models. Assessment in women's studies is rooted in a dialogue of content knowledge and learning process. Content is composed of pertinent disciplinary knowledge and feminist concepts, methods, and theory. Feminist assessment is also student-centered, participatory, and sensitive to the dynamics of collaborative learning in local contexts and cultures. When researchers surveyed programs around the country, they expected that standardized tests would dominate. Instead, they found a sophisticated and varied conception of assessment across campuses. Generally speaking, programs look for both demonstrated improvement on traditional measures and a record of experiences over time. They also rely on multiple methods and sources of information.

Because feminist pedagogy is shaped by feminist philosophy and informed by relationships between teachers and students, a variety of quantitative and qualitative approaches are used. Quantitative measures include analysis of enrollment figures, statistical data, and questionnaires. Qualitative methods include participant observation and textual analysis. Feminist ethnography, in particular, entails close examination of data such as transcripts, observations of class discussions, and interviews with teachers and students. Illuminative evaluation, which encompasses ethnographic and phenomenological modes grounded in experience, measures the success or failure of innovative projects. Portfolios evaluate progress over time.

The Human Development and Social Relations Program (HDSR) at Earlham College (Richmond, Indiana) is based in a different interdisciplinary field—human development and sociocultural systems. Yet, again, there are parallels. In HDSR, faculty from sociology/anthropology, psychology, philosophy, and education cooperate in offering a core sequence of psychology and social anthropology courses. The courses introduce students to theories, methods, and empirical data in disciplines related to specific problem areas. After the lower-division core, students deepen their understanding of a particular discipline or content area at the upper division. They can align their choice of courses with personal interests, career goals, or graduate study. The program culminates in a senior seminar, and students do field study in a domestic or international setting.

The designated learning outcomes in HDSR resemble those in many general education programs, including development of sensitivity to values and ethical judgments, and the ability to manage ambiguities, contradictions, and congruencies. Multiple instruments are used, including comprehensive exams, field-study reports, a problem analysis, and a reflective essay. In addition, the program conducts an alumni survey and does longitudinal tracking of employment and graduate school admissions. Information from these tools also supplies feedback for improving the quality of the curriculum. Added information comes from course evaluations, curriculum development/assessment workshops, steering committee meetings, brainstorming, reflections in Senior Seminar, and anecdotal information from present students and graduates (Field, Lee, and Field 1994).

Common Lessons

A number of insights emerge from this comparative picture of K–12 and college. The first is theoretical. The negotiated character of interdisciplinary knowledge is apparent in the dialogue of content and process that characterizes integrative learning. Interdisciplinarity may be thought of as a form of strategic knowledge that engages domain-specific knowledges. Domain knowledge is the realm of knowledge about a particular discipline or field. Strategies are procedures and processes that operate within and across domains. The bulk of research has been done on conventional disciplines, perceived as well-structured domains. What happens, though, in an ill-structured domain and when experts grapple with ill-defined tasks? As research on expertise has extended beyond well-defined boundaries, it has become more difficult to assign default values to the labels "novice" and "expert." This is especially the case when learning tasks have no clear-cut paths to solutions or standard responses. Furthermore, subject-matter research reveals that absolute distinctions dissolve when competent or proficient performance involves "real-world" or "common-sense" knowledge (Alexander 1992, 38, 40). As these dimensions continue to press on the educational system, interdisciplinary outcomes will become more important.

The second insight is practical. A number of guidelines for formulating a sound assessment plan may be derived from current practices.

Guidelines for Appropriate Assessment Plans

- Articulate goals for assessments early in the process, asking what kind of learning is valued.
- Compare program goals with goals of the larger institution, the school district, and/or pertinent professional groups.
- Consider the culture of the institution, its mission, and its political dynamics.
- Utilize multiple methods and perspectives, both quantitative and qualitative, conventional and creative.
- Incorporate locally designed qualitative approaches.
- Contextualize any standard instruments within the local plan.
- Incorporate feedback loops that lead to improving teaching, learning, curriculum design, and support systems.
- Begin with a few potentially useful assessment activities in route to a fuller program.
- Engage in ongoing data collection and review of the assessment plan.
- Include students in dialogue about assessment outcomes and measures.
- Do not confuse assessment of student learning with teacher evaluation.

Bill Moore (1995), coordinator of student outcomes assessment for the Washington State Board for Community and Technical Colleges, urges everyone across K–16 to "Think big, but start small." Beginning with small empirical approaches is a sounder strategy than creating an elaborate conceptual plan, especially one that requires more expertise and resources than are available. Assessment must also be organic. If mechanical devices such as tests and a priori measures are used, they must be contextualized locally. Local development accounts for unique understandings of interdisciplinarity that exist in different knowledge domains, institutional missions, and student populations. One of the hallmarks of a successful program, Field and Stowe (2001) add, is a sincere effort to improve teaching, learning, and the curriculum, not simply provide accountability to external bodies. A sound plan also allows for unintended and serendipitous learner outcomes in cognitive, affective, and developmental domains. Since integrative thinking is often elusive, data on unanticipated outcomes may be as instructive as data on intended outcomes.

The story of the School of Interdisciplinary Studies at Miami University (Ohio) illustrates many of these principles. Initially, the program adopted a single model of assessment based on nationally normed standardized tests. Over time, a variety of approaches were introduced, including portfolio analysis, structured interviews, ethnographic observations, pre- and post-testing using ACT COMP, plus a nationally normed questionnaire with student self-reports. Data on graduate school exams and admissions, supplemented by a nationally normed alumni instrument, provide external evidence. In shifting from a model that told "how well" the curriculum was working to a model that describes "what is happening," teachers discovered the power of descriptive assessment to tell a story of growth, change, and unexpected outcomes. Karl Schilling (2001) urges that the process be interdisciplinary. Assessment is a diagnostic problem-solving endeavor. At Miami University, techniques and philosophies from a number of disciplines were combined to create a more holistic framework for understanding and describing students' experiences. His evaluation of their respective advantages and disadvantages is a helpful guide to considering portfolios, structured interviews, free writing, ethnographic study, alumni surveys, the Cooperative Institutional Research Profile, and the College Student Experiences Questionnaire.

Every interdisciplinary program, Schilling uges, should develop a compelling story about itself that is supported by an array of information and data that help improve the quality of education. Like Heidi Jacobs, Rebecca Burns, and Bill Moore, Schilling urges that good assessment be grounded in classroom practice. It is inseparable from teaching and learning. A good assessment plan, Clarke and Agne add, moves across four levels. First, it gives focus to student learning by informing and guiding students and parents. Students need results that show them and their parents [and, by extension, college counselors, graduate admissions officers, and employers] what they have learned and what they need to learn. Second, it gives focus to teaching by providing feedback on day-to-day activities. All teachers need results that let them adjust daily plans to meet student needs and to evaluate the effectiveness of classroom strategies. Third, it improves support systems. Administrators and program managers need results that enable them to allocate special services, evaluate the systems that run a school [or college], and recommend adjustments in curriculum. Fourth, it influences policy and planning. Board members and the teaching community need results that help to evaluate whole programs and inform the public about quality of education (1997, 296–97).

Echoing T. Dary Erwin, Field and Stowe point out that in a "culture of evidence," everything is constantly on the table—from outcomes and curriculum to pedagogy and underlying philosophies. They warn against being unduly prescriptive and advise periodic review at all levels, from data to the overall plan. Review allows for adjustments in inputs and reflection on the process of assessment itself. Finally, results should be communicated to all stakeholders, including the peer community of teachers and scholars. The need to make the case public raises the third insight that emerges from our comparative look at K–12 and college. There is a political dimension to assessment, readily apparent in the question of what to do about the standards movement.

The Standards Debate

The present moment is as rich with possibility as it is fraught with danger. New discipline-based content standards and some state mandates for K–12 reinforce the authority of disciplines. At the same time, endorsements of interdisciplinarity have mounted in number and intensity. The tension inherent is this apparent contradiction is evident in an influential report, *America 2000: An Education Strategy.* The need to master essential disciplinary knowledge and information is affirmed in the call for consensus on subject matter and content standards measured by national tests. Yet the Goals 2000 project also endorsed "interdisciplinary frameworks" and thematic teaching of "big ideas." Integration is also a topic of discussion at local and state levels, as well as in subject- and discipline-based professional groups. It is even part of standards documents. In the Standards for Excellence in Education Project (SEE), overseen by the Council for Basic Education, standards for theater and visual arts incorporate a broad range of cultural, historical, and aesthetic understandings. The National Standards for Arts Education document calls for both disciplinary and interdisciplinary competence.

Interdisciplinarity is strongly endorsed in science as well, though there are several sets of standards. The 1988 report on *Science for All Americans* criticized teaching scientific principles in isolation. It endorsed a thematic approach and applying academic concepts to real-world contexts. The National Center for Improving Science Education advocated teaching conceptual themes, and the National Science Teachers Association called for an integrated science program to replace the high school "layer cake" curriculum that stacks biology on top of general science, physics, and chemistry. The SEE Project urges greater awareness of interdisciplinary relations in science, and the National Research Council

(NRC) encourages four general categories of content: science as inquiry, science subject matter, scientific connections, and science and human affairs. Project 2061, sponsored by the American Association for the Advancement of Science, also supports explicit connection making, applying scientific concepts to real-world situations, and studying themes such as energy, evolution, patterns of change, scale and structure, systems, and interactions. Project 2061, though, illustrates the complicated politics of standards. When the current standards movement gained force, Project 2061 began to emphasize narrower benchmarks of subject mastery. (See Cobb 1994 for a fuller discussion of national standards.)

At the college level, endorsements of interdisciplinarity abound. Integration is a major imperative in general education reform and is receiving growing attention in the disciplines. In a study sponsored by the Association of American Colleges and Universities (AAC&U), 12 learned societies examined the current state of the major. The picture differs by discipline. Economics and philosophy, for instance, have been more resistant to interdisciplinary developments than literary studies and political science. In the sciences significant variations arise from the inability of any one campus to provide a full range of subdisciplines, exposure to new technologies, courses exploring social and ethical implications, field experiences, and applications in problem solving. Yet learned societies in the AAC&U study were unanimous in calling for more opportunities to explore connections with other disciplines and the world beyond the academy, especially at the capstone level (*Reports from the Fields* 1991).

In addition to the AAC&U study, professional organizations from art and political science to the professions continue to call for connected learning. Integration of knowledge and multidisciplinary perspectives are among the top priorities endorsed by the American Society for Engineering Education. In its report on *Engineering Criteria 2000*, the accreditation Board for Engineering and Technology includes the capacity for multidisciplinary teamwork as a target goal for future professionals. The International Association for Management Education predicts interdisciplinary activity will reach a new level in pedagogy as more problem-oriented courses are developed, as well as multidisciplinary units in undergraduate business and graduate M.B.A. programs.

Even with the current level of endorsement, turning recommendations into reality is a formidable challenge. Judith Rényi faults proponents of interdisciplinarity for their absence in forums where standards were defined. For every endorsement, we can just as easily find evidence of states that are moving away from interdisciplinarity (2000, 45). Opposition to integration, James Beane noted earlier, must not be underestimated either, nor should the popular slogan heralding an "emerging curriculum" obscure the fact that it has been emerging for over 100 years. At the same time, thinking about assessment is changing.

Recognition that standardized tests alone cannot do the job is widening. The definition of effective and thoughtful learning is also being widely linked with a range of performances that demonstrate understanding, not just with tests focused on recognition and recall. In the assessment community, three broad shifts have occurred as well: from quantitative to qualitative approaches, from summative to formative evaluation, and from reliance on teacher inputs to emphasis on student learning outcomes. Comparably, in program assessment the focus has changed from judging the worth of programs to providing feedback for ongoing improvement of the curriculum (Farmer and Napieralski 1997, 597, 601–2).

As more teachers choose a result-oriented approach to instruction that emphasizes learning, Rebecca Burns predicts, they will employ a wider variety of assessment methods. They will make instructional decisions based on student needs and assessment data. They will move away from teacher-dominated mimetic instructional methods, curricula limited to facts and information, segregation of disciplines, and separation of school learning from applications. With assessment moving to center stage in educational reform, John Clarke adds, the marriage of "performance" and "standards" is a rare opportunity to gather around a common cause. Competing forces are being brought into confluence, forcing parties on both sides of the debate to focus on shared goals (e-mail 1.15.98). The crux of the matter, Agne and Clarke suggested earlier, is the metaphor of alignment. What is the preferred alignment of common standards for "performance," a word now being used in both disciplinary and interdisciplinary contexts? The composite term "performance standards" may have the power to bridge disciplinary and interdisciplinary teaching in a new way.

If the case for interdisciplinarity and integrative approaches is to be fully persuasive, however, claims of successful results must be matched by evidence. Studies of the mechanisms by which curriculum integration, teamed instruction, and interdisciplinary study achieve their effects are needed across K–16. Burns calls for more research on the acquisition of higher-order thinking skills in studies that consider broad measures of learning, including portfolios and performances. Beane, in turn, calls for more work to advance the understanding and practice of curriculum integration. In addition to more empirical and longitudinal research, claims must also be tested in the context of different institutional settings, content foci, and types of learners. Only then will assessment be fully "authentic."

Conversations across the borders of subjects and disciplines are not mere niceties. They are crucial issues that cannot be thought through if armed only with "canalized" standards (Wolf 1994, 98). Critics of integration and interdisciplinarity charge that the purity of disciplines will be destroyed, their depth compromised, and core concepts watered down. Yet "integrity," Beane admonishes, may well be a code word for "subject boundaries." Boundaries are not walled off by an internal consistency and logic that prevents integrative approaches (1997, 47). On the contrary, interdisciplinarity and integration have become so important because our needs and interests do not fit neatly within the boundaries of classification. Newer assessments, Agne and Clarke believe, can be proactive tools of reform in all contexts, pressing educators in all subjects, disciplines, and interdisciplinary fields across K–16 toward new forms of teaching and learning.

Epilogue

Imperatives for Dialogue on Interdisciplinarity K–16

Julie Thompson Klein

This book began with a striking fact. At the start of the twentieth century, the word "interdisciplinary" was not even in the English language. At the start of the twenty-first century, it is pervasive in education and research. Yet the discourse of K–16 remains dominated by subjects and disciplines. The current momentum for interdisciplinarity and the strong parallels across K–12 and college suggest it is time to widen that discourse. Five imperatives should be at the forefront of dialogue and collaborative work. (Contributors' insights from e-mail exchanges over the course of creating this book are incorporated.)

1. The existing bank of ideas, strategies, and materials must be shared.

Learning is a two-way street. The K–12 literature is rich in model units and graphic tools that can be used in college. In turn, the college literature contains program models, course syllabi, and reports on the changing disciplines and interdisciplinary fields that will be useful in K–12. Several immediate areas for conversation emerged in this book. The first is general education and core curriculum, where common themes and skills will be excellent focal points. The second area is common subjects and disciplines. Here, new approaches to traditional subjects and the teaching of new topics and materials will be productive points of intersection. The third is interdisciplinary fields, especially American cultural studies and studies of science, technology, and the environment. In addition to these content areas, assessment and pedagogical strategies are major topics for dialogue and joint research.

The strategy of team teaching exemplifies the untapped links that exist across K–16. Neither Rebecca Burns nor James Davis, who wrote on the subject, had read the literature on the other side of the K–12/college divide. Yet they discovered that they framed the topic similarly, as degrees of collaboration and integration along a continuum. They also share the same conviction, that assessment must be a collaborative activity focused on integration and synthesis, not an afterthought or individual responsibility. They have a common philosophical view as well. Interdisciplinary studies is not simply about coordinating the knowledge gained through disciplines. It is also about creating new ways of knowing, teaching, and learning. Interdisciplinary work and team teaching, Davis comments, are reactions. In college, they are a reaction to specialization and traditional modes of teaching. In K–12, they are a reaction to traditional subject-oriented teaching and the inadequacies of present schooling arrangements. In both cases, moreover, the origins lie in the ideas of core curriculum and general education.

2. Professional groups across K–16 need to be proactive in fostering dialogue.

Dialogue is not just the business of individuals. Systematic effort is required. Networks and professional organizations for teachers and administrators exist in K–12 and college. However, their members rarely interact. Creating a genuine continuum, John Clarke exhorts, will require a sustained effort if a sense of shared purpose is to emerge, let alone the structure for a shared profession. Organizational alliances across K–16 might take several forms:

- appointing liaisons to counterpart professional groups,
- exchanging information in newsletters and on listservs,
- hosting special K–16 sessions at annual meetings,
- identifying common projects, such as producing classroom materials in common areas.

Organizations that serve a K–16 audience are already positioned to foster dialogue. The College Board, for instance, bridges high school and college. Its program of Advanced Placement courses is a ready platform for conversations and curriculum projects, especially in subjects with an interdisciplinary orientation such as biology, language and literature, the arts, environmental studies, world history, and geography. Other groups can also play a key role. In K–12, the Association for Supervision and Curriculum Development is a major publisher of classroom materials and, in college, the Association for Integrative Studies serves the needs of teachers in a broad span of fields. Such groups can cosponsor research and publication projects in content areas and on strategies for curriculum development, teaching, and assessment. They can present joint responses to national reports and debates. They can keep their readers and members updated on new developments in particular subject-, discipline-, and interdisciplinary-based organizations. And, they can foster links with kindred groups, such as the National Middle School Association and the college-level Association for General and Liberal Studies (AGLS).

3. An interdisciplinary articulation is needed so students can move successfully across the K–16 continuum.

It is also time to think in terms of an interdisciplinary articulation. One of the convictions driving K–16 discourse is that students will move successfully along the continuum if they follow a coordinated sequence of learning. Interdisciplinarity must be considered in this regard. Beth Casey calls for an interdisciplinary "preculture" that will enable students to move toward integrative study as they progress along the continuum of school and college. Teachers at all levels should be aware of students' prior experiences with integrative learning and, vice versa, with expectations at later points. Articulation does not mean a rigid sequence of courses or stages of development. Variations of cognitive development and individual learning styles mean that students learn differently. For that reason, William Newell urges, teachers at all levels will benefit from knowing what works in different settings and with different students.

At the same time, echoing Heidi Jacobs's opening definition of learning characteristics along the K–16 continuum, curriculum designers should be alert to the context from which the learner arrives and to which the learner departs. Otherwise, she warns, we are working in a vacuum. Here again, content areas, assessment, and pedagogies can be focal points for dialogue and collaborative projects. Increased interest in learning communities in college, Casey adds, means that high school students should become familiar with collaborative learning and learning communities. Yet college teachers also need to be familiar with the kinds of collaborations students have already experienced in K–12. The same is true of team teaching, James Davis notes, not only to prepare students for the experience of team teaching in college but also to know what students have encountered previously.

4. Educators must become activists.

Widening the discourse is also a political task. Even in a climate of renewed interest, opposition continues across K–16. Resistance to the whole language approach, teaching mathematics in the context of real-world problems, constructivist and project-based learning, and making greater space in the curriculum for integration and interdisciplinary fields are flashpoints. Resistance often stems from lack of familiarity, polarized thinking, and skepticism about change. Misinformation and doubt must be countered with evidence and convincing arguments in all forums where assumptions about what is "basic" and "essential" become fixed in standards for eligibility, admission, and certification. Teachers and administrators in both K–12 and college need to work across the organizational and political levels of local campuses and communities, district school boards, and state boards and commissions of education.

An example from the classroom illustrates the importance of activism. A group of teachers and administrators in Perry, Arkansas, developed a fused approach to teaching global studies. They worked productively across K–16, including a partnership with the International Center at the University of Arkansas. Despite wide support, groups of parents and teachers opposed to the change became increasingly resistant as the program came into place. Organizing parent discussion groups in the community and presentations from a variety of speakers and experts helped to reduce the strain. So did a volunteer program that brought nonsupportive community members into the school to work on new planning units (Clarke and Agne 1997, 68–72).

Activism is both an individual and a collective responsibility. Individuals who serve on local, regional, and national committees are well positioned to inform debate. Most educators, it is safe to say, are also parents or may be at some point. When interdisciplinary initiatives arise that affect their children, whether in K–12 or college, they should contribute their expertise. In the spirit of the Education Trust's K–16 Councils, they should encourage formal interactions across schools and colleges in their areas. Wineburg and Grossman's (2000) collection of case studies is rich in models of school-university collaborations. Proponents of integration must also be more proactive in the standards and assessment movement. The "interdisciplinary lobby," Judith Rényi rightly admonishes, was not present when governors met with George Bush in 1989, when the U.S. Office of Educational Research and Improvement (OERI) sent out requests for proposals for standards projects, or when Goals 2000 funds were being spent (2000, 45).

5. Teachers should be prepared for interdisciplinary teaching at all points of the career life cycle, including ongoing professional development.

Interdisciplinarity has become more central to knowledge. It should not be peripheral to teacher education. Future teachers should have some experience with interdisciplinarity in their own studies and when student teaching in schools. Ongoing professional development is equally important. The majority of teachers engaged in integrative approaches still learn on the job. They also tend to retain an identity with their original disciplines and, a sobering reality sounded repeatedly in Wineburg and Grossman (2000), they do not necessarily have adequate knowledge of their own disciplines, let alone the complexity of interdisciplinarity.

No matter what levels of experience they have, all teachers will benefit from an interdisciplinary critical colleagueship. Brian Lord (1994) developed the concept of "critical colleagueship" in the context of subject-area standards, but it can apply here as well. The traditional teacher-training model is at odds with many reforms. Conceptualization of the teaching profession centers on a reductive set of behaviors, skills, and a toolbox of knowledge and strategies. Yet, Lord emphasizes, teaching is an uncertain craft defined by complex relationships and fluid situations that create mismatches between teacher preparation and student needs. Critical colleagueship is a form of ongoing professional development that fosters self-reflection, collegial dialogue, and critique. Through greater reflectiveness and sustained learning, teachers are able to think more deeply and experiment more thoroughly with novel approaches.

Critical colleagueship is all the more necessary today, as educators grapple with changing disciplines and interdisciplinary fields. The shared intellectual values of teaching and learning at the heart of critical colleagueship are crucial across the entire curriculum: being open to new ideas, being willing to reject weak practices and flimsy reasons, accepting responsibility for acquiring and using relevant information, being willing to seek out the best ideas and the best knowledge, relying on organized and deliberative investigation instead of learning by accident, and assuming collective responsibility for creating a professional record of research and experimentation. Critical colleagueship is in many respects a local activity. Yet, Lord adds, "collective generativity" is also required. Local practices and judgments must be informed by broader communities at both regional and national levels.

****

The most important lesson to emerge from this book is that there is no "best" way of doing things. A K–16 example provides a fitting conclusion, since it illustrates the variety of possibilities for creating integrative experiences. Teachers from K–12 and college participated in a two-week institute, the Truckee River Community Project. The theme was "Water in the West." Institute activities focused on language arts, with readings, journal writing, workshops conducted by Nevada writers, and culminating projects. Participants also took a field trip on the river, visited the Lahontan Reservoir in order to learn about the region, and prepared teaching materials for fall classes.

A striking variety of plans resulted:

- teachers from an elementary school developed a month's worth of activities related to the river, then expanded the project to a year-long thematic study of communities for the entire school; subsequently they revised their material for publication in *Teaching Nevada: An Interdisciplinary Approach;*
- a middle school teacher helped students map out a bicycle tour that traces the passage of pioneers throughout the region;
- a middle school media specialist and a high school English teacher compiled a Nevada water and desert bibliography for young readers;
- a teacher in a new interdisciplinary high school linked the water theme to a larger team focus on communities and survival;
- a literacy teacher at a Job Corps center incorporated Nevada interdisciplinary materials into her program;
- a college instructor based a writing course on Nevada issues and the theme of water. (Tchudi and Lafer 1993)

Forging a K–16 dialogue will not be easy. The term "school-college partnerships," Dan Tompkins observed in a report from the American Association for Higher Education, implies a marriage. Unfortunately, the relationship has been a stormy courtship at best. Resistance stems in part from the disinclination of college educators to work with schools. When they do, their K–16 work is usually not rewarded in universities. Furthermore, even in the same discipline, shared language is lacking. Members of a college English Department talked about discourse, subjectivity, and deconstruction. Their school counterparts spoke of rubrics, benchmarks, and performance outcomes (*Making a Place* 1999). Educators on both sides of the K–12/college divide are also busy, even overwhelmed, with pressing issues in their own parts of the continuum. The price of not forging a dialogue, however, becomes greater with every passing year.

A Beginning Library

In their book *Interdisciplinary Education: A Guide to Resources* (1999), Fiscella and Kimmel provided the first comprehensive bibliography of resources across the K–16 continuum on foundations; curriculum; faculty, teacher, and team development; pedagogy and student support, and administration. One of the questions educators in both K–12 and college always ask, though, is more preliminary: "Where should I start"? The following recommendations constitute a basic library for individuals, schools, colleges, and K–16 projects.

K–12 Literature

- Beane, J. 1997. *Curriculum Integration: Designing the Core of Democratic Education*. New York: Teachers College Press, Columbia University.
- Beane, J. 1993. *A Middle School Curriculum: From Rhetoric to Reality*. 2nd ed. Columbus, Ohio: National Middle School Association.
- Burns, R. C. 1995. *Dissolving the Boundaries: Planning for Curriculum Integration in Middle and Secondary Schools*. Charleston, W.Va.: Appalachia Educational Laboratory
- Clarke, J. H., and R. M. Agne, eds. 1997. *Interdisciplinary High School Teaching: Strategies for Integrated Learning*. Boston: Allyn and Bacon.
- Ellis, A., and C. Stuen. 1998. *The Interdisciplinary Curriculum*. Larchmont, N.Y.: Eye on Education.
- Fogarty, R. 1993. *Integrating the Curricula: A Collection*. Palatine, Ill.: IRI/Skylight Publishing.
- *Integrated Curriculum*. 1995. Alexandria, Va.: Association for Supervision and Curriculum Development. An ASCD resource packet.
- *Interdisciplinary/Integrated Curriculum*. n.d. ERS Info-File #128. Arlington, Va.: Educational Research Services.
- Jacobs, H. H., ed. 1989. *Interdisciplinary Curriculum: Design and Implementation*. Alexandria, Va.: Association for Supervision and Curriculum Development.
- Klein, J. T,. and W. H. Newell. "Strategies for Using Interdisciplinary Resources." Forthcoming in *Issues in Integrative Studies*.

- Vars, G. F. 1993. *Interdisciplinary Teaching: Why and How*. Rev. ed. Columbus, Ohio: National Middle School Association.
- Wineburg, S., and P. Grossman, eds. 2000. *Interdisciplinary Curriculum: Challenges to Implementation*. New York: Teachers College Press.

College Literature

- Davis, J. R. 1995. *Interdisciplinary Courses and Team Teaching: New Arrangements for Learning*. Phoenix, Ariz.: American Council on Education, and the Oryx Press.
- Edwards, A. F. 1996. *Interdisciplinary Undergraduate Programs: A Directory*. 2nd ed. Acton: Mass.: Copley.
- Fiscella, J., and S. Kimmel. 1998. *Interdisciplinary Education: A Guide to Resources*. New York: The College Board.
- Haynes, C., ed. 2002. *Innovations in Interdisciplinary Teaching*. Westport, Conn.: Greenwood Press.
- Klein, J. T. 1999. *Mapping Interdisciplinary Studies. The Academy in Transition 2*. Washington, D.C.: Association of American Colleges and Universities.
- Klein, J. T., and W. G. Doty, eds. 1994. *Interdisciplinary Studies Today. New Directions in Teaching and Learning 58*. San Francisco: Jossey-Bass.
- Klein, J. T., and W. H. Newell. 1997. "Advancing Interdisciplinary Studies." In *Handbook of the Undergraduate Curriculum: A Comprehensive Guide to Purposes, Structures, Practices, and Change*, edited by J. G. Gaff and J. L. Ratcliff, 393–415. San Francisco: Jossey-Bass.
- Newell, W. H., ed. 1998. *Interdisciplinarity: Essays from the Literature*. New York: The College Board.

References

- ASCD. 1995. *Integrated Curriculum*. Alexandria, Va.: Association for Supervision and Curriculum Development. An ASCD Select packet. Cited authors listed below.
- Brandt, R. 1991. "On Interdisciplinary Curriculum: A Conversation with Heidi Hayes Jacobs." *Educational Leadership* (October): 24–26; ASCD, 85–87.
- "Curriculum Integration: Modest Efforts to Link Disciplines Gain Support." 1990. *ASCD Update* 32 (1): 1–2; ASCD, 75–76.
- Gehrke, N. J. 1991. "Explorations of Teachers' Development of Integrative Curriculums." *Journal of Curriculum and Supervision*. 6 (2): 107–17; ASCD, 125–35.
- Krovetz, M., et al. 1993. "Beyond Show and Tell." *Educational Leadership* (April): 73–76; ASCD, 117–20.
- Tchudi, S., and S. Lafer. 1993. "How Dry Is the Desert? Nurturing Interdisciplinary Learning." *Educational Leadership* (September): 76–79; ASCD, 113–16.
- Williams, R., C. Bidlack, and D. Winnett. 1993. "At Water's Edge: Students Study Their Rivers." *Educational Leadership* (September): 80–83; ASCD, 109–12.
- Willis, S. 1992. "Interdisciplinary Learning: Movement to Link the Disciplines Gains Momentum." *[ASCD] Curriculum Update* (November): 1–8; ASCD, 77–84.
- Ackerman, D. B. 1989. "Intellectual and Practical Criteria for Successful Curriculum Integration." In *Interdisciplinary Curriculum: Design and Implementation*, edited by H. H. Jacobs, 25–37. Alexandria, Va.: Association for Supervision and Curriculum Development.
- Aikin, W. 1942. *The Story of the Eight Year Study*. New York: Harper and Row.
- Alberty, H. 1960. "Core Programs." In *Encyclopedia of Educational Research*. 3rd ed., 337–341. New York: Macmillan.
- Alexander, P. 1992. "Domain Knowledge: Evolving Themes and Emerging Concerns." *Educational Psychologist* 27 (1): 33–51.
- Alexander, W.M. (with K. McAvoy and D. Carr). 1995. *Student-Oriented Curriculum: Asking the Right Questions*. Columbus, Ohio: National Middle School Association.
- Allison, V., D. Beecher, and S. Jemmett. 1998. *Implementing School-wide Interdisciplinary Teaming Within a Junior High School*. Unpublished manuscript.

- Angelo, T. A., and K. P. Cross. 1993. *Classroom Assessment Techniques: A Handbook for College Teachers.* San Francisco: Jossey-Bass.
- Apple, M.W. 1990. *Ideology and Curriculum.* 2nd ed. London and Boston: Routledge and Kegan Paul.
- Apple, M.W. 1993. *Official Knowledge: Democratic Education in a Conservative Age.* New York and London: Routledge.
- Apple, M.W. 1997. *Cultural Politics and Education.* New York: Teachers College Press.
- Apple, M.W., and J.A. Beane, eds. 1995. *Democratic Schools.* Alexandria, Va.: Association for Supervision and Curriculum Development.
- Applebee, A., R. Burroughs, and G. Cruz. 2000. "Curricular Conversations in Elementary School Classrooms: Case Studies of Interdisciplinary Instruction." In *Interdisciplinary Curriculum: Challenges to Implementation,* edited by S. Wineburg and P. Grossman, 93–111. New York: Teachers College Press.
- Armstrong, F. 1980. "Faculty Development through Interdisciplinarity." *The Journal of General Education* 32(1): 52–63.
- Astin, A. 1993. *What Matters in College? Four Critical Years Revisited.* San Francisco: Jossey-Bass.
- Ausubel, D. 1968. *Educational Psychology: A Cognitive View.* New York: Holt, Reinhart and Winston.
- Barr, Robert B., and J. Tagg. 1995. "From Teaching to Learning: A New Paradigm for Undergraduate Education." *Change* (November/December): 13–25.
- Barstow, D. 1997. "Visualizing Earth." In *Hands-On!* 20(1): 1, 21–24. Cambridge, Mass.: Technical Education Resource Center.
- Bartolo, L. M., and T. F. Smith. 1993. "Interdisciplinary Work and the Information Search Process: A Comparison of Manual and Online Searching." *College and Research Libraries* 54(4): 344–53.
- Bates, M. J. 1996. "Learning about the Information Seeking of Interdisciplinary Scholars and Students." *Library Trends* 45(2): 155–64.
- Baxter Magolda, M. 1992. *Knowing and Reasoning in College: Gender-Related Patterns in Students' Intellectual Development.* San Francisco: Jossey-Bass.
- Beane, J. A. 1995. "Curriculum Integration and the Disciplines of Knowledge." *Phi Delta Kappan* 76 (8): 612–22.
- Beane, J. 1997. *Curriculum Integration: Designing the Core of Democratic Education.* New York: Teachers College Press.
- Beane, J. 1980. "The General Education We Need." *Educational Leadership* 35 (4): 307–08.
- Beane, J. 1990 /1993. *A Middle School Curriculum: From Rhetoric to Reality.* Rev. ed. Columbus, Ohio: National Middle School Association.
- Beane, J. 1994. Keynote presentation at the second annual national conference on curriculum integration, Scottsdale, Ariz., January 14.
- Beane, J. 1997. "Perhaps This Time." In *Interdisciplinary High School Teaching: Strategies for Integrated Learning,* edited by J. H. Clarke and R. M. Agne. Boston: Allyn and Bacon.
- Beane, J. 1993. "Problems and Possibilities for an Integrated Curriculum." *Middle School Journal* 25(1): 18–21.
- Beane, J., ed. 1995. *Toward a Coherent Curriculum.* Alexandria, Va.: Association for Supervision and Curriculum Development.
- Bellack, A. A., and H. M. Kliebard. 1971. "Curriculum for Integration of Disciplines." In *The Encyclopedia of Education,* edited by L.C. Deighton, 585–90. New York: Macmillan.

- Bernstein, B. 1975. *Class, Codes, and Control, Volume 3: Towards a Theory of Educational Transmissions.* 2nd ed. London: Routledge and Kegan Paul.
- Bingham, N. E. 1994. "Organizational Networking: Taking the Next Step." In *Interdisciplinary Studies Today*, edited by J. T. Klein. and W. G. Doty, 85–91. *New Directions in Teaching and Learning* 58. San Francisco: Jossey-Bass.
- Black, S. 1997. "Branches of Knowledge." *The American School Board Journal* 184(8): 35–37.
- Boix-Mansilla, V., W. C. Miller, and H. Gardner. 2000. "On Disciplinary Lenses and Interdisciplinary Work." In *Interdisciplinary Curriculum: Challenges to Implementation*, edited by S. Wineburg and P. Grossman, 17–38. New York: Teachers College Press.
- Bond, H. M. 1935. "The Curriculum and the Negro Child." *Journal of Negro Education* 4: 159–68.
- Boston, B. O. 1996. *Connections: The Arts and the Integration of the High School Curriculum.* New York: College Entrance Examination Board.
- Boyer, Ernest L. 1987. *College: The Undergraduate Experience in America.* New York: Harper.
- Bradley, E. M. 1988. "The Effectiveness of an Interdisciplinary Team Organization in a Selected Middle School Setting." Ph.D. dissertation, State University of New York at Buffalo.
- Brameld, T. 1944. "Progressive Education on the Firing Line." *Current History*, 95–100.
- Brantlinger, E., et al. 1996. "Self-Interest and Liberal Educational Discourse: How Ideology Works for Middle-Class Mothers." *American Educational Research Journal* 33: 571-98.
- Brazee, E., and J. Capelluti. 1995. *Dissolving Boundaries: Toward an Integrative Middle School Curriculum.* Columbus, Ohio: National Middle School Association.
- Brazee, E. N., and Capelluti, J. 1994. "The Middle Level Curriculum: Getting Where We Need to Be!" *Journal of the New England League of Middle Schools* 7 (1): 1–6.
- Brodhagen, B. L. 1995. "The Situation Made Us Special." In *Democratic Schools*, edited by M. W. Apple and J. A. Beane, 83–100. Alexandria, Va.: Association for Supervision and Curriculum Development.
- Brodhagen, B., G. Wilbacher, and J. Beane. 1992. "Living in the Future: An Experiment with an Integrative Curriculum." *Dissemination Services on the Middle Grades* 23(9): 1–6.
- Brooks, J., and M. Brooks. 1993. *In Search of Understanding: The Case for Constructivist Classrooms.* Alexandria, Va.: Association for Supervision and Curriculum Development.
- Bruner, J. 1986. *Actual Minds, Possible Worlds.* Cambridge, Mass.: Harvard University Press.
- Buckeley, W. M. 1997. "Hard Lessons." *The Wall Street Journal* (November 17): R4.
- Burns, R. C. 1995. *Dissolving the Boundaries: Planning for Curriculum Integration in Middle and Secondary Schools.* Charleston, W.Va.: Appalachia Educational Laboratory.
- Burns, R. C. 1994. *Interdisciplinary Teamed Instruction: Development and Pilot Test.* Charleston, W. Va.: Appalachia Educational Laboratory. ERIC document #ED 384 456.
- Burns, R. C. 1998. "Interdisciplinary Teamed Instruction: A Strategy for Comprehensive School Reform." Unpublished manuscript.
- Caine, R., and G. Caine. 1991. *Making Connections: Teaching and the Human Brain.* Alexandria, Va.: Association for Supervision and Curriculum Development.
- Casey, B. A. 1994. "The Administration and Governance of Interdisciplinary Programs." In *Interdisciplinary Studies Today*, edited by J.T. Klein and W.G. Doty, 53–67. *New Directions in Teaching and Learning* 58. San Francisco: Jossey-Bass.
- Casey, B. A. 1986. "The Quiet Revolution: The Transformation and Reintegration of the Humanities." *Issues in Integrative Studies* 4: 71–92.

- Cavanagh, R. F., and G. B. Dellar. 1996. *School Culture Questionnaire*.
- Citizens for Excellence in Education. 1992. *Reinventing America's Schools: A Practical Guide to Components of Restructuring and Non-Traditional Education*. Vol. 2. Costa Mesa, California: Citizens for Excellence in Education.
- Clark, B. 1987. *The Academic Life: Small Worlds, Different Worlds*. Princeton, N.J.: The Carnegie Foundation for the Advancement of Teaching.
- Clarke, J. 1990. *Patterns of Thinking: Integrating Learning Skills in Content Teaching*. Boston: Allyn and Bacon.
- Clarke, J. H., and R. M. Agne. 1997. *Interdisciplinary High School Teaching: Strategies for Integrated Learning*. Boston: Allyn and Bacon.
- Clarke, J., and A. Biddle. 1993. *Teaching Critical Thinking: Reports from Across the Curriculum*. Englewood Cliffs, N.J.: Prentice Hall.
- Clarke, J., et al. 1998. *Dynamic Change in High School Teaching: A Study of Innovation in Five Vermont Professional Development Schools*. Providence, R.I.: The Educational Lab at Brown University.
- Cobb, N., ed. 1994. *The Future of Education: Perspectives on National Standards in America*. New York: The College Board.
- Cognition and Technology Group of Vanderbilt University. 1990. "Anchored Instruction and Its Relationship to Situated Cognition." *Educational Researcher* 19(6): 2–6.
- Commission on Reorganization of Secondary Education. 1918. *Cardinal Principles of Secondary Education*. Washington, D.C.: U.S. Government Printing Office.
- Cotton, K. 1995. *Effective Schooling Practices: A Research Synthesis 1995 Update*. Portland, Oregon: Northwest Regional Educational Laboratory.
- Daniel, W.G. 1932. "The Curriculum." *Journal of Negro Education* 1: 277–303.
- Daniel, W.G. 1940. "The Aims of Secondary Education and the Adequacy of the Curriculum of the Negro Secondary School." *Journal of Negro Education* 9: 465–473.
- Davis, J. R. 1993. *Better Teaching, More Learning: Strategies for Success in Postsecondary Settings*. Phoenix, Ariz.: The American Council on Education and the Oryx Press.
- Davis, J. R. 1995. *Interdisciplinary Courses and Team Teaching: New Arrangements for Learning*. Phoenix, Ariz.: The American Council on Education and the Oryx Press.
- DeGarmo, C. 1895. *Herbart and the Herbartians*. London: Heineman.
- Delpit, L. 1995. *Other People's Children: Cultural Conflict in the Classroom*. New York: New Press.
- DeWachter, M. 1982. "Interdisciplinary Bioethics: But Where Do We Start? A Reflection on Epoché as Method." *Journal of Medicine and Philosophy* 7: 275–87.
- Drake, S. 1993. *Planning Integrated Curriculum: The Call to Adventure*. Alexandria, Va.: Association for Supervision and Curriculum Development.
- Educational Research Service. Citations from ERIC Info File #128, "Interdisciplinary/Integrated Curriculum," are available in a loose packet from the Educational Research Service in Arlington, Virginia. They are also available in their original publication venues.
- Fogarty, R. 1991. "Ten Ways to Integrate Curriculum." *Educational Leadership* 49 (2): 61–65.
- Educom Review. 1997. Group interview of Deming and others with editor. *Educom Review* 32: 4, 24.
- Edwards, A. F., Jr. 1996. *Interdisciplinary Undergraduate Programs: A Directory*. 2nd ed. Acton, Mass.: Copley.
- Ellis, A., and C. Stuen. 1998. *The Interdisciplinary Curriculum*. Larchmont, N.Y.: Eye on Education.

- Epstein, J. L., and D. J. MacIver. 1990. *Education in the Middle Grades: National Practices and Trends.* Columbus, Ohio: National Middle School Association.
- The Evergreen State College. 1990. Institutional self-study. Olympia, Wash.: The Evergreen State College.
- Farmer, D. W. and E. A. Napieralski. 1997. "Assessing Learning in Programs." In *Handbook of the Undergraduate Curriculum,* edited by J. G. Gaff and J. L. Ratcliff, 591–607. San Francisco: Jossey-Bass.
- Farmer, J. 1997. "Using Technology." In *Handbook of the Undergraduate Curriculum,* edited by J. G. Gaff and J. L. Ratcliff, 476–92. San Francisco: Jossey-Bass.
- Faunce, R. C., and N. L. Bossing. 1951. *Developing the Core Curriculum.* New York: Prentice-Hall.
- Fazenda, I. C. A. 1995. "Critical-Historical Review of Interdisciplinary Studies in Brazil." Translated by C. H. Cavichiolo and P. A. Fish. *Association for Integrative Studies Newsletter* 17(1): 1, 2–9.
- Field, M., and D. Stowe. 2002. "Transforming Interdisciplinary Teaching and Learning Through Assessment." In *Innovations in Interdisciplinary Teaching,* edited by C. Haynes. Westport, Conn.: Greenwood Press.
- Field, M., R. Lee, and M. L. Field. 1994. "Assessing Interdisciplinary Learning." In *Interdisciplinary Studies Today,* edited by J. T. Klein and W. B. Doty, 69–84. *New Directions in Teaching and Learning* 58. San Francisco: Jossey-Bass.
- Fiscella, J., and S. Kimmel. 1999. *Interdisciplinary Education: A Guide to Resources.* New York: The College Board.
- Fogarty, R. 1991. *The Mindful School: How to Integrate the Curricula.* Palatine, Ill.: Skylight Publishing.
- Fosnot, C. T. 1989. *Enquiring Teachers, Enquiring Learners: A Constructivist Approach for Teaching,* New York: Teachers College Press.
- Freeman, C. C., and H. J. Sokoloff. 1995. "Toward a Theory of Thematic Curricula: Constructing New Learning Environments for Teachers and Learners." *Education Policy Analysis Archives* 3(14): 1–11.
- Fullan, M., and A. Hargreaves. 1991. *What's Worth Fighting For: Working Together for Your School.* Andover, Mass.: The Regional Lab for Improvement, Northeast and Islands.
- Gabelnick, F., et al. 1990. *Learning Communities: Creating Connections Among Students, Faculty, and Disciplines.* San Francisco: Jossey-Bass.
- Gaff, J. G. 1980. "Avoiding the Potholes: Strategies for Reforming General Education." *Educational Record* 61(4): 50–59.
- Gaff, J. G. 1999. General Education: The Changing Agenda. *The Academy in Transition* 3. Washington, D.C.: Association of American Colleges and Universities.
- Gaff, J. G. 1991. *New Life for the College Curriculum.* San Francisco: Jossey-Bass.
- Gaff, J. G. 1994. *Strong Foundations: Twelve Principles for Effective General Education Programs.* Washington, D.C.: Association of American Colleges and Universities.
- Gardner, H. 1991. *The Unschooled Mind.* New York: Basic Books.
- Gardner, H., and V. Boix-Mansilla. 1994. "Teaching for Understanding in the Disciplines and Beyond." *Teachers College Record* 96(2): 198–218.
- George, P. S., and L. L. Oldaker. 1985. *Evidence for the Middle School.* Columbus, Ohio: National Middle School Association.
- Gilligan, C. 1982. *In a Different Voice.* Cambridge, Mass.: Harvard University Press.

- Goodson, I., ed. 1985. *Social Histories of the Secondary School Curriculum: Subjects for Study.* London and Philadelphia: Falmer.
- Gross, T. L. 1988. *Partners in Education: How Colleges Can Work with School to Improve Teaching and Learning.* San Francisco: Jossey-Bass.
- Grossman, P., S. Wineburg, and S. Beers. 2000. "Introduction: When Theory Meets Practice in the World of School." In *Interdisciplinary Curriculum: Challenges to Implementation,* edited by S. Wineburg and P. Grossman, 1–16. New York: Teachers College Press.
- Grubb, W. 1991. *The Cunning Hand, The Cultured Mind: Models for Integrating Vocational and Academic Education.* Berkeley, Calif.: National Center for Research in Vocational Education.
- Hammerness, K., and K. Moffett. 2000. "The Subjects of Debate: Teachers' Clashing and Overlapping Beliefs about Subject Matter During a Whole-School Reform." In *Interdisciplinary Curriculum: Challenges to Implementation,* edited by S. Wineburg and P. Grossman, 134–52. New York: Teachers Gallery Press.
- Hawley, W. D. 1993. "New Goals and Changed Roles: Re-Visioning Teacher Education." *Educational Record* 74(3): 27–31.
- Haycock, J., and N. Brown. 1993. "Higher Education and the Schools: A Call to Action and Strategy for Change." Washington, D.C.: American Association for Higher Education. ERIC microfiche #ED 369 356.
- Haynes, C., ed. 2002. *Innovations in Interdisciplinary Teaching.* Westport, Conn.: Greenwood Press.
- Haynes, C. 1996. "Interdisciplinary Writing and the Undergraduate Experience: A Four-Year Writing Plan Proposal." *Issues in Integrative Studies* 14: 29–58.
- Hendershott, A. B. and S. P. Wright. 1997. "The Social Sciences." In *Handbook of the Undergraduate Curriculum,* edited by J. G. Gaff and J. L. Ratcliff, 301–19. San Francisco: Jossey-Bass.
- Hershberg, T. 1988. "The Fragmentation of Knowledge and Practice: University Sector and Public Sector." *Issues in Integrative Studies* 6: 1–20.
- Hirsch, E. D. 1987. *Cultural Literacy: What Every American Needs to Know.* Boston: Houghton Mifflin.
- Hopkins, L. T. 1941. *Interaction: The Democratic Process.* New York: D. C. Heath.
- Hopkins, L. T., et al. 1937. *Integration: Its Meaning and Application.* New York: D. Appleton-Century.
- Hursh, B., P. Haas, and M. Moore. 1983. "An Interdisciplinary Model to Implement General Education." *Journal of Higher Education* 54 (1): 42–49.
- Iannozzi, M. 1997. "Portland State University." *Exemplars* (August). Philadelphia: Pew Higher Education Round Table and the Knight Collaborative.
- *IGE: Program Assessment.* n.d. Pomona: The Interdisciplinary General Education Program. Pomona: California State Polytechnic University.
- Informal Committee of the Progressive Education Association on Evaluation of Newer Practices in Education. 1941. *New Methods vs. Old in American Education.* New York: Teachers College Press.
- Jacobs, H. H., ed. 1989. *Interdisciplinary Curriculum: Design and Implementation.* Alexandria, Va.: Association for Supervision and Curriculum Development.
- Jacobs, H. H. 1997. *Mapping the Big Picture: Integrating Curriculum and Assessment K–12.* Alexandria, Va.: Association for Supervision and Curriculum Development.
- Jenkins, F. C. 1947. *The Southern Study: Cooperative Study for the Improvement of Education.* Durham, N.C.: Duke University Press.

- Jensen, E. 1998. *Teaching with the Brain in Mind*. Alexandria, Va.: ASCD Publications.
- Jervis, C., S. Bull, G. Sauter, and P. Turner. 1997. "Perspectives on Interdisciplinary Teamed Instruction as a Tool for School Change." Unpublished manuscript.
- Katenbach, J., and D. Smith. 1994. *The Wisdom of Teams*. New York: Harper Business.
- Katz, S. 1996. "Restructuring for the Twenty-First Century." In *Rethinking Liberal Education*, edited by N. H. Farnham and A. Yarmolinsky. New York: Oxford University Press.
- Kimmel, S. 1999. "Interdisciplinary Information Searching: Notes for Researchers." In *Interdisciplinary Education: A Guide to Resources*, edited by I. Fiscella and S. Kimmel, 293–309. New York: The College Board.
- Klein, J. T. 1993. "Blurring, Cracking, and Crossing: Permeation and the Fracturing of Disciplines." In *Knowledges: Critical Studies in Disciplinarity*, edited by E. Messer-Davidow, D. R. Shumway, and D. J. Sylvan, 185–211. Charlottesville: University Press of Virginia.
- Klein, J. T. 1996. *Crossing Boundaries: Knowledge, Disciplinarities, and Interdisciplinarities*. Charlottesville: University Press of Virginia.
- Klein, J. T. 1990. *Interdisciplinarity: History, Theory, and Practice*. Detroit, Mich.: Wayne State University Press.
- Klein, J. T. 2001. "The Interdisciplinary Variable: Then and Now." In *Reinventing Ourselves: Interdisciplinary Education, Collaborative Learning and Experimentation in Higher Education*, edited by B. L. Smith and J. McCann, 391–418. Bolton, Mass.: Anker Press.
- Klein, J. T., and W. H. Newell. 1997. "Advancing Interdisciplinary Studies." In *Handbook of the Undergraduate Curriculum*, edited by J. G. Gaff and J. L. Ratcliff, 393–415. San Francisco: Jossey-Bass.
- Klein, J. T., and W. H. Newell. "Strategies for Using Interdisciplinary Resources." Forthcoming in *Issues in Integrative Studies*.
- Kliebard, H. M. 1986. *The Struggle for the American Curriculum: 1893–1958*. Boston: Routledge and Kegan Paul.
- Kovalik, S., with K. Olsen. 1997. *ITI: The Model, Integrated Thematic Instruction*. 3rd Ed. Kent, Wash.: Susan Kovalik and Associates, Books for Education.
- Kockelmans, J., ed. 1979. *Interdisciplinarity and Higher Education*. University Park: The Pennsylvania State University Press.
- Kohlberg. L. 1981. *The Philosophy of Moral Development*. San Francisco: Harper and Row.
- Krogh, S. 1990. *The Integrated Early Childhood Curriculum*. New York: McGraw Hill.
- Larson, C., and F. LaFaston. 1989. *Teamwork: What Must Go Right/What Can Go Wrong*. Newbury Park, Calif.: Sage.
- Lawton, D. 1975. *Class, Culture, and Curriculum*. Boston: Routledge and Kegan Paul.
- *Learning A Living: A Blueprint for High Performance*. Washington, D.C.: U.S. Department of Labor.
- Lee, V. E., and J. B. Smith. 1994a. *Effects of High School Restructuring and Size Gains in Achievement and Engagement for Early Secondary School Students*. Madison, Wisc.: Center for Organization and Restructuring of Schools.
- Lee, V. E., and J. B. Smith. 1994b. "High School Restructuring and Student Achievement." *Issues in Restructuring Schools: Issue Report* No. 7. Madison, Wisc: Center on Organization and Restructuring of Schools.
- *Library Trends*. 1996. Special issue on "Navigating Among the Disciplines: The Library and Interdisciplinary Inquiry." 45(2): 129–366.

- Lickona. T. 1983. *Raising Good Children*. New York: Bantam Books.
- Lord, B. 1994. "Teacher's Professional Development: Critical Colleagueship and the Role of Professional Communities." In *The Future of Education: Perspectives on National Standards in America,* edited by N. Cobb, 175–204. New York: The College Board.
- Lounsbury, J. H., ed. 1992. *Connecting the Curriculum Through Interdisciplinary Instruction.* Columbus, Ohio: National Middle School Association.
- Macdonald, J. B. 1971. "Curriculum Integration." In *The Encyclopedia of Education,* edited by L. C. Deighton, 590–593. New York: Macmillan.
- Maeroff, G. 1993. *Team Building for School Change.* New York: Teachers College Press. *Making a Place in the Faculty Rewards System for Work with K–12: A Project Report of Four Universities.* 1999. Washington, D.C.: American Association for Higher Education.
- Manley, J. C., and N. Ware. 1990. "How Do We Know What We Have Done? Assessment and Faculty Development within a Learning Community." In *Rethinking the Curriculum: Toward an Integrated, Interdisciplinary College Education,* edited by M. E. Clark and S. A. Wawrytko, 243–52. Contributions to the Study of Education 40. New York: Greenwood.
- Martinello, M., and G. Cook. 1992. "Interweaving the Threads of Learning: Interdisciplinary Curriculum and Teaching." *Curriculum Report.* 21(3): 1–6.
- Martin-Kniep, G., D. M. Feige, and L. Soodak. 1995. "Curriculum Integration: An Expanded View of an Abused Idea." *Journal of Curriculum and Supervision* 10(3): 227–49.
- Martin-Kniep, G. O., D. M. Feige, and L. C. Soodak. 1995. "Curriculum Integration: An Expanded View of an Abused Idea." *Journal of Curriculum and Supervision* 10(3): 227–49.
- Merenbloom, E. Y. 1991. *The Team Process: A Handbook for Teachers.* Columbus, Ohio: National Middle School Association.
- Meriam, J. L. 1920. *Child Life and the Curriculum.* Yonkers-on-Hudson, N.Y.: World Book.
- Mickelson, J. M. 1957. "What Does Research Say About the Effectiveness of the Core Curriculum?" *School Review* 65: 144–60.
- Miller, J. H. 1997. "Cultural Studies and Reading." *ADE Bulletin* 117 (Fall): 15–18.
- Miller, M. A., and A-M. McCartan. 1990. "Making the Case for New Interdisciplinary Programs." *Change* (May–June): 28–36.
- Moffett, J. 1992. *Harmonic Learning: Keynoting School Reform.* Portsmouth, N.H.: Boynton/Cook.
- Moore, B. 1995. Consulting materials on assessment. Olympia: Washington State Board for Community and Technical Colleges.
- Musil, C. M., ed. 1992. *Students at the Center: Feminist Assessment.* Washington, D.C.: Association of American Colleges and National Women's Studies Association.
- Nagel, N. G. 1996. *Learning Through Real-World Problem Solving.* Thousand Oaks, Calif.: Corwin.
- National Association for Core Curriculum. 1991. *Bibliography of Research on the Effectiveness of Block-Time, Core, and Interdisciplinary Team Teaching Programs.* Kent, Ohio: National Association of Core Curriculum.
- National Education Association. 1893. *Report of the Committee on Secondary School Studies.* Washington, D.C.: U.S. Government Printing Office.
- National Education Association. 1895. *Report of the Committee of Fifteen on Elementary Education, with the Reports of the Sub-Committees: On the Training of Teachers; On the Correlation of Studies in Elementary Education; On the Organization of City School Systems.* New York: American Book.

- Newell, W. H. 1994. "Designing Interdisciplinary Courses." In *Interdisciplinary Studies Today*, edited by J. T. Klein and W. G. Doty, 35–51. New Directions for Teaching and Learning 58, San Francisco: Jossey-Bass.

- Newell, W. H., ed. 1998. *Interdisciplinarity: Essays from the Literature*. New York: The College Board.

- Newell, W. H. 1990. "Interdisciplinary Curriculum Development." *Issues in Integrative Studies* 8: 83–85.

- Newell, W. H. 1988. "Interdisciplinary Studies Are Alive and Well." *The National Honors Report* 9(2): 5–6.

- Newell, W. H. ed. 1986. *Interdisciplinary Undergraduate Programs: A Directory*. Oxford, Ohio: Association for Integrative Studies.

- Newell, W. H. 1983. "The Role of Interdisciplinary Studies in the Liberal Education of the 1980s." *Liberal Education* 69(3): 245–255.

- Newell, W. H., and J. T. Klein. 1996. "Interdisciplinary Studies into the 21st Century." *Journal of General Education* 45(2): 152–169.

- Nowicki, J. J., and K. Meehan. 1997. *Interdisciplinary Strategies for English and Social Studies Classrooms: Towards Collaborative Middle and Secondary Teaching*. Boston: Allyn and Bacon.

- Oberholtzer, E. 1937. *An Integrated Curriculum in Practice*. New York: Teachers College Press.

- Panaritis, P. 1995. "Beyond Brainstorming: Planning a Successful Interdisciplinary Program." *Phi Delta Kappan* (April): 623–28.

- Pascarella, E. T., and P. T. Terenzini. 1991. *How College Affects Students: Findings and Insights from Twenty Years of Research*. San Francisco: Jossey-Bass.

- Pate, E., E. Homestead, and K. McGinnis. 1996. *Making Integrated Curriculum Work: Teachers, Students, and The Quest for a Coherent Curriculum*. New York: Teachers College Press.

- Perkins, D. N. 1991. "Educating for Insight." *Educational Leadership* 49 (2): 4–8.

- Perkins, D. N. 1989. "Selecting Fertile Themes for Integrated Learning." In *Interdisciplinary Curriculum: Design and Implementation*, edited by H. H. Jacobs, 67–76. Alexandria, Va.: Association for Supervision and Curriculum Development.

- Perkins, D. N., and Solomon, G. 1989. "Are Cognitive Skills Context Bound?" *Educational Researcher* 18(1): 16–26.

- Perry, W. G. 1970. *Forms of Intellectual and Ethical Development in the College Years: A Scheme*. Troy, Mo.: Holt.

- Piaget, J. 1932. *The Moral Judgment of the Child*. Glencoe, Ill.: Free Press.

- Pickard, D., D. Travis, and D. Lang. 1994. "Designing a District Model to Promote Curriculum Integration." *ERS Spectrum* (Summer): 34–40.

- Pinker, S. 1996. *How the Mind Works*. New York: Norton and Co.

- Popkewitz, T. S., ed. 1987. *The Formation of School Subjects: The Struggle for Creating an American Institution*. New York: Falmer.

- Powell, R. R., and G. Skoog. 1995. "Students' Perspectives of Integrative Curricula: The Case of Brown Barge Middle School." *Research in Middle Level Education Quarterly* 19(1): 85–114.

- Powell, R. R., G. Skoog, and P. Troutman. 1996. "On Streams and Odysseys: Reflections on Reform and Research in Middle Level Integrative Learning Environments." *Research in Middle Level Education Quarterly* 19(4): 1–30.

- Powell, R. R., G. Skoog, P. Troutman, and G. Jones. 1996. "Standing on the Edge of Middle Level Curriculum Reform: Factors Influencing the Sustainability of a Non-Linear Integrative Learning Environment." Paper presented at the annual meeting of the American Educational Research Association, New York.

- Rényi, J. 2000. "Hunting the Quark: Interdisciplinary Curricula in Public Schools." In *Interdisciplinary Curriculum: Challenges to Implementation*, edited by S. Wineburg and P. Grossman, 39–56. New York: Teachers College Press.

- Report of Harvard Committee. 1945. *General Education in a Free Society*. Cambridge, Mass.: Harvard University Press.

- Reports from the Fields. 1991. *Liberal Learning and the Arts and Sciences Major 2*. Washington, D.C.: Association of American Colleges.

- Resnick, L. B. 1989. "Learning in School and Out: The 1987 Presidential Address." *Educational Researcher* 1(9): 13–19.

- Roszak, T. 1997. "Class Wars: Are Computers the Saviors of Education? It Depends on Whom You Ask." Debate with Seymour Papert. *The Wall Street Journal* (November 17): R 32, R 35.

- Roth, K. 2000. "The Photosynthesis of Columbus: Exploring Interdisciplinary Curriculum from the Students' Perspectives." In *Interdisciplinary Curriculum: Challenges to Implementation*, edited by S. Wineburg and P. Grossman, 112–33. New York: Teachers College Press.

- Rugg, H. 1936. *American Life and the School Curriculum*. Boston: Ginn and Co.

- SCANS, The Secretary's Commission on Achieving Necessary Skills. 1992.

- Schilling, K. L. 2001. "Interdisciplinary Assessment for Interdisciplinary Programs." In *Reinventing Ourselves: Interdisciplinary Education, Collaborative Learning and Experimentation in Higher Education*, edited by B. L. Smith and J. McCann, 344–54. Bolton, Mass.: Anker Press.

- Schneider, C. G. 1996. "The Arts and Sciences Major." In *Handbook of the Undergraduate Curriculum*, edited by J. G. Gaff and J. L. Ratcliffe and Associates, 235–61. San Francisco: Jossey-Bass.

- Schroeder, C. C. 1993. "New Students—New Learning Styles." *Change*, 25(4): 21–26.

- Scott, D. K., and S. M. Aubrey. 1993. "Transforming Scholarship." *Change* (July/August): 38–44.

- Seabury, M. B., ed. 1999. *Interdisciplinary General Education: Questioning Outside the Lines*. New York: The College Board.

- Searing, S. 1992. "How Librarians Cope with Interdisciplinarity: The Case of Women's Studies." *Issues in Integrative Studies* 10: 7–25.

- Searing, S. 1996. "Meeting the Information Needs of Interdisciplinary Scholars: Issues for Administrators of Large University Libraries." *Library Trends* 45(2): 315–42.

- Selman, R. 1980. *The Growth of Interpersonal Understanding*. New York: Academic Press.

- Seymour, D. 1988. *Developing Academic Programs*. Washington, D.C.: AAHE-ERIC Higher Education Report.

- Siskin, L. S. 2001. "Restructuring Knowledge: Mapping (Inter)Disciplinary Change." In *Interdisciplinary Curriculum: Challenges to Implementation*, edited by S. Wineburg and P. Grossman, 171–90. New York: Teachers College Press.

- Siu-Runyan, Y., and V. Faircloth, eds. 1995. *Beyond Separate Subjects: Middle School Curriculum for the 21st Century*. Norwood, Mass.: Christopher-Gordon.

- Sizer, T. 1984. *Horace's Compromise: The Dilemma of the American High School*. Boston: Houghton Mifflin.

- Smith, M. 1921. "An Educational Experiment: The Community Project." *Survey* 46: 301–304.

- Smith, M. 1927. *Education and the Integration of Behavior. Contributions to Education 261.* New York: Teachers College Press, Columbia University.
- Stella II. 1995. *Stella II Builds Understanding Across the Curriculum.* Hanover, N.H.: High Performance Systems Inc.
- Stemberg, M. 1991. "Advancing the Social Sciences Through the Interdisciplinary Enterprise." *The Social Science Journal* 28(1) 1–14.
- Stiggins, R. J. 1998. *Student Centered Classroom Assessment.* Saddle River, N.J.: Prentice Hall.
- Stevenson, C., and J. F. Carr, eds. 1993. *Integrative Studies in the Middle Grades: Dancing Through Walls.* New York: Teachers College Press.
- Stoehr, J., and S. Buckey. 1997. *Getting Started: Projects for the Integrated Curriculum.* Tucson, Ariz.: Zephyr.
- Sylwester, R. 1995. *A Celebration of Neurons.* Alexandria, Va.: Association for Supervision and Curriculum Development.
- Tchudi, S., and S. Lafer. 1993. "How Dry Is the Desert? Nurturing Interdisciplinary Learning." *Educational Leadership* 49(2): 76–79.
- Vars, G. F., ed. 1969. *Common Learnings: Core and Interdisciplinary Team Approaches.* Scranton, Pa: Intext.
- Vars, G. F. 1996. "The Effects of Interdisciplinary Curriculum and Instruction." In *Annual Review of Research for School Leaders, Part II: Transcending Traditional Subject Matter Lines: Interdisciplinary Curriculum and Instruction,* edited by P. S. Hlebowitsh and W. G. Wraga, 147–64. Reston, Va.: National Association of Secondary School Principals and New York: Scholastic Press. For the most recent bibliography on effects, contact *The Core Teacher* at NACC/1640 Franklin Ave, Suite 104/Kent, OH 44240-4324; or e-mail GVarsNACC@aol.com.
- Vars, G. 1991. "Integrated Curriculum in Historical Perspective." *Educational Leadership* 49(2): 14–15.
- Vars, G. F. 1987/1993. *Interdisciplinary Teaching: Why and How.* Columbus, Ohio: National Middle School Association.
- Vermont Department of Education. 1995. *Vermont's Framework of Standards and Learning Opportunities.* Montpelier: Vermont Department of Education.
- Vickers, J. 1997. "'[U]nframed in open, unmapped fields': Teaching and the Practice of Interdisciplinarity." *Arachne: An Interdisciplinary Journal of the Humanities* 4(2): 11–42.
- Wesley, C. H. 1941. "Education for Citizenship in a Democracy." *Journal of Negro Education* 10: 68–78.
- White, M. F. 1996. "Specialization, Territoriality, and Jurisdiction in the Growth of Knowledge: Librarianship and the Political Economy of Knowledge." *Library Trends* 45(2): 343–63.
- Wiggins, G. 1989. "Teaching to the (Authentic) Test." *Educational Leadership* 46(7): 41–47.
- Wineburg, S., and P. Grossman, eds. 2000. *Interdisciplinary Curriculum: Challenges to Implementation.* New York: Teachers College Press.
- Wineburg, S., and P. Grossman. 2000. "Scenes from a Courtship: Some Theoretical and Practical Implications of Interdisciplinary Humanities Curricula in the Comprehensive High School." In *Interdisciplinary Curriculum: Challenges to Implementation,* edited by S. Wineburg and P. Grossman, 57–73. New York: Teachers College Press.
- Wisconsin Department of Public Instruction. 1996. *Doing Curriculum Integration.* Madison, Wis.: Wisconsin Department of Public Instruction. VHS tape.

- Wolf, D. P. 1994. "Curriculum and Assessment Standards: Common Measures or Conversations." In *The Future of Education: Perspectives on National Standards in America*, edited by N. Cobb, 85–106. New York: The College Board.
- Wraga, W. G. 1997. "Patterns of Interdisciplinary Curriculum Organization and Professional Knowledge of the Curriculum Field." *Journal of Curriculum and Supervision* 12 (2): 98–117.
- Wright, G. S. 1958. *Block-Time Classes and the Core Program in the Junior High School. Office of Education Bulletin* 1958 (6). Washington, D.C.: U.S. Government Printing Office.
- Wright, G. S. 1963. *The Core Program: Unpublished Research*, 1956-1962. Washington, D.C.: U.S. Government Printing Office.
- Wrightstone, J. W. 1936. *Appraisal of Experimental High School Practices*. New York: Teachers College Press, Columbia University.
- Wrightstone, J. W. 1938. *Appraisal of Newer Elementary School Practices*. New York: Teachers College Press, Columbia University.
- Wrightstone, J. W. 1935. "Evaluation of the Integrated Curriculum in the Upper Grades." *Elementary School Journal* 35: 583–87.
- Young, J. H. 1991/1992. "Curriculum Integration: Perceptions of Preservice Teachers." *Action in Teacher Education* 13(4): 1–9.
- Zemsky, R. (1989) *Structure and Coherence: Measuring the Undergraduate Curriculum*. Washington, D.C.: Association of American Colleges.